P9-CKK-517

Henry Clay
and the
American System

Henry Clay
and the
American System

Maurice G. Baxter

Editorial and Sales Offices: Lexington, Kentucky 40508-4008

Library of Congress Cataloging-in-Publication Data

Baxter, Maurice G. (Maurice Glen), 1920-
    Henry Clay and the American System / Maurice G. Baxter
      p.   cm.
    Includes bibliographical references and index.
    ISBN 0-8131-1919-7 (acid-free)
    1. Clay, Henry, 1777-1852.   2. United States—Economic policy—To
1933.   3. United States—Economic conditions—To 1865.   4. United
States—Politics and government—1815-1861.   I. Title.
E340.C6B39   1995
973.6'3'092—dc20
[B]   94-48090

This book is printed on acid-free recycled paper meeting
the requirements of the American National Standard
for Permanence of Paper for Printed Library Materials.

Contents

Preface

In the formative period of this republic, one of the most prominent persons in American politics was Henry Clay of Kentucky. From 1807, when the young senator came to Washington, until 1852, when he died in a hotel room there, he participated in many important events. Known as a skillful pacificator, he fashioned three great compromises of fundamental sectional differences. During his tenure in the House of Representatives (1811-1825), he advanced the role of speaker to that of an influential policymaker. At first a Jeffersonian Republican, then a highly visible leader of the Whig party, a senator, and a presidential aspirant during the thirties and forties, Clay advocated an economic nationalism called the American System. I have focused on that aspect of his career.

This is a biographical perspective upon economic history. It explores the character and impact of Clay's program for growth of the United States in a political setting, as distinguished from existing studies of economic theory or econometric analysis. On numerous issues, whether concerning tariff, banking, public land, or transportation, the positions taken in congressional debate as well as during elections usually involved the meaning and applications of the Constitution, in a broad sense. So I have paid attention to this aspect but have sought to integrate it with other relevant factors. Hopefully, the result will be an improved understanding not only of the life of Clay as a colorful pathmarker but also of the dynamics of general history.

Acknowledgments

I am greatly indebted to the editors of *The Papers of Henry Clay* (11 vols., University Press of Kentucky, 1959-92) for their superb contribution of source materials and editorial annotations, upon which I have drawn heavily in this study, as my citations will indicate. At the Press, I received excellent advice and support. Lois Crum improved the final version with expert copyediting. Theresa Schaefer prepared a first-rate index. James Birchfield of the Special Collections in the King Library at the University of Kentucky kindly helped in making available prints of Clay portraits. And William Henning, curator of the University Art Museum, provided a valuable print. As always, Cynthia Lewis Baxter was much involved in the enterprise.

Henry Clay. Engraving of oil portrait by John Neagle, c. 1843. Courtesy of the University of Kentucky Library, Special Collections.

1

Jeffersonian Nationalist

At the beginning of the nineteenth century the new western state of Kentucky offered splendid opportunities to an ambitious young lawyer in the fast-growing town of Lexington. Near the house of Henry Clay at Mill and Second Streets were signs of a go-ahead community: shops of weavers, tailors, blacksmiths, and saddlers, as well as establishments of distillers and hemp manufacturers. A flourishing trade with the East, the South, and foreign countries passed through the great Ohio-Mississippi River system. The basic industry of agriculture, especially in this fertile bluegrass region, was thriving too. Here, as in other frontier areas, interest in land was intense. Optimism stimulated speculation and settlement; indeed it had done so as early as Revolutionary days when Virginians had blocked out large, if hazily bounded, grants in their transmontane county.[1]

In 1800 Clay was only twenty-three. But he had definitely begun his ascent to prosperity and a favorable reputation. Within months after emigration from his native Virginia, he had secured admission to the bar and had begun a profitable practice. And he had married the eighteen-year-old

daughter of Thomas Hart, a leading merchant-capitalist involved in a variety of enterprises. The Clays lived next door to
the Harts and would become a family of social standing in
their own right.

This connection merely enhanced his prospects, which
depended chiefly on his unusual personal qualities. He was
tall, thin, and sandy-haired, with an expressive face. His personality, at times emotional and always engaging, would be a
never-failing asset. Intellectually, he was quick and resource-
ful. In an era of golden oratory he would be in the front rank
because of his ability not only to arouse but to instruct an audience on almost any subject.

Given his circumstances, it was natural for him to move
into politics without delay. His background was Jeffersonian
Republican of the Virginia school. As a youth he had been a
student and assistant of Thomas Jefferson's mentor, Chancel-
lor George Wythe, in Richmond. He admired James Madison's
leadership in party conflicts with the ascendant Federalists
over domestic and diplomatic issues. Soon after settling in
Lexington, he took part in a lively debate over changing the
state's constitution, which, he thought, ought to be more democratic. Arrayed against the administration of John Adams, he
spoke out ardently against the Sedition Act of 1798 as violating state and individual rights. Now, during Jefferson's
presidency, he would be a steady supporter of Republican principles and policies.

Like Jefferson himself, Clay tempered his subscription to
states' rights and limited government with a firm belief in positive efforts to forward economic development. For the republican "experiment" to survive, the economy must support it.
Though identified as agrarians, Jeffersonians such as Clay
sought national strength and true independence by also
encouraging commerce and manufacturing. Perhaps there was
some ideological inconsistency. Nevertheless, constitutional
amendment and recourse to state and private action would be
available.

Clay's own rapid advance on the Lexington scene illustrates the relationship of political and economic elements of
early American society. His involvement in numerous undertakings in addition to a law practice helps to explain the for-

mation of his political ideas. His lifelong commitment to agriculture began with acquisition of hundreds of acres of land, much of it near town, where his crops of hemp and grain, his stock of horses and other animals, and his increasing number of slave laborers justly classified him as a border-state planter. The Clay family, including several children, occupied a handsome new mansion on the property known as Ashland. And he owned many parcels of land elsewhere, some as distant as Illinois and Missouri. But he had several other interests. He was a stockholder and proprietor of the hemp and cotton spinning mill on Silver Creek in Madison County. He was a director, as well as attorney, for the two banks then organized in the state. His property included many lots, houses, and even a tavern in town. As a trustee, he had a strong commitment to the administration of Transylvania University in Lexington. In light of the breadth of his personal concerns, well beyond those of a mere lawyer or farmer, there is little wonder that he expounded the merits of a growing, diversified economy, fostered by government.[2]

So he did not wait very long before entering current political contests. At age twenty-six he won the first of seven annual elections to the Kentucky House of Representatives. Nor did the young legislator pause before taking a position of leadership. He quickly became the chief spokesman for a Republican majority against the dwindling Federalist ranks in the debates, which were sometimes less than decorous. His counterpart was Humphrey Marshall, a cousin of Chief Justice John Marshall and a bitter opponent in the House or on the dueling field.

An early legislative conflict, however, involved a fellow Republican, Felix Grundy, against whom Clay would be repeatedly arrayed in future years at the national capital. This battle concerned the state's policy on banking. In 1802 the legislature had incorporated the Kentucky Insurance Company in response to the hazards of a lively traffic on the western rivers. But in addition to regulations in the charter on that subject, there was a provision authorizing the corporation to operate as a bank—to make loans and issue notes. For a while it was the only bank in Kentucky and was yielding large dividends to its stockholders.

a John Taylor-ish "old republican"?

artificial ⟶

Representative Grundy took a staunch agrarian position in attacking the company as a privileged instrument of merchants to the disadvantage of honest farmers. Such banks were inconsistent, he declared, with the principles of a simple republican economy. Not so, Clay retorted. For desirable development, the state must have adequate capital and credit. Over three sessions Grundy sought to repeal or severely amend the company charter. Besides his economic defense, Clay contended that revocation would amount to a breach of contract violating vested rights. He managed to turn back a repeal but had to maneuver cleverly to do so. As a bluff, he introduced a bill to enforce state collection of old payments from occupants of lands in the Green River area, for whom Grundy was speaking. At length, both he and Grundy agreed to withdraw their bills. Clay's victory was not complete, because Grundy had previously succeeded in getting an amendment to the charter requiring a larger reserve for note issues.[3]

Shortly afterward the legislature set up a second corporation, the Bank of Kentucky, in which the state would hold half the stock and appoint not only half the directors but the president as well. A mixed corporation, of which there were to be many in the period, it had a rough road ahead and would not last out its chartered lifetime. But Clay was quite satisfied with its organization; in fact, he became a director and often an active one. In his view, such financial institutions were indispensable to the commonwealth's prosperity.[4]

An equally important facility was a good transportation system or, as then expressed, internal improvements. During the first decade of the nineteenth century, Kentucky and the rest of the western country suffered from slow, expensive movement of the products they bought and sold. For some purposes, it was nearly prohibitive to ship goods to and from the Atlantic coast. Though westerners used the long route down the river system to New Orleans and thence by sea, more so after the Louisiana Purchase (1803) had assured access to that port, the downriver barges were slow and upriver keel boats were hardly practical. In 1810 Kentucky was the most populous trans-Appalachian state, and the annual value of its own downstream shipments amounted to $1,182,000 out of a western total of $2,600,000. The next year the steamboat came to the Mississippi Valley and promised to increase that trade decidedly—if river channels were clear and if falls and rapids were neutralized. At Louisville the latter problem was most acute. During much of the year river boats at the falls there had to unload and reload cargoes, with all the cost and delay that involved. For a long while, the slow and expensive project of a canal and locks dragged on.[5]

In his second legislative session (December 1804), Clay had reported a committee recommendation to charter a company for this work. A year later it was obvious that adequate capital would have to come in substantial amounts from stock subscriptions not merely by Kentucky but by neighboring states and the national government. Always, it seemed, the cost would be underestimated. But Clay shared the prevailing opinion in the West that a canal would be a key to progress.[6]

The growth of manufacturing in Kentucky drew political attention too. Clay's hemp crops contributed to the state's development of an active industry turning out several products. In addition to rope and sailcloth, a fabric for bagging southern cotton became an important output. Throughout his legislative career, Clay never neglected to pursue whatever was necessary to benefit this industry. He deserved his occasional title, the prince of hemp. In the legislature he guided a charter for the Madison Hemp and Flax Spinning Company to passage in 1808. Holding stock in the corporation and briefly acting as a proprietor, he also assisted it as an officeholder.[7]

In the years after 1807 during a critical phase of the Napoleonic wars, Britain and France invoked severe restrictions on neutral maritime trade. The United States reacted with an embargo on trade and other countermeasures, and eventually declaration of war in 1812. The West, as well as the maritime East, suffered economically. States such as Kentucky lost much of their agricultural exportation to Europe and the West Indies (one reason for advocating military response to Britain). But as in the Northeast, reduced imports brought an impetus to western manufacturing. Clay was alive to this dimension of national events and introduced resolutions not only approving Jefferson's embargo but also urging Kentuckians to use only goods made in America. Specifically, he proposed that legislators on a certain day wear clothing of domestic rather than foreign manufacture.

During a name-calling exchange his long-term Federalist adversary Humphrey Marshall attacked the resolutions so heatedly that, with equal heat, Clay challenged Marshall to a duel. Fortunately the encounter ended with no loss of life, the challenger suffering only a minor wound. Notwithstanding this personal unpleasantness, Clay was convinced he spoke for a large majority on the necessity to attain economic self-sufficiency as a nation.[8]

He interrupted his state legislative service briefly in early 1807 when he went to Washington to fill out the term of a senator who had resigned. The attraction of doing so was largely his own financial interest. He had been involved in land speculation himself and in extensive litigation as a lawyer about unclear land grants, defective titles, and delinquent taxes. So he traveled to the capital and argued such cases before the Supreme Court while attending the Senate.[9] Again in sessions of 1810 and 1811 he replaced another senator. It was a time of difficult diplomacy, soon leading to American entrance into war, of decisions that the young war hawk would influence. He also moved energetically into congressional discussions about important domestic issues, allowing him to draw upon his state experience.

Clay found an even stronger movement in Washington than in Frankfort, Kentucky, for internal improvements. The idea that action by the national government should develop vital lines of transportation was gaining ground. But did Congress have the power to enter upon an extensive program for better roads and waterways? Here was a difficult question the Republican administration confronted.

President Jefferson did not have the slightest doubt that such projects were highly desirable for eastern commerce and western expansion, for manufacturing and agriculture in the country as a whole. Yet he could find no specific constitutional authority, whether in commerce, defense, or postal clauses of the document, for direct federal involvement. He had relaxed his strict constructionism somewhat in approving Secretary of Treasury Albert Gallatin's plan for the National Road in connection with the congressional law of 1802 on statehood for

Ohio. Since that measure preceded actual admission of Ohio and therefore concerned a territory, over which there was a larger scope of national power than over a state, and since the Ohio legislature had entered a kind of compact, Jefferson felt comfortable about this legislation. The procedure would devote 5 percent of federal land sales in Ohio to build the National Road to and through that state. Later, the policy would be extended to Indiana and Illinois. Still, this undertaking seemed to be a special case, not a precedent for other improvements. They would require an amendment to the Constitution, and Jefferson had recommended such a course.[10]

This was the status of national internal improvements when Clay arrived in the Senate in early 1807. He soon had an opportunity to show his enthusiastic approval of a measure for the federal district, a bridge across the Potomac to Alexandria. His speech was a full-scale, animated argument, favorably impressing some colleagues if not convincing those who thought the existing Georgetown ferry was sufficient. At the moment, opponents prevailed by one vote, but the bridge's sponsors would win passage at the next session.[11]

Concurrently, Clay was at work chairing a committee on aiding construction of a canal at the Ohio River falls. He brought to the task his experience in getting a canal charter from the Kentucky legislature. It was a matter of money, which, he found, must be provided by several states in the region as well as by Congress. He now made a good case for the large benefits to the national economy from facilitating western commerce. Nevertheless, he had to go slowly, to ask only for a commission to study the practicability of a canal. The Senate approved by a good margin, but the House did not.[12]

In pressing for help on the Ohio canal, Clay allied with senators advocating other plans, one of them a Chesapeake-Delaware canal. James Bayard sought to subsidize a twenty-mile connection of rivers flowing into those bays, particularly a goal of Philadelphia shippers as access to the Chesapeake. The formula, similar to many in the future, would use federal land grants to subscribe stock in a private company. Public land would furnish capital for a mixed governmental-private undertaking. Another member of the Senate, John Quincy Adams, voted against these proposals because, with some reason, he suspected logrolling by a coalition of local interests to raid the treasury. Adams urged a more systematic, general approach to improvements, but his motion to that effect failed.[13] After the Senate postponed acting on the Chesapeake-Delaware request, another member's motion for requesting a comprehensive report by the secretary of treasury did pass.[14]

Gallatin complied with this request enthusiastically. His report of April 1808, a year later, was a detailed survey of existing land and water routes and became a classic blueprint for future development. With information elicited from public officers and persons active in all fields of transportation, such as Benjamin Latrobe and Robert Fulton, Gallatin laid out a nationwide program. He recommended a continuous north-south inland waterway paralleling the Atlantic coast, linking bays and sounds from Maine to Georgia with canals. To develop east-west communication, he would improve river systems on either side of the mountains and build turnpikes, joining the nation's sections into one network. He would urge adoption of some currently contemplated projects, including Clay's canal at the Louisville rapids and another from the upper Hudson River to Lake Erie.

The secretary's geography and his economic diagnosis were very good, much better than his thoughts on how to execute the grand design. He estimated it would cost $16,600,000. And since some states would not benefit as much as others, he would distribute an additional $3,400,000 to them for local purposes. Raising the total to $20 million seemed manageable: appropriate $2 million annually for ten years, to be obtained from proceeds of public-land sales. Quite practical, he thought, since the treasury's yearly surplus then amounted to $5 million. Of course, his figures on construction were unrealistic—in the report itself he remarked on costs of road building in Connecticut, amounting to a million dollars for each hundred miles. Furthermore, the surplus of funds represented revenue from customs, which had been unusually large because foreign commerce had expanded during the war in Europe. This revenue would soon shrink with adoption of an American embargo, and fiscal problems would continue on through the War of 1812.[15]

There was also the constitutional problem. Jefferson's messages had warned Congress that an amendment empowering national action was required. Gallatin recognized the difficulty and mentioned the options of state consent or governmental subscription to stock of private companies. Whether any of these solutions was politically possible was unclear. In any event, Jefferson and Gallatin had made a convincing case for the value of internal improvements—to stimulate economic growth, to hold the Union together, even to help public finance by boosting the value of the public domain.[16]

These were valid arguments for the long run, but now few positive steps could be taken. Often discussed, a constitutional amendment made no progress. Legislation decidedly lagged, owing to diplomatic and subsequent military priorities. In 1810 Clay's colleague in the Senate, John Pope, sought to pass a bill with many features of Gallatin's report, financed by governmental land grants and subscription of company stock. Peter Porter of New York, whose political views were identical to those of his friend Clay, delivered an extensive speech forcefully putting the case in the House, but all was in vain. That was true not only of his efforts but those by DeWitt Clinton and others from New York who were lobbying for aid to dig the Erie Canal. Internal improvement advocates could get only modest appropriations to build a section of the National Road from Cumberland, Maryland, toward Ohio.[17]

The Republican administrations of Jefferson and Madison were also reacting to the transformation of manufacturing then under way. They favored policies supporting industry mainly to achieve national economic independence at a time of disrupted foreign commerce and of possible involvement in war. Near the close of his presidency early in 1809, Jefferson emphasized the desirability of an "equilibrium" of manufacturing, agriculture, and commerce. He warned against the danger posed by an aggressive Federalist commercial interest, understandable in view of his irritation with its vexing opposition to the recent embargo legislation.[18] His successor, Madison, in annual messages to Congress recommended protecting manufactures that had developed during the Napoleonic wars when imports from Europe had declined. He especially had in mind more assistance to cotton textiles from the tariff.[19]

Accordingly, the House Committee on Manufactures reported its approval of the president's view and of pleas from a number of petitioners.[20] For more information the House also asked Secretary Gallatin to report on the general status of manufactures, indicating the extent to which they had been established and providing a plan to protect those requiring protection. After a year-long process of collecting data, the secretary forwarded his admittedly incomplete findings in April 1810. He described the trend toward mechanized production in factories and the roles of labor and capital. Then he suggested that some products were in sufficient quantity to meet the domestic demand, but that many others still needed protection by higher customs rates or governmental bounties or loans. He particularly pointed to textiles, which had received a stimulus from the reduction of European imports. He also included in this category not only iron manufactures but iron itself, a surprising situation in a country with such rich resources. In fact, that was true of other raw materials. Throughout the document the theme of fostering diversification was evident, to the degree of endorsing the goal of a balanced economy and a home market in the manufacturing sector for the country's output of food, fiber, and ores. Despite a strong effort, Gallatin concluded that he had been unable to supply all the desired information. He advised use of the coming census of 1810 to fill the gaps.[21]

Census takers did compile a large body of detail, though results were still incomplete and defective. To make the report more intelligible, the House directed preparation of a digest, which fell to Tench Coxe, former assistant to Alexander Hamilton in the Treasury and dedicated promoter of manufacturing. His report of 1813 surveyed a wide range of industries and tabulated the annual value of production by each, with textiles the largest. He took the liberty of amending, substantially upward, the total annual value of all manufactures from $120 million to $173 million.[22]

After Clay returned to the Senate in early 1810, he was quite aware of this rising interest in economic development. During debate on the military appropriations bill, he vigor-ously supported an amendment instructing the secretary of the Navy in purchasing supplies to give preference to domestic over foreign hemp products (rope and sailcloth). He spoke as he would throughout his career for this important interest back home. Kentucky's dew-rotted hemp, however, was handicapped in competition with the superior water-rotted variety from abroad. As long as the European war continued, the domestic market did make gains, but in the future Clay and other hemp planters would have to improve their methods.

Clay's specific argument about hemp rested on a broader exposition of economic self-sufficiency. He rejected the familiar warning that America must avoid commitment to industrialization or suffer the social ills so apparent in British manufacturing centers. All the nation needed to do, he said, was to produce only what it needed at home and not strive for a world market. Then the United States would be as happy as a self-reliant family household, unhurt by outside exploitation. Besides, the American setting and character differed so much from Britain's that he perceived no risk. His criticism of what he called economic colonialism must have caused his fellow senators to smile: "For many years after the [Revolutionary] war, such was the partiality for her [British] productions, that a gentleman's head could not withstand the influence of solar heat unless covered with a London hat—his feet could not bear the pebbles or frost of this country unless protected by London shoes—and the comfort or adornment of his person was only consulted when his coat was cut out by the shears of a tailor 'just from London.'" His most memorable words were "Others may prefer the cloths of Leeds and of London, but give me those of Humphreysville [Connecticut]."[23]

Tariff policy became unavoidably entangled with diplomatic and financial aspects over the next several years. As the United States invoked commercial restrictions on belligerent nations in Europe, another possible action was to raise tariffs to an extreme height. A 50 percent proposal came to the Senate at the time of Macon's Bill Number Two in 1810. Clay favored the idea, but it failed passage.[24] Then when war against Britain was declared in 1812, all rates were doubled for the duration to obtain badly needed revenue. This policy aided American business somewhat, but its principal significance was probably to whet the appetite of protectionists afterward.[25]

Another issue upon which many Jeffersonian Republicans moved away from their original strict-constructionist position concerned banking. In 1811 the twenty-year charter of the Bank of the United States (BUS) would expire. Its usefulness to the government as a public depository and as a provider of currency in its circulation of notes, as well as its relationship to the economy in credit and exchange operations, recommended it to persons of both political parties. This was true of Gallatin, who endorsed recharter with President Madison's acquiescence. A year in advance of the date of expiration, the Senate discussed a renewal bill. Though Clay did not speak on the measure, he showed some dissatisfaction with the institution by proposing restrictions on it. He was not completely negative, however, and voted against terminating the bank. The Senate deferred action.[26]

An all-out debate followed at the next session. William Crawford, chairman of the Senate committee, reported for recharter with generous praise of a constructive role of the BUS. He reflected sentiment of a sizable number of fellow Republicans. Still, the final vote was going to be close, not on strict party lines. Some members of Crawford's party adhered to pure Jeffersonianism to oppose renewal, and others apparently opposed because they disliked Gallatin or because they were influenced by competing state-bank opinion.

Clay was among those Republicans who argued against the national bank bill. One of his reasons was practical and concerned the situation in Kentucky. His professional and political connections with the Kentucky Insurance Company and the Bank of Kentucky, both of which had complaints against the BUS, probably had an effect. Then the legislature had instructed the state's senators to oppose recharter. The other reason was ideological. In his set speech during the senate debate in February, he advanced a constitutional argument similar to the well-known Jeffersonian opinion on the original chartering in 1791.

He contended that establishing this corporation could not be justified as an implied power, necessary and proper to carry out congressional powers enumerated in Article I, section 8, of the Constitution, such as authority to tax, to pay debts, or to regulate commerce. Just as Jefferson had written twenty years earlier, the power to set up a corporation had been denied in the federal convention of 1787. As for the present, Clay could not agree that the bank was performing any of these necessary functions. Here he recounted a humorous anecdote: "Like the Virginia justice you tell the man, whose turkey had been stolen, that your book of precedents furnishes no form for his case, but then you will grant him precept to search for a cow, and when looking for that he may possibly find his turkey! You say to this corporation, we cannot authorise you to discount—to emit paper—to regulate commerce, &c. No! Our book has no precedents of that kind. But then we can authorise you to collect the revenue, and, whilst occupied with that, you may do whatever else you please!"[27]

The senator joined colleagues in depicting the specter of a privileged corporation—it was truly an exploitative monopoly, he declared. Worse still, foreigners, mainly British citizens, owned 70 percent of its stock. And now that the United States faced arrogant British policies paralyzing maritime commerce and perhaps instigating a war, the danger was even greater.

The senate vote was seventeen to seventeen, whereupon Vice President George Clinton broke the tie. It was said that Clay wrote or at least contributed to Clinton's statement explaining the decisive blow. To cap the bank's defeat, its request for an extension of time to wind up its operations was not granted. Clay was chairman of the committee recommending rejection.[28]

At this juncture, early in 1811, attention to domestic issues was declining as diplomatic and military concerns became dominant. Elected to the House, Clay began his long service as Speaker later that year and played a leading role in pressing for war against Britain, declared in June 1812. Two and a half years of conflict, marked by political discord and military stalemate, ended with negotiations at Ghent, to which Clay went as one of the peace commissioners.

In addition to discussions about postwar boundaries, resulting in no changes of antebellum lines, two economic subjects were considered by the treaty makers: (1) British access to and use of the Mississippi River from Canada, and (2) American "liberty" of fishing in waters off Newfoundland. Both privileges dated back to the treaty of the Revolution (1783), but the present war may have terminated them. The first seems to have been a symbolic question, since the Canadian boundary did not extend as far south as the source of the Mississippi, thus making access rather impractical. Clay staunchly opposed any concession, however, for he knew how sensitive his fellow westerners were about this great commercial artery. The second subject, the Atlantic fisheries, was an important interest of New England, also viewed as at risk and perhaps with better reason. Clay's colleague John Quincy Adams of Massachusetts, with concurrence of two others of the five American commissioners, insisted that both rights, access to the Mississippi and the fisheries, be renewed by express provision. Clay vehemently opposed what he saw as an unacceptable bargain to benefit New England at western expense. Then followed moves and countermoves, culminating in deletion of any mention of either matter in the Treaty of Ghent (1815). Adams would get his fishing rights in a subsequent agreement (1818), but the whole episode left him and Clay with hard feelings toward one another.[29]

A follow-up move was to negotiate a British-American commercial convention. It was desirable to obtain one because earlier provisions had lapsed. Both sides wished to stimulate trade with one another, for it was complementary in many ways. So Clay went to London in spring 1815 for this purpose, joined by Bayard, Gallatin, and Adams, the new minister to Britain.

Throughout the talks, Clay tried to get British acknowledgement of neutral maritime rights against impressment of sailors and spoliations of ships and cargoes, rights claimed by the United States before and during the late conflict. To the extent of persuading his English counterparts to discuss these matters, he succeeded; but that did not produce any explicit commitment, just as nothing had been gained in the Treaty of Ghent.

Clay and his colleagues did sign a commercial convention, assuring freedom of each nation from discrimination in tonnage duties on its ships and in import rates on goods carried by those ships. This was a modest retreat from long-standing navigation laws of the two signatories. Britain managed to retain some of its system by way of imperial preference, since the United States benefited only in trade with Britain proper and with its possessions in India, but not with its West Indies islands and other colonies. The breakthrough toward equal shipping rights did, however, provide a model for future treaties.[30]

At its next session, in 1816, Congress debated a bill putting the trade agreements into effect. Because of a continuing ban of American ships from the West Indies, there were understandable objections to allowing nondiscriminatory entry of British ships arriving in the United States on indirect routes from their home country, including stops at those Caribbean colonies. Clay said very little during this discussion in the House, but he entered briefly a debate on the relationship of commercial treaties and congressional statutes under the Constitution. Some opponents of the agreement contended that a treaty had no effect unless supplemented by a statute. Others thought Congress could enact a law nullifying a treaty. Clay reasoned that a statute was permissible, though unnecessary, to execute the treaty; but he thought in this case the House ought to enact one, repeating the terms of the convention. Anglo-American trade would, however, create many problems in the future.[31]

2

The American System

The decade after the Treaty of Ghent, from 1815 to the middle twenties, was a time of emerging economic trends. The end of the European war, in which the United States had long been entangled, diplomatically and then militarily, meant that the nation could now direct more attention to domestic affairs. Westward migration into the Ohio and Mississippi Valleys populated several new states from the Great Lakes to the Gulf of Mexico. The South strengthened its plantation system and its institution of slavery to produce an ever larger output of cotton. And the Northeast was industrializing and urbanizing at a startling pace.

Politically, a current of nationalism moved men and events. Though the peace commissioners had failed to assure neutral maritime rights or to acquire territory, at least the republic had passed through the ordeal without loss and with pride in standing ground against powerful Britain. This psychological impact, although difficult to measure, contributed to a surge of nationalism. One beneficiary was the Republican party, now dominant over the Federalists, who were associated with an unpatriotic, narrow-minded opposition to the war. Nationalism competed with the old agrarian tradition, and the triumphant Jeffersonians became advocates of such nationalist policies as a national bank, a protective tariff, and even federal internal improvements.

Through most of these postwar years, Clay was Speaker of the House. Exceptions were the congressional session (1814-15) when he was abroad on the peace commission and a three-year period (1821-23) when he did not seek reelection to the House. Otherwise, he presided over the lower chamber until he became John Quincy Adams's secretary of state in 1825. So he was at the center of political debate and decision making when these nationalist tendencies arose. Since the two presidents, Madison (1815-17) and James Monroe (1817-25), did not exercise strong leadership on Capitol Hill, and since the earlier two-party system had disintegrated, Clay's role was all the more influential.

To be sure, he never disclaimed his Jeffersonian roots—he often declared that Madison's report to the Virginia legislature in 1799 on broad states' rights exactly expressed his own political creed. Nevertheless, on specific issues he, as well as many others of the day, seemed to be confirming a Hamiltonian creed of expansive nationalism. He was attuned to prevailing sentiment, but he also drew upon his own experience. Where he seemed inconsistent with an earlier position, for example on a national bank, he insisted that conditions, not his basic ideas, had changed.

In the session of 1816, Clay and like-minded congressmen sought governmental encouragement to industrialization then under way. Several industries—iron, flour, glass, leather, textiles—had benefited from reduced imports during the war. Further impetus came from a large pool of investment capital, a plentiful supply of fiber, food, minerals, and lumber, a good source of labor for the new factories, and advances in technology for mechanized, efficient production.[1] The industry undergoing the most spectacular change was that of cotton textiles. Francis Cabot Lowell and other merchants of New England established mills with new machines to spin yarn and weave cloth. They employed large numbers of women and children in paternalistic environments. By avoiding urban locations, they hoped to sidestep the social ills that afflicted British mill areas, notably Manchester.[2]

With such progress in industrialization came a feeling that public policy ought to be more positive. And the most obvious positive assistance to enterprise in its infancy was believed to be a protective tariff. The largest share of foreign goods now came, as usual, from Britain. In 1815, the first year of resuming commerce, British imports amounted to $85 million. The next year they soared to $151 million, bringing on the charge that Britain was "dumping" goods at unfairly low prices to smother American producers.[3] A widely reported remark of Lord Henry Brougham in Parliament added credence to that complaint: "It is well worthwhile to incur a loss upon the first exportation, in order by the glut, to *stifle in the cradle*, those rising manufactures, in the United States, which the war had *forced* into existence, contrary to the natural course of things."[4]

Enactment of a tariff would not be a novelty, for Congress had legislated on the subject almost every year since the adoption of the Constitution. The first measure, in 1789, shaped and sponsored by Representative Madison, announced in its preamble an objective of encouraging and protecting American manufactures. Of course another, more pressing reason for the enactment was a desperate need for revenue, so sadly lacking during Confederation days. The average rate of 8 percent represented a compromise for the moment between the two principles of revenue and protection, but it was only the beginning of a continuing interaction. A significant point, however, is that at this time there was little if any constitutional objection to the protective option.[5]

Among early advocates of a tariff to foster American manufactures, Tench Coxe of Pennsylvania stands out. As a young, aggressive publicist, Coxe tried to persuade the constitutional convention of 1787 to frame a document that would promote economic growth and national self-sufficiency. He put forward a rationale that would have a long political life. Industrialization, he said, would result in a balanced economy, with mutual benefits to agriculture, commerce, and manufacturing. This was the essence of the home-market argument. Then when Representative Madison was guiding the tariff bill to passage in 1789, Coxe supplied him with large amounts of information and with anti-British, protectionist reasons for a

schedule of formidable rates. Coxe became assistant secretary
of treasury under Hamilton and contributed significantly to
the secretary's well-known Report on Manufactures.

Coxe's later publications in 1794 and in 1814 (the digest
of the census of 1810) were undoubtedly known to politicians
like Clay.[6] It was probably through materials such as those of
Coxe and of later popular writers that Clay equipped himself
with some everyday concepts of political economy.

At the beginning of this postwar session, in early 1816,
the House centered its attention on fiscal policy. A public debt
of $120 million represented heavy borrowing during the con-
flict, even though Congress had laid excise and direct land
taxes and doubled tariff rates. Now the question was how
much the government should rely upon taxes and how much
upon import duties. Through January, Clay repeatedly
stepped down from the Speaker's chair to urge reduction of
taxes. He was pleased that the direct levy on land would be
phased out the following year and that reliance on other taxes
would diminish in comparison with proceeds from public-land
sales and especially from the tariff. His aim was to strengthen
the argument for a high tariff to protect manufactures by dependence upon it also as the major source of revenue.[7]

In an earlier message President Madison had recommended that Congress consider "means to preserve and promote the manufactures which have sprung into existence, and
attained an unparalleled maturity throughout the United
States, during the period of the European wars."[8] On February
13, 1816, the House Committee on Commerce and Manufactures responded to a stream of petitions by textile manufacturers with a report describing the status of that industry and the
desirability of governmental assistance. Statistics in the document revealed enormous growth. Mills had used only five hundred bales of cotton in 1800 but ninety thousand in 1815. Total
capital in the industry amounted to $40 million; and the labor
force rose to one hundred thousand persons, nine-tenths of
them women and children. To encourage further development
in face of a menacing British competition, the committee called
for higher import rates.[9]

The same day, Secretary of Treasury Alexander Dallas
reported on revising the tariff. He envisioned three levels of

imposts: (1) high rates on goods that this country made in sufficient quantity to satisfy domestic demand; (2) lower but protective rates on goods that, if encouraged, could be produced in sufficient quantity; and (3) still lower rates, for revenue only, on goods that American manufacturers could not supply. For textiles in category 2, the secretary recommended ad valorem duties of $33\frac{1}{3}$ percent, much higher than the prewar level but lower than that of wartime.[10]

In late March, with adjournment approaching, the House began debate on a bill presented by William Lowndes, chairman of the Ways and Means Committee. Some rates in this version were lower than than those recommended by Dallas— that on cotton textiles would be 25 percent. Clay entered into discussions on numerous features of the bill; but like others, he showed the greatest interest in the section on textiles. He tried several times to restore the $33\frac{1}{3}$ percent in the Dallas report or at least 30 percent for three years before a reduction to Lowndes's 25 percent. Here he encountered resistance from Daniel Webster, who was concerned about an adverse effect of protectionism on New England shipping. At last Webster got the better of him, and the final vote was for 25 percent for three years, then 20 percent on cottons. Woolens received the same treatment, and Clay was no more successful on the hemp rate.[11]

Despite his aversion to full-scale protection, Webster did respond to needs of New England's manufacturers. On hand was Francis Lowell, who lobbied effectively for his textile companies in Massachusetts. Webster later recalled, "I was much with him, & found him full of exact practical knowledge, on many subjects."[12] The subject about which Lowell was most knowledgeable was inexpensive cotton sheeting, in which his mills specialized, though in competition with low-priced imports from British India. So Lowell got Webster's help for adding a provision to the bill placing a minimum value of twenty-five cents per square yard on such goods for purposes of assessing ad valorem. As time passed, this minimum system would virtually prohibit imports of cheap cottons (with actual value far below twenty-five cents) and would be the favorite target of antiprotectionist complaint.[13]

In light of future events, the position of John Calhoun is noteworthy. Then in his nationalistic phase, Calhoun spoke warmly in support of these textile rates. The true policy, he said, must be a regard for all elements of the economy: manufacturing, commerce, and agriculture. What benefited one benefited the others. Cotton manufacturing required an ever larger quantity of southern fiber. Mill workers were consumers of other agricultural products. Foreign and domestic commerce carried and profited from the output of industry. Factories operated successfully when there was a good market for their goods. Besides, a self-sufficient nation would not be at risk of foreign exploitation or wars. And the values of the republic, the liberty of its citizenry, and the perpetual union of its states would be enhanced. Liberty and union, he declared, were inseparable. In his postnationalist years he would hear his adversary Webster utter the same sentiment.[14]

Now Clay and Calhoun were kindred spirits. The home-market idea, national economic independence, the favorable impact of industrialization, and governmental promotion of these conditions all had become basic concepts of the Speaker's ideology. When the tariff bill passed, he could be heartened at least by the commitment it made to economic growth and could hope for further progress in fulfilling that commitment.

The statute of April 1816, however, turned out to be only moderately protective—rates on many imports, including cottons, were actually lower than they had been during the war. The levy on hammered iron would be even less than the prewar level. Raw wool, sugar, hemp, and a number of other items did not get the kind of protection Clay had sought. And generally, the ad valorem system allowed circumvention by the much reviled auctions to undercut American competitors at port cities. To say all this is simply to recognize a persistent characteristic of all tariff history, its open-ended, always controversial presence in the nation's politics.[15]

Dissatisfaction with the new rates and with weaknesses in collecting customs soon induced movements for more protection. In a number of cities, societies for promoting manufactures were forming, holding conventions, and petitioning Congress. Their memorials complained about imports flooding the market, consequent problems of American producers, and an inadequate law just adopted. Lobbyists and propagandists visited Washington during the session of 1817-18.[16] Modest help came from President Monroe's annual message, briefly calling attention to the value of manufactures. "Their preservation," he said, "depends on due encouragement" by Congress.[17]

A bill passed for postponing reduction of the duty to 25 percent on cottons and woolens until 1826. Other measures raised the schedule on selected products, such as glass, iron, and other metals. A drive for still more decisive action seemed to be gaining ground.[18]

An added factor was the downturn of economic conditions in 1819. Banks had overextended and were unable to resume specie payment for their notes. The new Bank of the United States had failed to provide the dependable base expected of it, had also overextended, and then had suddenly attempted to retrench. Merchants, farmers, and land speculators had been caught up in this cycle of expansion and contraction. As a result price levels declined sharply and would remain lower for a long time. Unemployment of labor and bankruptcy of businesses spread discouragement across the land. Protectionists reacted by blaming the continued unfavorable balance of foreign trade, which, they concluded, only a higher tariff could correct. Their logic might have been questionable, but tariff revision seemed necessary anyhow because the Treasury needed more revenue, as Secretary William Crawford had explained.[19]

So in April 1820 the House began consideration of a bill for these purposes. As Speaker, Clay had attended to the necessary groundwork of committee appointments and of planning the strategy. It was now near the end of the session, and the legislators' thoughts had focused month after month on the Missouri Compromise. Henry Baldwin, a western Pennsylvania protectionist, presented a report for upward revision, nearly doubling many ad valorem rates, increasing those on textiles from 25 to 33 percent, and raising specific duties on forged iron, hemp, and other goods. Baldwin also brought in two more bills that would tax sales of imports at auctions and would replace the existing credit system at customs houses with a cash basis.[20]

During a week-long debate, both sides of the issue spun out the familiar arguments and a few new ones on protection. Baldwin and Louis McLane probably made the strongest case for encouraging manufacturing while reconciling it with commerce and agriculture on home-market grounds. In opposition, John Tyler and Philip Barbour—both Virginians—spiritedly defended the agrarian position. High rates, they contended, unjustly subsidized industry and raised consumer prices, amounting to an exploitative tax. And they drew upon political economists, such as Adam Smith, to argue for maximum freedom of international trade. Tyler and Barbour urged Congress not to force an undesirable structure upon this country, whose interests had been agricultural and commercial and ought to continue to be.[21]

Clay entered the discussion in support of Baldwin's report. He pressed for nurturing manufacturing at a time when American agricultural exports and foreign commerce generally had fallen off. No longer would Europe provide the kind of market prevailing in the prewar period, he warned. But to soften opposition, he sought to reconcile all elements of the economy, thereby achieving national self-sufficiency. To make his point, Clay drew a parallel comparing what he wished for the country and what an individual household could do. Consider the situation of Isaac Shelby, an early Kentucky settler and governor, he remarked. Shelby's family produced most of their own clothing and other articles instead of loitering at a crossroad tavern or otherwise wasting their money: a happy scene. One could have asked Clay, however, why the Shelbys did not patronize local merchants and manufacturers to promote a balanced economy. As for his opponents' dependence upon Smith's doctrine of noninterference by government, Clay convincingly showed that foreign nations did not practice what they preached. Britain, for instance, was heavy-handed in laying high, if not prohibitive, rates on imports, particularly by their corn laws as a barrier to American grain.[22]

The outcome in this session of 1820 was postponement of Baldwin's bill in the Senate by a margin of two votes after passage by the House. A sectional breakdown of the vote demonstrates the alignment of the country's interests and opinions: the mid-Atlantic states and the Northwest were solidly for protection, New England was divided between adherence to commerce and to manufacturing, and the South was decidedly opposed to Clay's prescription for prosperity.[23]

Although the Kentuckian did not occupy the Speaker's chair for the next three sessions (1821-23), the effort for tariff reform persisted. Clay himself reiterated his home-market argument at a dinner at Lexington upon leaving Congress. "The old system of applying so large a portion of our labor to production [of agricultural goods] for foreign markets, which have ceased to exist," would not do, he warned.[24]

One of the most active protectionist publicists was Mathew Carey. This Irish-American bookseller and pamphleteer of Philadelphia widely disseminated the principal arguments of the cause and later passed the torch to his son Henry, an influential economist for decades.[25] Equally active in spreading the word was the Baltimore editor Hezekiah Niles, whose *Weekly Register* (1811-36) carried commentaries on the issues and an endless stream of documents. It was highly useful not only to contemporary politicians but to future historians as well.[26] In the early twenties both Carey and Niles were emphasizing revision of the tariff even more than usual. Clay acknowledged their help and benefited from their popularization of a theory of national self-sufficiency.[27]

Now in the twenties a depression still beset the country and provided reasons for congressional relief to industry. Actually, there were both negative and positive symptoms. Prices remained low in comparison to the level of 1816, the financial disorder of the panic of 1819 resisted recovery, and businesses continued to close their doors. Yet if the census of 1820 and other surveys are even rough indicators, there was substantial growth. At Lexington, Clay could see expansion wherever he looked: textile mills, cotton-bagging factories, ropewalks, distilleries, iron and lead works, and many other enterprises. The annual value of Kentucky's production was at least $2 million. The figure for the leading state in the Union, Pennsylvania, was about $4.8 million. Representatives of new companies, as well as old ones that had experienced trouble, were sending lobbyists to Washington.[28] The large Lowell-Appleton cotton-textile combination, however, was comparatively disinterested in further protection because the tariff of 1816 seemed to be an effective barrier to cheap Indian imports, hitherto in competition with its specialty of coarse cottons.

What help could this movement expect from the Monroe administration? Secretary of Treasury William Crawford saw no constitutional or economic difficulty in raising rates either for added revenue or for added protection. He had not yet joined southern opposition to that policy.[29] And the president, like Madison before him, reminded Congress to consider the interest of manufacturing as an offset to foreign supply of American necessities. At last, in his communication of December 1823, Monroe referred to the fact that other nations had not opened their ports freely, and the United States must respond proportionately, but with the "greatest caution."[30]

After the tariff bill of 1820 failed to pass, further attempts stalled. The chairman of the Committee on Manufactures for part of this time was Philip Barbour, a states'-rights Virginian hostile to high tariffs. And of course any protective measure had poorer prospects when it lacked Clay's supervision and eloquent support. The outlook brightened when he returned to Washington in December 1823 and resumed the post of Speaker. Another favorable development was the reapportionment of congressional representation, with protectionist states, such as New York, Pennsylvania, and Ohio, gaining twenty-three seats.

Memorials, executive documents, and lobbyist activity again provided raw material for the House Committee on Manufactures in drawing up a tariff report. On January 9, 1824, Chairman John Tod of Pennsylvania presented it for consideration, though debate did not begin for another month. Then Tod described the recommendations in his bill. There were two categories of rates, he explained: (1) on imports not competing with domestic goods and therefore subject to imposts for revenue, and (2) on imports to be protected against foreign competition. Some rates would be ad valorem, more would be specific. Generally, he continued, the bill did not move in a new direction but merely extended present policy, adopted in 1816. The purpose of raising the level of protection would be to help American farmers and laborers and also to strengthen national economic independence. Levies on wool-

ens, wool, iron, cotton bagging, glass, and spirits were some
that fell into the second category. To calm his colleagues' worries, Tod cited protective precedents going back to Hamilton
and Jefferson. In any case, he said, such a measure would
raise essential revenue.[31]

Over the next two months the House gave much attention to the bill. Speeches were long-winded, probably soporific.
Nevertheless, they reflected basic economic concerns and con-
tours of political thinking in those days. In the absence of an
operative two-party system, the divisions of opinion had
become more sectional (South, Middle Atlantic, New England,
West) and economic (commerce, agriculture, and manufacturing). Clay and like-minded spokesmen for the manufacturing
interest now seemed to have the advantage.

For several weeks discussion of Tod's report consisted
mainly of reactions to particular rates, with voting on adjustments up or down. Then Barbour spoke strenuously against
the general principles of protectionism, spurring Clay to defend them.[32] His speech, extending over two days, would be
perhaps his best-known exposition of economic nationalism.[33]

He began, as he often did, by describing the poor condition of the country, which urgently required remedy. The depression persisted in every part of the economy, he declared:
decline of the carrying trade in foreign commerce, disordered
agricultural markets, bankruptcies in large numbers, unemployed labor. "What is the cause of this widespreading distress, of this deep depression, which we behold stamped on
the public countenance? We are the same people. We have the
same country. . . . The sun still casts its genial and vivifying
influence on the land." The cause, he felt, was the sharp contraction of postwar demand for American goods abroad, a situation that would not change. European restrictions of
American imports, especially the British corn laws, appeared
unyielding. Admittedly, the quantity of cotton exports had
risen rapidly, yet lower prices provided less income to
planters.[34]

Predictably, Clay's cure for the malady was development
of a home market for domestic products. "Let us counteract
the policy of foreigners, and withdraw the support we now
give to their industry, and stimulate that of our own country."

Legislation, as in the present bill, was therefore essential. It would establish "a genuine American System."[35] This term would become a staple in the political vocabulary of the antebellum era. Clay did not invent it, for Hamilton had used it more than a quarter century earlier. Later Jefferson did also. And in a different context, Clay himself had employed the expression in a congressional speech in 1820, urging recognition of Latin American independence and a common commercial interest with that part of the hemisphere.[36] But now it became synonymous with a protective tariff and later would extend to other policies. The American System rested on the idea of harmonizing all segments of the economy for their mutual benefit and of doing so by active support from an intervening national government.

In several respects, Clay thought, the United States could adopt the British model of industrialization, helped substantially by restrictions upon foreign trade except for an indispensable flow of American cotton to its thriving textile mills. The South, he believed, should not fear British retaliation on cotton if the proposed tariff bill passed, for that country would never overlook its own interest. Here he countered arguments widely advanced against the pending bill. The Kentuckian insisted he did not wholly admire British behavior, though he would borrow some of its developmental strategy.

Again the Speaker encountered antiprotectionist reliance upon Adam Smith's political economy. These opponents contended that this new science had demonstrated the undesirability of forcing enterprise into a pattern. It was much better to allow capital and labor to take an unhindered direction to a natural and ideal order. Clay responded that British regulations abounded. So this nation, Clay said, must not unilaterally implement Smith's dictum of governmental nonintervention.

Still another objection to protection, assuming importance for the first time, was constitutional. In the early nineteenth century customs receipts supplied most of the revenue needed by the treasury, and some antiprotectionists reasoned that tariffs could not constitutionally have any other purpose. Not so, Clay declared. Congress had the delegated powers to lay imposts on imports and to regulate interstate and foreign commerce. Absent any specific limitation of these powers, he said, they were plenary, thus including authority to nourish American industry. There were precedents going back to the first tariff law of 1789 with its preamble about protection of manufactures. And there had been an embargo and additional commercial regulations in the cause of neutral maritime rights before the late war, which the courts had upheld as constitutional.[37] Nevertheless, the time was approaching when the constitutionality of a protective tariff, as well as other controversial subjects of politics, would become the focus of inflamed disagreement.

Clay's argument drew upon practical illustration and generalization more than upon the abstract wisdom of political economy. So he dipped into history for proof. He referred to the record of several nations to show that some, Britain and France notably, prospered as a result of promoting industry while others, Spain for instance, did not. In addition to illustrating again the effectiveness of British policies, he went so far as to quote Napoleon's recollections of his French policy of economic development. This example must not have strengthened his case. On the other hand, his negative classification of Spanish torpidity seemed apt in view of the recent upheaval dismembering its empire in Latin America.[38]

Clay's speech of March 30-31 had followed several weeks of debate on the bill. Most of the general principles he had propounded were familiar themes: the home-market idea, the mutual advantages to all economic interests and geographical sections, the superior evidence of experience compared to theory. Others did emphasize more heavily the beneficial impact of industrialization both upon factory labor and upon agricultural labor, each complementing the other. Andrew Stewart and Silas Wood, as well as others from the Atlantic states, took this line of reasoning.[39]

On the other side, the recently elected congressman from Massachusetts, Daniel Webster, immediately launched a lengthy refutation of the Speaker's points, one after another. He saw no need for most of the proposed rates, because the country was not afflicted with all the economic ills Clay gloomily perceived. Though prices had declined and business had slowed, the New Englander saw widespread prosperity and happiness. All that was necessary was to allow free enterprise to work. Avoid putting the burden of a higher tariff on shipping, depend upon the freedom of an active foreign commerce, and do not interfere with productive individualism, the basis of a true American System. Unlike Clay, he believed Britain was indeed moving toward free trade, necessarily at a deliberate pace. Nevertheless, Webster was not doctrinaire, for he did favor moderate protection of woolen and cotton manufactures, while attacking increases on iron and hemp, a position balancing commercial and manufacturing interests in Massachusetts. It would not be long before he would tip the balance toward higher tariffs.

Webster reiterated what he had drafted in a vigorous memorial of Bostonians to Congress against the bill of 1820, so narrowly rejected. In fact, that document now attracted some attention, impossible four years earlier because it had arrived in Washington after congressional adjournment. It had been an even stronger statement than the present speech, for it not only protested on economic grounds but had doubted the constitutionality of such governmental intervention. How Webster would later prefer to forget that foray![40]

A good many other opponents expressed views on general principles similar to those of Webster. The chief difference within their ranks was sectional. Whereas he was a spokesman for commercial New England, southerners foresaw harmful effects upon agriculture. Britain would retaliate by cutting its demand for their exports, they predicted, and the domestic market would not compensate for the loss. Far better to supply raw materials to Europe and to purchase imported manufactures, a natural process. This was, of course, another endorsement of Smith's economics. Among those speaking for the planter interest were George McDuffie and James Hamilton, both of South Carolina, in addition to Barbour.[41] Though believing a protective tariff violated the Constitution, Clay's adversaries had not fully developed that argument. Near the close of House debate, the volatile John Randolph of Virginia launched a scorching attack on the tariff's threat to the South. His diatribe mixed hyperboles and Latin phrases with hints of strong remedies for an injustice. As it developed, this forensic battle was a preface to the alarming story of political sectionalism.[42]

Protracted debate moved back and forth between general principles and particular rate changes. On each provision, local interests strongly influenced positions the representatives took—Pennsylvanians on iron, Louisianans on sugar, Kentuckians on hemp, and so forth. This has been true, of course, throughout history. But principles and interests did interact at least in the rhetoric enveloping the House. Steadily, protectionists of the Atlantic and western states (Clay's forces) gained in their duel with their southern and New England adversaries.

One would have expected the subject of textiles, especially cottons, to be prominent, yet that was not the case. Relatively few words were spent as this schedule emerged nearly unchanged. Most cottons would remain at 25 percent, and minimum valuation would still screen out cheap material from India. Woolens would rise to $33\frac{1}{3}$ percent two years later; but a lower rate, 25 percent, was allowed on cheaper goods, a palliative to southerners supplying clothes to their slaves. Even so, the bill would do something for wool growers, who got 30 percent for their product, substantially weakening woolen protection because of costs to the mills. More would soon be heard about this matter.[43]

Somewhat more attention went to iron, increasingly central to industrialization. The chairman of the reporting Committee on Manufactures, John Tod of Pennsylvania, did not miss the opportunity to strengthen iron manufacturing in that state and received special help from his colleague James Buchanan, who brokered mutual assistance of iron and hemp contingents in Congress. Hammered bar, a basic American output, rose to ninety cents a hundredweight (112 pounds), twice the level adopted in 1816. Members from New England's maritime districts, such as Webster, strenuously complained about increased costs of this metal, which was essential to shipping.[44]

Early in debate on the bill, a lively discussion about raising the rate on spirits to 15 percent had begun. An East-West split on the issue appeared, with Clay and other westerners favoring it to benefit grain growers and whiskey distillers in opposition to easterners who feared that commerce in liquor imports from the West Indies would suffer. Opponents said that even the exising specific rate was twice the value of spirits. Despite this argument, Clay got the increase. He may have been helped a little by scattered feeling that a stiff duty might encourage temperance.[45] During discussion of the impost on molasses he urged further assistance to grain distillers. Emphasizing the sharp increase in sales of rum distilled from West Indies molasses, he carried an upward revision over mercantile protests.[46]

The most extended argument on a particular rate concerned cotton bagging, the hemp product of special importance to Clay. This fabric was in greater and greater demand as the output of cotton doubled every ten years up to the Civil War. As a hemp planter himself, the Kentuckian could speak confidently about the state of the industry; and his powerful leadership made a higher tariff on cotton bagging likely. At several junctures he took the floor to describe the difficulties requiring correction. Foreign competition from Scottish producers had hurt domestic marketing badly, in part because the American process of dew rotting had not yet been replaced by the superior method of water rotting. He thought the shift was quite practical—he had made progress at Ashland. He could not deny, however, that ever since he had been involved in congressional consideration of the problem fifteen years earlier, the American disadvantage had persisted. Actually, he took better ground when he pointed to continued hard times as a reason for relief. And of course he did not overlook the staple goals of national independence and security, derived from economic self-sufficiency.[47]

Speeches on cotton bagging came mainly from opponents of more protection, naturally from southerners who fought an added cost of shipping their vital cotton crop. James Hamilton and George McDuffie of South Carolina took the lead in attacking what they felt to be an unfair sectional imposition in behalf of the Kentucky hemp industry. In fact, declared Charles Mercer of Virginia, the expense amounted to a tax on cotton that they exported and therefore violated the constitutional clause (Article I, section 9) prohibiting export taxes.[48] Although an innovative theory, it was soon to be replaced by others more persuasive.

After the House focused on this issue for two weeks, it approved an increased rate by the margin of a few votes. Final congressional action later set the level at $3\frac{3}{4}$ cents per square yard, about double what it had been.[49]

The committee had also recommended increasing the impost on the raw material itself, hemp, a prime interest of the Speaker. Strong protest came from members watching out for the merchant marine because of resulting higher prices of cordage. In his set speech, Webster emphasized what he felt was a huge injustice in boosting the hemp duty 50 percent to two cents a pound. Again Clay prevailed, though the law, as enacted, cut the increase slightly to $1\frac{3}{4}$ cents.[50]

The House discussed and lightly amended the report from the Committee of the Whole over ten days until approval on April 16 in a close ballot, 107-102. A month later, after a few senate and conference-committee adjustments, the bill passed.[51] In the end, Clay could be very pleased with the outcome, a definite endorsement of the protective principle and of his proclaimed American System. He portrayed the measure as moderate, as a reconciliation of interests. Perhaps there was truth in that view, yet those who had lost out in this debate on economic policy did not concur.

Two sections of the nation showed substantial opposition. New England, divided between commercial and manufacturing opinion, voted against the bill, twenty-three to fifteen, despite a trend toward industrialization. The South was still less reconciled. The vote of southern representatives was seventy to six against the Kentuckian's bill.[52] Secretary of War Calhoun did not comment on the tariff publicly, probably because he was the prospective vice president and was seeking an alliance with one of the presidential hopefuls. Nevertheless, he had already perceived how unattractive Clay's economic nationalism was to the South, whose plantation-slave system seemed to gain little from it. So he privately supported and advised opponents of the American System, such as fellow Carolinians McDuffie and Hamilton, during congressional debate.[53]

Just how Clay's program would affect the current presidential election was unclear. Senator Andrew Jackson, who was making spectacular gains in the ongoing contest, had

voted for the bill on grounds of national economic independence and defense, not to mention expected voter approval in states like Pennsylvania. In a letter to a person there, published in April 1824, he applauded a "home market," created by employment of factory labor as consumers of agricultural goods. "It is therefore my opinion," he ventured, that a "judicious tariff is much wanted."[54] Another candidate, Secretary of State John Quincy Adams, was a well-known nationalist, undoubtedly favoring protectionism but cautious about expressing his views. Secretary of Treasury William Crawford, also an aspirant, had favored a higher tariff in his departmental capacity; yet he was seen to be the foremost heir of the Virginia school of states-rights politics. Clay summed up the electoral implications of the battle over the tariff when he wrote that though all candidates approved more protection, "the difference between them & me is, that I have ever been placed in situations in which I could not conceal my sentiments."[55] His characteristic optimism led him to select a positive position as the most promising route to popular approval.

3

Postwar
Issues

Other developmental policies besides the tariff attracted political attention during these postwar years. Congress passed measures on banking, internal improvements, and other subjects, reflecting an expansive, optimistic nationalism. Counterforces of states-rights sectionalism opposed them and indeed overtook the nationalist trend by 1825.

An important reason for the narrower outlook must have been the impact of a depression, first felt as a financial panic in 1819 and persisting for several years. The basic industry of the country, agriculture, had expanded rapidly after the war in both the North and the South; but European markets could not or would not absorb a desirable amount of American products. The problem of oversupply extended also to the domestic market for manufactures, largely due to a flood of European imports, now that tariff barriers were lower than during wartime. Businesses failed, disappointed in getting much relief from debt moratoria and bankruptcy laws. Western farmers who had too confidently bought large acreages at government land offices on lenient terms lost mortgaged property. Labor was hard pressed—many workers unemployed. An economic malaise lingered well into the twenties.[1]

Sober analysis of the causes of these difficulties laid a good deal of blame upon the financial system, especially the banks. Since 1811, after congressional failure to recharter the first Bank of the United States, both private and public sectors had to rely upon state-chartered corporations. Undeniably, these institutions had not performed well in a lightly regulated, disordered setting. The number of banks had soared in the five years before 1816 from 88 to 260, while their note circulation increased dramatically from about $23 million to $99 million. Conditions deteriorated so seriously after the British raid upon Washington in 1814 that bank offices across the country, except in conservative New England, stopped redemption of their paper in specie. Meanwhile at the capital, the Treasury had endless trouble in raising funds through loans and taxes to maintain the war effort. The patchwork of unstable, diverse state institutions hindered more than helped.[2] Well before the peace treaty, the Madison administration sought establishment of a new national bank. The problem was that it wanted one that would be a virtual arm of the treasury in marketing large amounts of government securities and in operating on a specie basis only as long as it suited the president. Such a plan encountered strong congressional opposition, and another bill for more independence from the government fell to Madison's veto in January 1815.[3]

So in December, after Clay returned from diplomatic negotiations in Europe and again became Speaker, the House resumed the effort for a bank. He asked Calhoun, as chairman of a special committee, to make another attempt. This time the administration accepted Calhoun's view that the institution ought to be more conservative and less subject to executive dominance. Accordingly, Secretary of Treasury Alexander Dallas proposed a bank with less capitalization ($35 million) and with five presidential appointees on the board of twenty-five directors, the same ratio of public and private elements as in subscriptions to shares of stock. And unlike the earlier plan, which made it easy to suspend specie redemption of bank notes, the present one emphasized a stricter basis of currency.

Calhoun guided this kind of bill to passage by mid-March 1816. In his speeches, he focused on counteracting the vast increase of state banks and their overissued, unredeemable notes. He said very little about the proposed structure of the institution and peremptorily dismissed all constitutional questions as now settled by long practice since 1791.[4]

Strange to say, the staunchest opponent was the Federalist Webster, whose party had been the original advocate of a national bank. Some historians have not understood his reasoning. Webster himself claimed Hamiltonian orthodoxy by insisting he did not oppose a national bank per se, certainly not constitutionally. But he did object to the government's mingling with and manipulating this private corporation by holding some of its stock and appointing some of its directors.[5]

These objections did not impress Clay. Stepping down from his chair, he painstakingly explained why he entirely favored the pending measure despite having opposed recharter of the first Bank of the United States in 1811 as a senator. Five years ago, he said, the Kentucky legislature had instructed him so to vote, whereas now, as a representative, his immediate constituents favored a new charter. Furthermore, he had felt the old bank had abused its power by collaboration with the Federalist party, but he was confident the new one would not mix in politics. How wrong he would prove to be!

To those colleagues uncertain constitutionally, he set forth a view more frank and convincing. Though he conceded that, as a young senator, he believed the bank recharter was unconstitutional (a pristine Jeffersonian position), experience had changed his mind. The question had been and presently was: is a bank necessary now to carry out the powers of Congress? He saw an urgent need, both for assisting the government's fiscal operations and for supplying the people a uniform national currency instead of the bloated, variable paper now circulating. Citing the necessary and proper clause of the Constitution, Article I, section 8, he concluded that what may not have been necessary in 1811 had become so in 1816. Then there was the provision requiring tax payments to be "uniform," which depended upon a uniform currency.[6] The House passed the bill, eighty to seventy-one, the Senate concurred with unimportant amendments, and Madison signed it in early April 1816.[7] Through the twenty years of its charter, the bank would often be at the center of political contention, and Clay would be its leading advocate.

After enactment of the law for the Bank of the United States (BUS), Calhoun sought resumption of specie payment both for the mass of state bank notes already in circulation and for future issues of the new institution. With Secretary Dallas's recommendation, he reported a bill restricting payments to the national government to specie or specie-paying notes by the end of the year. This could induce a general circulation in these media. Though Calhoun lost his bill by one vote, he collaborated with Webster to adopt a resolution to the same end, imposing redemption in specie by February 20, 1817.[8] Compliance by national and state banks was slow but somewhat effective.[9]

Organized for business by January 1817, the BUS had an unsatisfactory record for quite a while. Unfortunately, its first president was the unqualified William Jones, former member of Monroe's cabinet, who committed numerous mistakes and allowed numerous abuses. Stockholders got loans from the bank, secured by their shares of the bank's stock, and could use the loans to pay for that stock. Inexplicably, Clay saw no harm in that. The discount policy was far too loose, fueling still more widespread speculation. Western branch offices issued notes, to be redeemed at any other branch, drawing specie from the East. And the BUS neither adequately assisted nor controlled the state banks, which lacked sound capital and often failed to resume specie payment. These mistakes probably contributed to the onset of a nationwide depression in 1819.[10]

Clay seemed far too tolerant. His correspondence with Jones remained friendly and supportive, as one can see in a series of letters about his becoming a BUS director. Plainly interested in being selected, the Kentuckian saw opportunities to advance the interests of his region and party. While commenting on a possible appointment, he also freely offered advice on BUS policy. Perhaps because he said he could attend board meetings only occasionally whenever he happened to be in Philadelphia, he was not chosen. Later he did receive an invitation to serve but declined. Only then he did feel uneasy about the appearance of bias on legislative matters concerning the corporation if he were a director.[11]

His relations with the institution were very close anyway. As soon as Congress issued the charter, he pressed for establishment of branch offices in Kentucky. With his encouragement, a group of his friends in Lexington traveled east to persuade Jones their town ought to have a branch. They were successful, and a few months later Clay's intervention helped Louisville get one, too.[12] He frequently exerted influence upon appointment of directors at these places. Though usually satisfied with such selections, he once complained that most of his recommended list had been passed over, resulting in a board dominated by Federalists. Republicans should make up the majority, he thought, with a few Federalists added. The bank should not be "a party institution," as its predecessor had been, he warned.[13] It is difficult to understand how apportioning party distribution on the board to reflect the political character of the state, as he urged, would have kept the BUS out of politics.

As time passed, Clay's relation to the bank became even closer, due largely to the depression and its impact upon the financial system. In any case, William Jones was reaching the end of his mismanagement after some months of futilely trying to tighten loose policies. In March 1819 Langdon Cheves, the South Carolina congressman who had had a friendly association with the institution since it was established, took over. He intensified the curtailment of credit, which had already begun—and did so with determination. Branch offices, such as those at Lexington and Louisville, were prohibited from redeeming notes issued at other branches. Their discounting and exchange operations were severely contracted. Transactions with state banks were stiffened, especially with respect to their paper circulation. Secretary of Treasury Crawford encouraged Cheves to press ahead.[14]

Clay observed the effects with mixed feelings. Though always in favor of sound, conservative banking, he saw essential capital drying up, which, he feared, would have the opposite effect of what Cheves intended. There would be a tendency for local banks to issue still more paper worth much less than face value. And already he saw movements under way for relief legislation to help hard-pressed debtors by postponing judicial executions against property that secured loans. While applauding the main office's effort to root out excesses, he urged Cheves to instruct the branches to provide sufficient currency and credit to meet the emergency, to forestall what he believed to be an injurious attitude toward the West. A troubling indicator, he argued, was the steady flow of specie eastward.[15]

A significant expansion of credit did not occur until 1823, when the BUS presidency again changed hands. Nicholas Biddle, a scholarly aristocrat, began his long tenure in that position with modest financial experience, only as a director on the main board; but he displayed an amazing ability to operate what amounted to the nation's central bank. At once, he readjusted Cheves's approach to intricate credit and currency problems by a liberalized policy on note issue and exchange, producing badly needed capital for industry at this stage of recovery. Yet he was a cautious, sound-money person fundamentally. Clay and Biddle saw eye to eye on this and other things. The politician and the banker would maintain a satisfying collaboration for many years.[16]

Clay had another BUS connection, representing it as a lawyer. He had a particular reason for taking on this work: to pay off a heavy debt of about forty thousand dollars, much of it owed to the bank.[17] Retiring from Congress for a term and returning to an extensive legal practice, he became chief counsel for the corporation's litigation in Kentucky and Ohio during the early twenties. He had his hands full, for there were hundreds of cases, mostly debt collections in these depression days. Besides appearing in court himself in a large portion of them, he oversaw other "solicitors." His income from this business apparently amounted to what he needed: three thousand dollars a year from the bank as chief counsel; more for appearing in specific cases; and a sizable amount of real estate in Ohio and Kentucky in addition to the cash. Enough, at least, so that when he resigned to become secretary of state in 1825, he was pleased not only with a high rate of favorable judgments but with his compensation.[18]

The kind of business he conducted, however, was usually not pleasant. Typically, it consisted of getting a court's order against a debtor, forfeiting the property that had secured a defaulted debt. What an emotional wrench when a farmer lost everything, house and land. Often payment by the unlucky borrower was utterly impossible. Predictably, public opinion in both states tended to be negative toward lawyers and banks, despite Clay's intention to soften the effects whenever he could. No wonder the bank seemed a pitiless creditor.[19]

In Kentucky, hostility toward the institution led to legislation in January 1819 taxing each of the two branches sixty thousand dollars annually. Other states adopted the same tactic. In the best-known instance, a Maryland tax had come to the Supreme Court *(McCulloch* v. *Maryland),* where a decision was expected within weeks. Clay strongly disapproved of his own state's action for being rash and unconstitutional. As he had argued in the congressional debate on chartering the bank, he believed Congress had an undoubtable power to establish it; and now a state could not "break" it by such a destructive tax. He directed the bank's efforts to oppose the measure in both state and lower federal courts; and in one case he successfully argued that the United States Circuit Court could enjoin Kentucky not to collect the levy.[20] In the end, the state Court of Appeals, though unpersuaded by the *McCulloch* decision in Washington upholding the charter, chose not to insist upon collection.[21]

The two BUS offices had reluctantly carried out orders from Philadelphia to get redemption of state-bank notes; and as they did, specie moved to the East. Because of a shortage of capital and the advent of the depression, a demand for relief shook the legislature at Frankfort. The response was a flurry of state banking laws, beginning in 1818 and continuing to the midtwenties. The Kentucky Insurance Company, which had been the earliest financial institution in the state, closed its doors in 1818 after an embezzling executive officer had ruined it.[22] And the Bank of Kentucky, still in business after many years as a mixed public-private operation, seemed unable to supply the needs of the economy.[23] So the legislators responded to the cry for a freer system by incorporating forty-six private banks, alloting one to each local district. The life of these paper mills, known as the "forty thieves," was short. In 1820 the legislature replaced them with the Bank of the Commonwealth, entirely state owned and administered by state appointees. It had many branches and issued a great deal of non-specie-paying paper, just what advocates of relief wanted.[24]

Other legislation supplemented banking restructuring to help desperate debtors. A so-called replevin statute of 1820 allowed them a year's extension before they had to forfeit property as a security on defaulted debts. If a creditor did not agree to accept Bank of Kentucky non-specie-paying notes at the new date, another year's extension was granted. This centerpiece of economic policy precipitated a political upheaval. For several years relief and antirelief parties battled one another over issues related to it. Though winning elections for governor and legislators up to 1824, the relief party did not retain ascendancy very long. In fact, by that time the replevin laws had been repealed. Perhaps a more serious setback came from the courts. A county circuit judge, James Clark, declared the statutes invalid, a retroactive deprivation of property in conflict with the contract clauses of national and state constitutions. Not only did the legislature fail to remove the bothersome judge, but the state Court of Appeals upheld his decision, whereupon the lawmakers passed a measure abolishing this court and establishing one pledged to relief. For a while Kentucky politics revolved around "Old Court" and "New Court" parties. The relief party lost the election of 1824, and the Old Court refused to leave office. Eventually the New Court gave up.[25]

What ought Clay, the state's foremost politico, to do in this treacherous situation? His personal reaction was to deplore radical overhaul of state banking and of debtor-creditor relations. Long associated with the Bank of Kentucky, he wrote and spoke to its officials and stockholders in behalf of a sound-money policy, yet somewhat liberalized to provide sufficient capital, so scarce during the depression.[26] As a lawyer he argued cases on the antirelief side. Still, he avoided embarrassing involvement in the conflict as much as possible, because it might both undermine his home base and damage his position in national affairs.[27]

Probably the most sensitive aspect for him proved to be the strain upon his relations with Amos Kendall and Francis Blair. Years before, upon arrival in the West as a young man,

Kendall had been helped by the Clay family—for a period he had tutored the children. As editor of the newspaper *Argus of Western America* he had until recently supported Clay; but during the relief war, he favored the policies of easy money and of replevin for debtors. For the time being he was on the fence, a New Court leader but a friend of Clay. Soon he would be very disappointed when Clay, as the new secretary of state in 1825, did not find an appointment for him. He then would go over to the Jacksonian movement; and in the future, as a principal adviser of President Jackson, he would be a thorn in his former mentor's side.[28] Likewise, Frank Blair, another ardent follower of Clay, became a prominent relief man—the clerk of the New Court among other things.[29] He, too, joined the Jacksonian, anti-Clay ranks a little later. His subsequent editorship of the Washington *Globe,* the main Democratic organ, would be a political irritant, to say the least. Generally, New Court adherents in Kentucky moved toward the rising Jacksonian Democratic party. Ironically, Jackson himself disliked relief measures such as those in this state.[30]

In Ohio as BUS counsel, Clay continued to handle a great deal of business, most of it involving delinquent debts. Economic distress persisted well into the twenties and, as in Kentucky, fueled antagonism toward the bank, depicted as a relentless creditor responsible for much that had gone wrong. Clay did favor all possible leniency toward debtors, principally postponement of final hearings.[31] Nevertheless, he seldom lost cases altogether. In late 1822 he told BUS President Cheves at the main office that he had obtained 211 favorable judgments on debts at Cincinnati, while losing only three or four on account of procedural mistakes. In other correspondence up to 1825, he reported similar success.[32]

The legislature responded to vigorous complaints with an act to expel the two branches at Cincinnati and Chillicothe from the state. In February 1819, just before the Supreme Court invalidated a Maryland tax, Ohio imposed an annual levy of fifty thousand dollars on each branch. At the same time, Clay also faced the nearly identical Kentucky tax. Though unconvinced by the *McCulloch* decision, the state Court of Appeals there decided not to resist the ruling for the bank. Ohio proved to be more determined. A protracted constitutional crisis brought angry expositions of state sovereignty, strange instances of officials being put in jail, and complex legal proceedings in the federal courts.

To carry out the state law, Auditor Ralph Osborn ordered forcible collection of the tax, if necessary. So in September 1819 his officers seized one hundred thousand dollars from the BUS branch in Chillicothe and headed for Columbus with it in a wagon.[33] Then upon the bank's petition, the federal Circuit Court issued an injunction against this procedure. The state refused to comply and retained the money. Osborn's two agents who had hauled off the funds spent three months in jail before being released by a local judge. At this point, March 1820, President Cheves asked Clay to take the question of the tax's validity into the federal courts. Thenceforward, he gave close attention to this litigation, stretching over four years. He filed civil and criminal suits in Ohio and defended the bank on Osborn's appeal to the Supreme Court at Washington.[34] Meanwhile he negotiated with the state's counsel, Charles Hammond, about compromises, all of whose proposals he finally rejected because the state wished to shape the settlement so as to get the bank's recognition of a tax power in exchange for return of the money that had been seized.[35]

Osborn's appeal to the Supreme Court required two hearings during the 1824 term. Clay felt confident that Chief Justice Marshall and his Court would reject Ohio's position that *McCulloch* v. *Maryland* was erroneous, an unconstitutional deprivation of the state's sovereignty. The crucial question concerned federal jurisdiction in cases such as this, brought by the bank.[36] At the second hearing in 1824 Webster and John Sergeant joined Clay in dealing with this point. Since their printed brief, the only known source indicating what the lawyers said, is a joint statement, Clay's particular contribution is unclear. Yet it must have been substantial, because of his long experience with the controversy.

Marshall's opinion for the Court accepted the BUS argument that it had standing as a party in federal courts and that an injunction against Osborn was therefore an available remedy. Clay could remember a case he had won in the federal Circuit Court in Kentucky on this very issue. He and his colleagues relied upon provisions in the BUS charter of 1816 (a United States law) for the institution's access to federal courts. They also prevailed, without much emphasis, against Osborn's claim that the state of Ohio, not he personally, was the actual defendant and therefore protected by the Eleventh Amendment, which forbids suits against states without their consent. Marshall ruled, superficially to be sure, that it was sufficient that the certified record of the case listed Osborn and not Ohio as the defendant.[37]

This case provides an interesting view of Clay the lawyer-politician, using his superior professional ability to forward the type of economy he nourished as a politician. In both legal and political areas, he wished to strengthen property rights beyond mere protection of vested interests, to stimulate the country's growth and enhance its welfare. In this instance the impact amounted to more than a reaffirmation of the bank's legitimacy, because opening the federal courts to that institution provided it with a favorable, much used forum in its interstate operations. The decision thereby reflected a current trend in modernizing the legal status of all corporations.

Still, Clay's close connection with the bank appeared to his critics to be cold-hearted service in behalf of wealth and privilege during a severe depression. Would his diligent advocacy in bank suits against hard-pressed debtors hurt his political prospects? The presidential election would follow in a few months. Though not general or definitive, a study of legal and voting records for 1824 in Ohio finds that districts where Clay filed many cases against debtors nevertheless supported him strongly for the presidency.[38]

As a lawyer, Clay also dealt with a difficult political and economic issue involving land titles. In 1789, when Virginia consented to Kentucky's separation, it stipulated that its previous land grants there be honored. Although this proviso seemed reasonable, it turned out to be wholly impractical. The process of distributing land had been very loose, in fact chaotic. Since the transmontane region had not been systematically surveyed, Virginia had no dependable idea of what it was doing; and parcel piled upon parcel, extending in unverifiable directions. Gaining statehood in 1792, Kentucky also granted large amounts, much of it the same as the Old Dominion tracts. The Kentuckians who occupied these areas by the 1820s were either squatters with no titles of ownership or persons with dubious titles, now challenged by Virginia claimants.

These circumstances led to the important case of *Green* v. *Biddle,* heard by the federal Supreme Court in 1821 and decided two years later. John Green had brought an action claiming an old land grant by Virginia as superior to Richard Biddle's occupancy of the property in Kentucky. The suit may have been fictitious, fabricated to get a large question of policy before the Court. At least there seemed to be no actual adversarial relationship of Green and Biddle. But the underlying question was real enough. It hinged upon Kentucky laws conferring substantial rights upon occupants threatened by such claimants—in this instance, the right to deduct sums spent on improving the tract and an immunity against payment of past rent to claimants.[39]

Proceedings in Court concerning this policy assumed an unusual character. Although attorneys appeared for Green, no counsel made an argument for the Kentuckian Biddle to defend the land-occupancy legislation. Justice Joseph Story delivered what he called a unanimous opinion against the validity of the statutes, although one member of the Court of seven was absent and others, including Chief Justice Marshall, probably abstained. A week later Clay went down to the judicial chamber in the Capitol basement in an attempt to turn the decision around. As an amicus curiae, he requested a rehearing to allow an argument by counsel for Kentucky's side because there had been none and because valuable interests of a great many persons were at stake. It was so ordered for the next term.[40]

Just before reargument Clay and George Bibb went to Richmond to address the Virginia legislature with an appeal to authorize a commission of the two states to settle the dispute, as set forth in the original compact of 1789.[41] A few days later they also put their case before the Supreme Court. Clay argued persuasively, centering on the Virginia-Kentucky compact. He pointed out that it had never received the assent of Congress, as the Constitution required of all interstate agreements. Furthermore, Virginia had so far refused to establish a commission, as provided. He contended that the compact, indispensable to the Old Dominion's position and to Story's opinion, was inoperative by its own language. At any rate, he attacked the document because it would diminish the essential sovereignty of Kentucky, which must be free of endless outside interference. Such states' rights reasoning, even by a nationalist, could reach receptive ears. The time for adjournment had arrived, however, and the Court postponed its decision until 1823.[42] Meanwhile Clay represented Kentucky in another effort to get Virginia's consent to a commission. He failed, much to his disgust, when a proposal to do so lacked one vote in that state's Senate.[43]

The one remaining hope for success collapsed when the Supreme Court refused to change its decision of 1821. Justice Bushrod Washington's opinion defined the states' compact as a contract, whose obligation Kentucky had impaired, the first time the Court applied the contract clause of the Constitution to an agreement between two states. The opinion did not accept Clay's contentions that Congress had not approved the compact or that a two-state commission instead of the judiciary should settle disputes on land grants.[44]

This outcome inflamed Kentucky. The decision was three to one for Virginia, since Justice William Johnson would have denied jurisdiction. With two of the seven members absent and the Chief Justice abstaining, less than a majority of the Court had weakened a fundamental right, Kentuckians complained.[45] Nonetheless, the state consistently did not comply with the decision. Then in another case the Court upheld a law limiting claims against occupants to a period of seven years, in effect neutralizing *Green* v. *Biddle*.[46] As for Clay, politics had demanded his responsiveness to opinion at home, where he had several problems: the relief contest, a tangle of banking, and the approaching presidential election. If it had not been for them, he might have opposed widespread, extralegal occupancy of lands by squatters. In fact it would not be long before he would take a strong stand in Congress against concessions of preemption to squatters on the public domain.

Among other economic policies, the development of transportation (internal improvements) remained a fundamental condition for growth. The War of 1812 had diverted national attention and resources from earlier modest beginnings; but as soon as peace arrived, a renewed effort got under way. An industrializing Northeast, an expanding cotton plantation system of the South, and an accelerated migration into the transmontane West required better ways of moving people and products. Furthermore, the handicap of primitive means of transporting troops and supplies during the war showed the need to strengthen this aspect of national defense. Petitions flowed into Washington to revive the spirit of Gallatin's prewar plan. Clay insisted that the country must have "a chain of turnpike roads and canals from Passamaquoddy to New Orleans, and other similar roads intersecting the mountains, to facilitate intercourse between all parts of the country, and to bind and connect us together." President Madison in his annual messages of 1815 and 1816 recommended congressional action, including, if necessary, a constitutional amendment. Since he approved a national-bank charter and a protective tariff, he seemed to have deserted strict constructionism.[47]

Calhoun set to work on the subject by moving for a House committee report; and a week later, as chairman of that committee, he proposed a plan. It called for creation of an internal improvements fund, composed of the bonus of $1.5 million received for chartering the bank and of projected dividends on government stock in that institution. In guiding his bill to passage, the South Carolinian was the complete nationalist. His speech emphasized its benefits to the economy, to military needs, and to governmental operations such as the postal service and fiscal functions. Do not worry about the constitutionality of federal internal improvements, he said, for at present he merely asked for a fund to be set aside. Nevertheless, he left no doubt that he thought a program would be valid. In words he would later prefer to forget, he told his colleagues (and Madison too) that the Constitution was "not intended as a thesis for the logician to exercise his ingenuity on. It ought to be construed with plain good sense."[48]

Clay was perfectly satisfied. Joining the discussion, he also downplayed specific applications of the fund. Let that be decided later.[49] He resisted amendments for distributing money to states according to their population and permitting them to share with Congress decisions on the projects. But he and Calhoun soon found they had to accept these amendments. Even so, the margin of House passage was thin, eighty-six to eighty-four.

The bill went to Madison on March 1, 1817, only three days before congressional adjournment. Yet the president had foreseen what happened, had made up his mind, and undoubtedly had drafted his decision, which was a veto. Expressing regret that he could not sign a desirable measure, he explained why constitutional clauses on commerce and general welfare did not authorize exercising such a broad power as now proposed.[50] Clay urged Madison to leave the decision to President-elect Monroe after inauguration—a strategy itself very questionable constitutionally. Obtaining no last-minute help, the Speaker could only wait until Monroe revealed his thinking at the next session.[51]

From the first day of his presidency, Monroe showed his reservations about immediate adoption of a program. In his inaugural on March 4, 1817, he did comment favorably on legislative action, though "proceeding always with a constitutional sanction."[52] Then in his first message to Congress in December, he was quite plain: only a constitutional amendment could clarify the long-standing disagreement about such a power. He urged that be done.[53]

Already irritated by the new administration, Clay was in no mood to follow this advice. He had ruffled feelings from the president's selection of John Quincy Adams as secretary of state, a post he reckoned his due. And now it was unbearable for Monroe to tell a coordinate branch of the government he disapproved a law not yet enacted. Was it possible that Clay translated his personal unhappiness into the area of policy? No doubt there was a degree of truth in such a suspicion. But the Kentuckian would have strongly advocated internal improvements in any event, for he had very settled views on that matter.

As Speaker, he appointed a committee, chaired by Henry St. George Tucker, to consider Monroe's recommendation of a constitutional amendment. Aligned with Clay, Tucker thought the House must be free of presidential intervention. Besides, he believed Congress had all the power it needed concerning roads and canals. His committee report, mainly a restatement of Gallatin's plan a decade ago, described a long list of potential projects and estimated their cost.[54]

Debate in the House centered on the constitutional aspect more than on an economic one. Proponents of a national program, Tucker, William Lowndes of the Ways and Means Committee, Charles Mercer, and Clay himself based congressional authority upon clauses of the Constitution empowering legislation to establish post roads, to provide for the common defense, and to regulate commerce among the states. To "establish," they reasoned, comprehended building new roads as well as delivering mail on those already built. Similarly, construction of roads and canals for military purposes was a means to accomplish the goal of national defense. And facilities for transporting goods, they contended, were closely related to interstate commerce. In short, it was a familiar conflict of broad and narrow interpretations, with Clay facing strong resistance, especially from Philip Barbour and Hugh Nelson, who were alarmed by a specter of centralization.[55]

Whatever the merits of his argument, Clay was willing to soothe opponents by requiring a state's consent for internal improvements within its boundaries—not that it was really necessary constitutionally, he explained. And to recruit more support, he agreed to put the bare constitutional questions to a vote before proceeding to specific projects.

On the basic power to appropriate money, Clay's cohorts won, ninety to seventy-five. But on federal powers actually to construct postal and military roads and canals and to improve interstate commerce, they lost by two votes. Since a number of persons had urged a provision for state consent, which the House decided to delete, it appears that those resolutions would have passed if nationalists had made that concession.[56]

In the next few years after this debate of 1818, other problems diverted attention from internal improvements: the protracted controversy about statehood for Missouri, relations with Spain concerning Florida and Latin America, and the impact of a depression. Nevertheless, Clay lost none of his interest in launching an extensive program. If for no other reason, he wished to strike back at Monroe, who appeared to be the main obstacle to movement on the issue. Not only had the president influenced recent House voting against constitutional power, he seemed to be altogether inconsistent by giving executive orders to build military roads. Why could he do this while Congress could not? Clay demanded to know how much had been spent currently on a military road from Tennessee toward Louisiana. Upon learning that the value of soldiers' labor on it was ten thousand dollars, he put through an authorization for that amount to establish the principle of legislative control. Monroe seemed unimpressed.[57]

Collaboration with at least one executive office was more positive. In compliance with a House request for information on desirable internal improvements, Secretary of War Calhoun reported in January 1819 on the importance of good facilities to move troops and materiel. The breadth of the country's interior and its long coastline required a network of transportation, he concluded. Portending what would happen, Calhoun recommended assignment of Army engineers and other military personnel to participate in these programs. But politician that he was, the secretary carefully avoided upsetting the president and did not discuss constitutional aspects of internal improvements.[58]

The most important federal internal improvement in this period, the National Road, gradually extended westward from Maryland toward the Mississippi Valley. It had originated in the law of 1802 enabling Ohio's admission to the Union and pledging 5 percent of proceeds from public-land sales in the new state for constructing the road—2 percent for the part leading to Ohio and 3 percent for the part within it. Later Congress made the same provisions for Indiana, Illinois, and Missouri. In addition to the fund from land sales, frequent congressional appropriations financed the ongoing work. By the time of the bonus-bill debate, 1817-18, construction had connected Cumberland, Maryland, and Wheeling, Virginia, on the upper Ohio River. All along, Clay had been the project's fully committed friend in Congress and had had much to do with selecting the route, particularly the site of Wheeling. His enthusiasm for expediting construction probably owed as much to his personal satisfaction in traveling between Kentucky and Washington on the road and the river as to his general commitment to developing the country's transportation. Clay spoke eloquently about the enormous savings in time and cost of travel the highway contributed, not merely to the deserving West but to the entire nation.[59]

Despite a narrow constitutional view of federal involvement in internal improvements, Monroe had no reservations about signing all appropriation bills for them. His record coincided with House votes in 1818, affirming full legislative power to provide funds but not to construct facilities. The crucial test of his ideas came in May 1822, when he received a bill to set up tollgates to pay for maintenance of the National Road. Ever since becoming president, Monroe had kept in his possession a long paper he had written on the question, and now he enclosed it with his message vetoing the bill. He defined the power to appropriate funds as virtually unlimited, but he categorically rejected any additional power to administer a road, including plans, acquisition of land by eminent domain, enforcement of a criminal code, and in this instance maintenance supported by tolls. These were functions, he said, belonging to the states. His reasoning ranged across constitutional history from colonial days to the present, as he examined various parts of the Constitution, notably postal, military, commercial, and financial clauses.[60] Monroe's persistent call for a constitutional amendment is strange in light of his fear of broad federal power. An amendment would merely countenance the danger.

Clay was not currently serving in Congress, though he could see that his presence would neither have prevented Monroe's veto nor have helped to override it. Furthermore, closely divided opinion on the subject forbade amending the Constitution. National internal improvements might have to depend only on federal grants and some indirect approach in collaboration with states or private enterprise, a strategy to which Monroe would gladly assent, as he demonstrated in legislation he signed in later sessions. Lacking a constitutional amendment, the nation would have to accept these limitations for much of the next century.[61]

As for the future of the National Road, construction continued, but at an uneven pace.[62] There were large gaps in the road west of Columbus and a primitive western part that stopped at Vandalia, the Illinois capital, instead of its projected terminal in Missouri. By 1842 Congress, having appropriated a total of $5 million, turned responsibility for it over to the states through which it passed.[63]

When Clay returned to Congress for the session of 1823-24, he had another opportunity to challenge the strict-constructionist position of the administration on internal improvements. He could not accept Monroe's tollgate veto during his absence as a conclusive definition of national power. The president himself helped set the stage for another congressional discussion when he recommended enactment of a measure to use Army engineers to survey potential routes for roads and canals. At the outset, Clay insisted that there would be no justification for governmental surveying if construction of future projects were not within governmental power. It was necessary, he said, to reexamine basic principles. So he and other representatives ran through the familiar arguments on whether Congress could go beyond appropriating funds to legislate upon construction and administration. The Speaker again expounded a broad doctrine resting on the postal, military, and commercial clauses of the Constitution, while Barbour, Randolph, and other states' righters reiterated contrary views. A bill did pass in April 1824 with a comfortable margin; yet it left the constitutional question close to where it had been, which meant Clay's valiant effort fell short.[64] In the future, Army engineers surveyed a great many areas for developing land and water transportation, but actual construction fell to states or private companies. Still, these surveys became a valuable public subsidy, substantially softening the severity of the presidential vetoes of 1817 and 1822.[65]

Within the limits of Monroe's formula of federal aid without involvement in actual construction, many projects received help in the twenties. An important area was waterways: clearing river channels for navigation, subscription to stock of canal companies (the Chesapeake-Ohio and the Chesapeake-Delaware), and land grants for canal routes (the Wabash-Erie and the Illinois-Michigan).[66] Clay was, of course, supportive, particularly for western undertakings. Like other politicians, his nationalist outlook did respond also to sectionalism. He often emphasized the justice of more liberality toward the West to counteract what he saw as a bias toward the East.[67]

Still another way to develop transportation involved distribution of proceeds from public-land sales for this purpose to the states. The idea was not new, for President Jefferson and Secretary Gallatin had referred to that possibility. And the Ohio enabling act of 1802 had pledged 5 percent of land proceeds in the new state for a national road. The same provision attached also to other western states upon admission. Then too, the Land Ordinance of 1785 had set aside a section in each township to establish schools. As an extension of these precedents, Maryland started a movement in 1821 for distribution of land proceeds to all states, not only to the West. The proposal got some positive reactions from other states and in Congress. From 1824 onward there were proposals for distribution, now linked to internal improvements. It offered an alternative to direct federal involvement, and Clay would tirelessly labor for it the rest of his career.[68] Concurrently, Thomas Hart Benton had shaped a competing formula, called graduation, which would sharply reduce land prices step by step to a free homestead level; but it had no internal improvements dimension.[69] Neither plan gained congressional approval for the time being.

Looking toward the election of 1824, Clay believed the fulfillment of his aspirations for the presidency could depend upon his congressional record, especially upon the issues of the tariff and internal improvements. On that basis he perceived his chances to be very good. As he returned to the House, resumed the speakership, and dominated the agenda, his position seemed strong. He had put forward an American System for economic growth by protecting domestic industry and by uniting the country with an extensive network of transportation. But he faced formidable opposition of several candidates at this moment when the old two-party system had faded. He had to admit that Secretary of State Adams also had a strong commitment to federal internal improvements. Though seen as a strict constructionist of the Virginia school, Secretary of Treasury Crawford had favored the survey bill and other national measures. Secretary of War

Calhoun promoted the same internal improvements plans as he had. Senator Jackson, the rising military hero, defied easy classification; yet he had voted for tariff and internal improvements bills. So at the end of the session in mid-1824, it was uncertain what the impact of Clay's advocacy of economic nationalism would have on this unusual election.[70]

4

Secretary
of State

The controversial election of 1824 did not meaningfully register popular will about economic issues, whose resolution Clay had thought would be so decisive. The collapse of the two-party system had led to sectional and factional support for several candidates and blurred, even more than usual, their positions on future policy. Then, with no candidate achieving a majority vote in the Electoral College, the decision went to the House. Here maneuvering to align a majority of state delegations pushed principles still further into the background. Clay himself missed obtaining enough electoral votes to be one of three (Jackson, Adams, and Crawford), upon whom the House would ballot. With less popular and electoral votes than Jackson, the Adams forces, headed by Clay and Webster, managed to recruit votes of thirteen out of twenty-four states, enough for victory. Few, if any, knowledgeable observers could say that Adams won the presidency because of his muted economic nationalism in a contest with the vague democratic appeals of Jacksonians.

Clay's contribution to Adams's election, followed by appointment as secretary of state, clouded the next four-year term, allowing a developing Jacksonian bloc in Congress to defeat administration measures. Clay would spend time repelling charges of a corrupt bargain when he preferred to attend to diplomatic business.[1] He felt the more frustrated because he and the president shared views on the tariff and internal improvements at home and on all matters of foreign affairs. Their personal relations, often cool and adversarial in the past, now became compatible. Though a seasoned diplomat and Monroe's secretary of state for nearly eight years, Adams gave Clay ample room to shape policy and manage his department, while collaborating with him constructively.[2]

Upon assuming office in March 1825, the new secretary understood that Latin America would be an area of major interest. It had been so ever since the Spanish colonies in Central and South America had fought a long war for independence. Early on, Clay had taken the lead in Congress to prod President Monroe and his secretary of state Adams into official recognition of the several Latin American republics. In the House during sessions of 1818 and afterward, he spoke warmly for that policy, which Monroe and Adams viewed as premature. Perhaps Spanish recovery of the vast area had become impossible; yet at this juncture Adams was negotiating a treaty to purchase Spanish Florida and did not want to antagonize Spain by recognizing independence of the new nations. Such caution did not appeal to Clay.

He had launched a spirited argument for bolder action. His resolution would appropriate funds for a minister to Buenos Aires, capital of the United Provinces of Rio de la Plata—if the president found it expedient, he added. These neighbors to the south, he declared, had made good their bid for freedom and promised to establish republican institutions similar to those of this country. They should have friendly encouragement from the United States. He emphasized these political dimensions but did refer to an economic reason for support. Valuable commercial avenues to and from Latin America would open, he predicted. Already exports flowed northward: precious metals, coffee, cocoa, sugar, and other tropical products. In return, this nation could market agricultural goods and manufactures there. And he predicted a strong stimulus to the American carrying trade, not the economic sector Clay would ordinarily underscore. At the moment, the

Kentuckian could not prevail against a determined opposition by the executive and its congressional followers. His resolution failed in a House vote of 115-45. He was so upset by this decisive vote that he did not leave the Speaker's chair for debate again the rest of the session.[3]

This was merely the opening phase of a sustained campaign. Clay regularly repeated his effort for recognizing the Latin American governments. Two years afterward, in 1820, he advanced the theme of two spheres, the Old and New Worlds, America and Europe. If the United States extended a helping hand to its fellow republics, the contrast would be clear, both politically and economically. As for commercial connections, "Let us become real and true Americans," he urged, "and place ourselves at the head of the American system." The call foreshadowed his use of the term in the later appeal for an economy at home balancing manufacturing, agriculture, and commerce. And the concept of two spheres, old and new, would soon find expression in the Monroe Doctrine of 1823, warning the Holy Alliance not to intervene in Latin America. Whether a Pan-American political or economic system would develop was unclear for some time. Nevertheless, Clay did make a point about commercial possibilities; and as secretary of state he would soon have an opportunity to exploit them.[4] At least in 1821, his repeated resolution supporting possible presidential recognition of independence passed the House, eighty-seven to sixty-eight.[5] This pronouncement of congressional sentiment not surprisingly coincided with the administration's decision that at last the time had come to commence diplomatic relations with these new governments. It did so over the next several years. Such was the situation when Clay became secretary in March 1825.

He let it be known promptly that the United States viewed Latin American independence as an accomplished fact. In his instructions to American ministers abroad, he emphasized the necessity for Spain to abandon a forlorn hope of recapturing its American empire. Better for that country to relax its old trade restrictions affecting America, he said, and stimulate general prosperity.[6]

Besides negotiations on commercial and political matters with individual nations on both sides of the Atlantic, Clay saw an opportunity to accomplish something on a collective basis. An invitation arrived from Colombia to participate in an inter-American congress at Panama for discussing common hemispheric problems. Adams agreed to request a congressional appropriation for sending delegates after Clay overcame the president's wariness of political, perhaps even military commitments. Unfortunately, the mission to Panama got entangled with politics at home. For months Jacksonian forces at the Capitol blocked approval of Adams's recommendation on partisan rather than diplomatic grounds. After much delay, one of the two American ministers arrived, too late for any effect.[7]

Clay's instructions for the Pan-American mission, however, demonstrated what he sought to accomplish in future hemispheric relations. Like the president, he disapproved any military involvement or any centralized governmental authority at the expense of American neutrality and national sovereignty. Instead, he urged the ministers to negotiate commercial treaties with individual nations at the congress in the absence of general agreement. In bilateral treaties the secretary wanted not only reciprocity of regulations by the signatory nations but also equal commercial concessions to others. Use the recent pact with Central America as a model, he directed.[8]

His diplomatic effort to promote Latin American commerce had been under way well before plans for the Panama Congress. And this also was not a new departure, for in the preceding administration Adams as secretary had pursued the same end with the same strategy if not with the same zeal. A treaty of 1824 with Colombia had opened trade on liberal terms, known as "the most favored nation," allowing the United States the same privileges for shipping and imports given to any other nation.[9] Now in 1825 under Clay's supervision, a treaty with Central America went further by establishing reciprocity, a preferable system that eliminated duties on United States goods and ships not levied on goods and ships of that federation itself.[10] The United States minister to Brazil negotiated a similar agreement except for special concessions to the former parent, Portugal.[11] An effort in Mexico by Joel Poinsett proved to be difficult because of that country's wish to grant more generous terms of trade to other Latin American nations. Here, as elsewhere, Clay pointed out the friendly help of the United States in warning off European intervention during the wars of independence. That lecture may have helped to induce a Mexican compromise. Nevertheless, ratification of the treaty came so late that it passed the deadline for taking effect.[12]

Just how much the secretary's policy affected commerce at the time is difficult to assess. For one thing, despite sustained attempts, he did not get agreements with other republics, such as Peru and the United Provinces of Rio de la Plata.[13] And continued turmoil broke up some states, such as Central America and Colombia, probably disarranging patterns of business. The best evidence shows no surge upward of United States-Latin American imports and exports through the 1820s. Annual totals were fairly stable. Yet they indicate a very substantial commerce, nearly a third of the volume of American trade with all of Europe. Clay's economic diplomacy seems justified, if for no other reason than to have prevented even more British dominance than existed.[14]

Of course, Clay would not neglect commercial relations with Europe. Here too, he could build upon policy already in place. Adams as secretary had negotiated several treaties with most-favored-nation clauses. Congress had enacted laws in 1815 and 1824 allowing reciprocal concessions in duties on tonnage and goods to any country abandoning discrimination that favored its own trade. Generally, reciprocity applied to direct commerce involving shipment of goods from one signatory to the other, not indirect routes or goods of a third nation. But Clay and Adams sought to broaden that rule to include indirect commerce, which a law of 1828 did cover. Like his predecessor, the secretary pursued a liberal policy by diplomacy backed up by congressional statutes. By 1830, the United States had trade pacts with much of northern Europe.[15]

Commerce with Britain continued to be decidedly the most important, in both exports and imports. On this subject Clay had personal experience, going back to his participation in producing the commercial accord of 1815. It had provided reciprocal privileges of nondiscriminating duties on ships and goods of the two signatories in direct trade. Renewed in 1818

and again in 1827 when Clay was in the cabinet, the treaty
left much to be done. The level of many British import duties
was very high—some prohibitive. But an encouraging situation had now developed. The president of the Board of Trade,
William Huskisson, proposed in Parliament a so-called free-
trade budget, including bold reductions of duties on imports:
from as high as 75 down to 10 or 15 percent on some commodities. He succeeded in passing some revisions. But duties
on agricultural goods, particularly in the corn laws, remained
high despite Huskisson's attempts. Though appearing to be a
free-trader, he would adjust his reformist convictions to retain
what he classified as moderate customs for even-handed
trade and for revenue. Just what he himself favored, Clay remarked.[16]

Another loose end in the agreement of 1815 created a
special problem, trade with the British West Indies colonies.
Clay and his colleagues had not been able to pierce the old
mercantilistic system to allow American ships access to these
islands. Since the Revolution, the United States had been an
outsider, though its exports (flour, lumber, livestock) moved
there and its imports (sugar, tropical products) were received
from there in large quantities by indirect routes, by British
carriers, and by evasion.

Dissatisfaction with the continued prohibition of American ships led Congress to consider measures that might break
down the barriers. In the House during the sessions of 1818
and 1820, bills did pass to shut off British vessels engaged in
this traffic between the United States and the West Indies
colonies either directly or indirectly. During debate Clay expressed his disappointment not to have fully opened commerce with the islands in the convention of 1815 and strongly
supported retaliation to press for correcting an injustice.[17]
Still more legislation followed. Britain seemed to give way in
a parliamentary statute of 1822, permitting American ships to
land and load goods in West Indies ports, providing the
United States abolished all discriminating rates on tonnage
and cargoes of British ships. Though proclaiming the commerce open the following year, President Monroe did not re-
scind the discriminating duties. And Congress stipulated that

these duties would stand until England eliminated an unfair, centuries-old system of imperial preference for its intercolonial trade. At this the British balked.[18]

So when Clay took over the State Department in March 1825, promising advances toward liberalization had stalled. A flurry of legislation by both sides had not settled the dispute; obviously they would have to rely upon diplomacy.

The secretary did not give the West Indies question high priority. Richard Rush, the outgoing minister to London, continued unproductive conversations with the Foreign Office, and his successor, Rufus King, spent another year in the same groove without fresh instructions. How far Clay could depart from past positions may have been a worry, especially since President Adams had structured them during the Monroe administration. In any case, Clay displayed an uncharacteristic hesitancy, which would turn out to be costly. Through the summer of 1825, he sent out queries on policy to several persons knowledgeable about maritime commerce. The answers inclined toward abandoning discriminatory duties and the American proviso on imperial preference. That is how Clay himself felt. At last the secretary concluded that the matter of imperial preference must be left to the empire itself, for somewhat like members of the American union, the colonies were internal parts of a unit.[19] Furthermore, he certainly could see after three years of legislation and diplomacy that England was not going to give in. Even the free-trader Huskisson would not touch either discriminating duties or imperial preference.[20]

Clay's instructions of June 19, 1826, to a new minister to London, Albert Gallatin, reflected this view, no longer resisted by the president. The document authorized the minister to recede from opposing imperial preference and merely obtain reciprocal elimination of discriminating duties.[21] That might have worked three years before, but now a different situation forbade success. Britain had increased the price of agreement in a statute of 1825 requiring the United States also to grant most-favored-nation status in this commerce, with unclear and possibly destabilizing impact upon other trade relations of the United States. And Foreign Secretary George Canning, sharing views of Huskisson and others, no longer had any interest in granting concessions or even in serious talk about concessions. In addition to differences of opinion, hostility toward Adams appears to have been a deterrent. Possibly rivalry of the two countries in Latin American affairs, such as on the Panama Congress, had an effect as well.[22]

When Gallatin arrived in England, he discovered to his dismay that an order in council had declared a prohibition of all American trade with the islands, effective the following January (1827). That occurred, and in March Adams proclaimed a similar interdiction of British intercourse. Over his year's stay in Britain, Gallatin received frequent instructions from the secretary on withdrawing or modifying previous demands and urging renewed negotiations. Canning became prime minister but soon died. The two sides had reached an impasse, and a completely frustrated Gallatin returned home in October.[23]

Notwithstanding this diplomatic failure, American-West Indies trade did not suffer as much as one might suppose. As it had in the past, it moved in large amounts by way of Nova Scotia and Caribbean islands of other European nations. Clay found consolation in the fact that the total value of goods held up well.[24] He employed an agent to visit various islands and report the status of this commerce, which, he learned, had recently increased.[25] True, American shipping suffered somewhat in the loss of direct imports from the British colonies, yet the situation had not deteriorated as much as had been portrayed by critics of the administration.

One sees unfortunate mistakes in handling the West Indies problem. Certainly inexcusable delays, especially in Clay's first year as secretary, were costly. Other matters consumed much of his time before he even sent off the Gallatin mission. The fall-out of the aberrant presidential election, the need to organize departmental administration, the fact that many points of policy had been set up by ex-Secretary, now President Adams (however defective they were) pushed this issue to the background. Then the decision to require British abandonment of imperial preference seriously weakened American chances for success. It was little help for him to know that he had dropped that objective after a year or so.

Nevertheless, in general, he had strengthened the nation's foreign trade as an important element of the American System, which, in his mind, must balance commerce with manufacturing and agriculture. Obviously he had more success with European and Latin American commercial relations than with the West Indies.

A little later, however, he would watch bitterly as the next administration of Andrew Jackson opened the trade in 1830 and did so after deprecating the Adams-Clay approach. Actually, Clay's Democratic successor as secretary, Martin Van Buren, achieved it more because of the passage of time and the cooling of tempers than because of superior diplomatic skill.

Although Clay gave a major share of his time as secretary of state to foreign affairs, he remained involved in the politics of economic policy. He and President Adams agreed on the main issues: federal internal improvements, terms of public-land sales, and protective tariffs. They were disappointed with progress on the first of these yet did get sizable congressional appropriations to assist road and canal construction. On land policy, competing proposals for downward "graduation" of prices and for "distribution" of public-land revenue to states took shape without resolution. But it was the tariff that became the chief domestic question addressed by the developing parties of Adams and Clay and of Jackson and Van Buren.

Halfway through the Adams administration, in early 1827, Congress considered a bill to raise ad valorem duties on raw wool and woolen textiles, subject to a scale of minimum valuations at custom houses exceeding actual value. Passed in the House, the bill was tabled in the Senate when Vice President Calhoun broke a tie vote, an ominous signal that the Carolinian was moving from his well-known nationalism to states-rights sectionalism.[26]

Soon Clay joined with friends in protectionist Pennsylvania to lay plans for a broadly based tariff policy to present at the next session. Working with leading persons in that state and with the zealous propagandists Mathew Carey and Hezekiah Niles, he favored calling a national convention at Harrisburg in July 1827 to formulate a concrete legislative plan. On his way home through western Pennsylvania in June, he spoke at several towns in defense of the American System, now a familiar term across the country. He looked upon the forthcoming meeting as a political response to the dangerous obstruction of Jacksonians. So the convention was understandably viewed as an administration tactic in the approaching presidential election.[27]

Delegates from thirteen northeastern and western states did gather to discuss the status of industry and the necessity of governmental encouragement of its growth. Politicians, including Chairman Rollin Mallary of the House Committee on Manufactures, mingled with private individuals from many parts of the economy to share information and ideas. While considering manufactures of iron, hemp, spirits, cottons, and other commodities, they emphasized wool and woolens, which they felt Congress had failed to support adequately. On wool, the convention urged gradual increase of rates to a nearly prohibitive level; on woolens, it sought levies even higher than the recently tabled bill.[28] At the convention's request, Niles reported its proceedings and recommended specific revisions to the national legislature.

Reflecting the position of the administration, Secretary of Treasury Richard Rush's annual report to Congress in December 1827 advanced an extensive argument for increased protection. Although Adams favored that policy, he did not publicly express his views. In his diary he reasoned that "measures of detail should be matured in Congress, and it is time for the President to act upon them when they are brought to him in the form of bills for his signature."[29] Political caution, however, more than constitutional principle probably induced his silence. Clay's incoming correspondence freely criticized the president's detachment, but the secretary loyally justified Adams's uncharacteristic deference as avoiding "a delicate topic." He predicted Jacksonian hostility to the American System would be exposed during the coming debate.[30]

Opponents of the administration controlled the House and put through a bill there with higher protective rates on some imports, especially raw wool, to please agricultural interests of the mid-Atlantic and Ohio Valley states, but with imposts on woolens lower than those sought by the Harrisburg convention. This action caused complaint by many New Englanders because it would result in comparatively greater costs of raw material for their mills. They charged that Jacksonians wanted the Northeast to reject the whole measure. Actually, that was the aim of southern Democrats but not of a northern contingent led by Van Buren. In the Senate his amendments to the bill for somewhat higher woolen rates contributed to passage of the so-called Tariff of Abominations (1828).[31]

Clay hoped that administration forces would benefit in the fall elections from their advocacy of a protective tariff and other features of economic nationalism. In that contest with the Jacksonians he relied upon a new party of which he had been a principal architect. Much as Van Buren had done in unifying the opposition, he had helped build a network of state organizations of politicians, newspaper editors, and financial contributors—all, he believed, who subscribed to the American System. The goal now was to reelect Adams. Yet he encountered insurmountable obstacles. Notwithstanding complete agreement with the secretary on policies, Adams would not electioneer and saw no need to revive a two-party system. A larger obstacle proved to be the dismaying popularity of Andrew Jackson. His personality, coupled with Van Buren's efficient organization, swept the presidential election of 1828. These factors, apparently more than positions on tariff or internal improvements, more even than a rising sectionalism or an invocation of democratic sentiment, contributed predominantly to Jackson's election.[32]

Nevertheless, the recent enactment of the Tariff of Abominations portended trouble for the new administration. Vice President Calhoun, responding to opinion in his South Carolina and the South generally, now saw nothing but injustice in Clay's protective system. He had collaborated with Van Buren in building a Jacksonian party and envisioned himself as successor to the Old Hero in the White House. But he felt the maneuvers in passing the tariff had been highly destructive to the South economically and constitutionally. So he drafted two documents, known as Exposition and Protest, arguing against Clay's brand of nationalism and contending an injured state had the right to nullify such legislation. There was an overtone too of secession from the Union.[33] Clay not only had lost an election but had to reckon with these disturbing possibilities.

5

Nullification

Early in his administration Jackson remained cautious about the tariff. Quite aware of political hazards, he preferred not to tamper with rates. If revenue produced a surplus, he suggested distributing it to the states after retiring the national debt, which seemed about to occur. It would be desirable, he said, to authorize distribution with a constitutional amendment. But he emphasized his firm belief that Congress did have full power to enact a protective tariff. In any case, he ventured his opinion that the existing tariff of 1828 had not had as much effect, either good or bad, as extremists asserted. He would advise them to quiet down for the sake of the general welfare.[1]

Here was a rare instance when Clay found some common ground with his adversary. Of course he could not concede that the level of rates made little difference; yet he did concur in a moderate approach. The present schedule appeared compatible with the goals of the American System, he thought. It would be enough to improve enforcement of the law, stopping the frauds and evasions that abounded. The largest problem bothering Clay and other protectionists centered on the auction system, which permitted sale of imports at low prices prior to payment of customs. Another vexation was assignment of goods to agents of foreign merchants at eastern cities.

These practices undermined a true ad valorem assessment.[2]

In its first session of the Jacksonian era, Congress took a modest step toward reforming procedures in collecting imposts. It did not stop there, as Clay wished, but lowered several rates, on salt, molasses, coffee, and tea. And through May 1830, foes of protection, notably George McDuffie of South Carolina, stimulated lively discussion in the House.[3]

A more exciting debate had been under way in the Senate, one that marked the initial stage of a growing constitutional crisis. The highlight was an oratorical duel between Robert Hayne of South Carolina and Webster of Massachusetts, though many senators spoke out in alignment with one or the other. Hayne laid out an argument for state sovereignty against what he saw as a consolidationist trend damaging to southern interest, especially measures for federal internal improvements and a protective tariff. Everyone could see he was reiterating the Exposition of 1828, composed by Vice President Calhoun, now presiding in this chamber. Webster explained his own metamorphosis from favoring low tariffs to favoring high tariffs and justified it with a classic statement of American nationalism.[4]

Calhoun himself was moving into the open as the foremost opponent of loose-constructionist politics. Shedding his nationalism of former times, he had signaled his states-rights transformation by breaking a senate tie vote to defeat the woolens bill of 1827. Then the next year, though he had not openly acknowledged authorship of the states-rights Exposition, it was well known that he had written it. His support of Jackson's presidential candidacy in 1828 had rested on his hope for downward revision of the tariff. But when the new chief executive seemed disinterested in replacing the protective system, when radical agitation back home intensified, and when Van Buren gained the advantage in their rivalry for the presidential succession, Calhoun decided he had to set forth his position to the public.

So at his up-country plantation in summer 1831 he drafted his widely noticed Fort Hill address, restating the doctrine of interposition, based upon state sovereignty and power to judge the validity of national legislation. He contended that the present high tariff was plainly unconstitutional, for it abused both revenue and commerce powers. Southerners were unfairly taxed, in effect, when they paid prices of consumer goods inflated to benefit northern manufacturers. The Carolinian did not mention secession as a remedy, should interposition fail to remove the evil.[5]

Soon afterward, in October, free-traders aimed another blow at protectionism. An editor active in their cause, Condy Raguet, helped bring delegates together at Philadelphia to influence the public and Congress. A majority of the two hundred persons attending were southerners, inclined in varying degrees to believe the tariff laws unconstitutional as well as unfair. And their resolutions said so. A northern wing wished to avoid that question and succeeded in having old Albert Gallatin draft the convention's memorial to Congress, emphasizing the ineffectiveness and inequity of protectionism but expressing no constitutional objections.[6]

Protectionists employed similar tactics. In the lead, Hezekiah Niles regularly and unreservedly promoted the American System in his *Weekly Register.* An admiring friend of Clay (he named a son after the Kentuckian), Niles published masses of information on industry, commerce, and public policy to support his argument. His special target was Britain, which he insisted was exploiting the United States commercially while merely talking about free trade. His fellow journalist Mathew Carey also propagandized with effect by way of essays and personal relations. The correctly conservative *North American Review* in Boston carried protariff articles by Edward and Alexander Everett.[7] State legislatures, such as those in Kentucky and Louisiana, in which Clay had particular interest, passed resolutions for nourishing "domestic industry."[8] Then in October 1831, shortly before a new Congress assembled and before the presidential election year arrived, a national convention met in New York, aiming to get the better of the recent free-trade assemblage. Niles worked hard to organize this effort. He served as secretary, and afterward his *Register* carried reports of proceedings and an address to the people. Memorials on the tariff went to Congress while it was considering a new bill.[9]

Clay had been the acknowledged leader of the opposition to the Jackson administration since it had come to power in early 1829. Though at home in Ashland most of the time, he maintained that position by an extensive correspondence with key figures across the country. Wherever he did travel in the West or South, he met large crowds, eager to hear his views expressed with characteristic eloquence. It seemed clear he would be the presidential nominee of the new National Republican party. Certainly he expected it.

He had a ready-made platform, the American System, of course. Two of his numerous speeches on that theme, in Ohio at Columbus and Cincinnati in summer 1830, were typical. Encouragement of industry helped everyone, he declared. That policy would ensure economic independence of the nation, essential in war or peace. What helped manufacturing helped the farmer and the mechanic, the merchant and the banker. A home market meant self-sufficiency.[10] At Natchez, Mississippi, he spoke to a large audience on his way up the river after his winter's visit in New Orleans. He emphasized benefits to the South. Cotton planters were badly mistaken, he argued, in thinking that a protective tariff raised prices of what they bought and lowered prices of their cotton. Just the opposite. Textile mills in the United States provided a valuable market for raw cotton, and industrial growth stimulated competition and lowered consumer prices. On these occasions he was aiming his message toward the South, the pivotal element in the approaching election, he believed.[11]

Ever since the Webster-Hayne debate in January 1830, Clay had portrayed Calhoun's nullification as an erroneous, very dangerous theory. No one state can block a decision of the majority, he contended, for otherwise that state would be legislating for the whole Union. Like Webster and Chief Justice John Marshall, he relied upon Article VI of the Constitution, making national law supreme over state law, together with Article III, giving the federal courts jurisdiction in cases involving the Constitution. Recalling his youthful opposition to the Alien and Sedition Acts of 1798, condemned by the Virginia and Kentucky Resolutions of Madison and Jefferson, he found no precedent in them for Calhoun's pretended Jeffersonianism now. Those resolutions of 1798, he reasoned, called upon all states, not one, to resist, yes nullify, federal constitutional infractions by repeal in Congress, by the turnover of power in an election, or, in the extreme, by resort to the natural right of revolution. So as the prospect of confrontation between nullifiers and unionists over the tariff became imminent, his position was clear.[12] He advised a political friend, "We ought to stand or fall upon our principles; and make no compromise or surrender them."[13] Time would tell.

If he took an unyielding stand against nullification, he did seem ready to make some adjustments in a new tariff. The treasury was reaching that unique condition of completely retiring the national debt. Once that obligation disappeared, he calculated, as much as $10 million (more than a third of the annual budget) would be eliminated from federal expenditures, allowing that much reduction of the tariff. He felt willing to abolish rates on imports not competing with American goods but wanted to continue protection of other domestic products.[14]

His prescription would soon be tested. The Kentucky legislature had elected him to the Senate for the new Congress beginning in December 1831. He was very visible, not only because he resumed his legislative leadership but because the National Republicans now nominated him for the presidency. After that unanimous action, the party convention approved an address, giving a resounding endorsement to the American System. It scolded Jackson for his opinions on the tariff, internal improvements, and banking.[15]

The president also had his eye on the approaching election. His annual message to Congress revealed a shift toward a states-rights position from his previously guarded pronouncements. He urged sizable reductions of the tariff to conciliate the restive South and to accommodate the commercial interest in the North. Though not elaborating those reasons, he did emphasize the decreasing need for revenue as the public debt disappeared.[16] Jackson wanted more drastic revisions than Clay.

The first month of the session yielded little progress by the Senate except to define the line of battle. As a member of the Committee on Manufactures, Clay skirmished with Samuel Smith, the eighty-year-old merchant-politician and chairman of the Finance Committee. They disagreed over committee reference of Clay's proposals. Since Smith supported the administration's effort for deep cuts in the tariff, Clay wanted his proposals to go to his own committee. On this procedural matter he won a significant vote, twenty-two to seventeen. He could see that a majority of the Senate shared his protectionist commitment.[17]

After these preliminaries the Kentuckian explained his plan for revision, which he offered as a resolution. With some precision he analyzed the status of the public debt, then $24 million and soon to be retired from a sinking fund. He would continue that process and still cancel the tariff on goods not in competition with American products. This he would do while retaining protective duties on competitive imports at or near the present levels. Surely the South would be satisfied, short of total surrender by the industrial interest. The debt could be retired if customs collection changed from a credit to a cash system and if home valuation (at American ports by American officials) replaced deceptive foreign invoices. And most important, he would preserve the principle of protection.

As Clay ranged across the whole subject, he developed an argument he would often advance later. Instead of accumulating an undesirably large surplus from the tariff, he wished the Treasury to begin transferring money from public-land sales to the states for internal improvements and other uses. Such distribution would not permanently fasten a high-tariff policy on the country, he insisted, because it would draw only from land sales. In his view, using revenue from customs for distribution would be unconstitutional. The distinction between the two sources, however, was quite hazy.[18]

Hayne, his principal opponent, moved a low-tariff amendment reducing rates to bare revenue needs and to the same percentage on all goods. The South Carolinian's argument corresponded exactly to that of Calhoun's Exposition of 1828. He portrayed the tariff's impact upon the South as destructive: low cotton prices and high consumer prices, amounting to an oppressive tax imposed by a heartless manufacturing class. It would be better for the United States to produce only what it could not buy more cheaply abroad, he contended.[19] As for parliamentary procedure, Hayne and those of like mind wished to refer Clay's resolution to the unfriendly Finance Committee and its antiprotectionist chairman Smith. This re-

fueled Clay's long-standing disagreement with the aged Mary-
lander. The two senators exchanged heated personal remarks,
highlighted by Smith's shouting that he could still defend himself.[20]

At the beginning of February, Clay had the floor for a
three-day set speech in a memorable defense of the American
System. The policy, he said, originated in the first years of the
republic. Washington, Hamilton, and Jefferson supported it
from 1789 onward in the form of protective legislation. He
then cited the laws of 1816 and 1824, further encouraging
manufacturing. And he displayed his pride in promoting the
latter statute, which had stimulated prosperity dramatically.
Deploring the constant call by opponents for free trade, he exclaimed, "It never has existed, it never will exist." Britain, the
principal supplier and customer of the United States, had not
adopted free trade despite much talk about it. Indeed, if Congress rejected protection, Britain would recolonize America
economically. At this point, Clay launched into a rather cruel
attack upon Albert Gallatin, who had recently written the memorial of the Philadelphia free-trade convention. "Go home to
your native Europe," he commanded, "and there inculcate
upon her sovereigns your Utopian doctrines of free trade, and
when you have prevailed upon them to unseal their ports, and
freely admit the produce of Pennsylvania and other States,
come back, and we shall be prepared to become converts, and
to adopt your faith."

The senator's main target was the South on blaming the
tariff for its economic distress. He cited statistics to show a
downward trend of prices since passage of the law of 1824.
This had been the predictable impact of protection, he said, because encouragement of industrial growth brought on healthy
competition and lower prices. Even if his primitive figures
were accurate, he did not make the qualification that many
other variables influenced price fluctuations. Nevertheless,
this led him into his stronger position, the desirable development of a home market, of a balanced domestic economy. The
exchange of agricultural and manufactured goods helped all
sections and classes, according to this familiar rationale.[21]

Until recently, Clay remarked, few persons had doubted
the constitutional validity of a protective tariff. Even Vice Presi-

dent Calhoun, who was presiding over the debate, had not doubted it. In 1816 he had strongly supported such a measure; and in 1828, when he drew up the South Carolina Exposition, Calhoun was merely restating what others, not he, believed about constitutionality, the senator observed. Definitely not, Calhoun interjected from the dais. He certainly did doubt it. And in 1816, he declared, Congress did not debate the constitutional issue. Well, that was because it was not debatable, Clay retorted.[22]

The Senate continued to discuss every facet of the tariff over the next several weeks. Mainly, the speeches made the same points about the bill as before. On the economic implications, Thomas Ewing and George Dallas did broaden the question by lecturing South Carolina not to blame the tariff for its troubles but to consider the fixation on one crop of cotton, a declining soil fertility, and the unproductiveness of slave labor. The last of these criticisms touched a highly sensitive nerve.[23]

On the other side, antiprotectionists—Willie Mangum, Felix Grundy, Isaac Hill, and others—encouraged Hayne to stay the course.[24] John Tyler of Virginia, the future president, made one of the strongest attacks upon the American System and its foremost spokesman. He charged that Clay wielded "an influence over the legislation of Congress, as I verily believe, more powerful and more controlling than any other man, or set of men, in this country, the manufacturers, and they alone, excepted."[25] And Thomas Hart Benton of Missouri had moved over from favoring to opposing protection. In his long-winded remarks, he traced the term and the policy of the American System back to *Federalist* 11 (1787) and later to Jefferson and Madison as well as Hamilton. But they had called only for a selective response to discriminatory commercial policies of particular countries, not for economic subsidies at home such as presently urged, Benton said.[26] Then several persons joined Hayne in opposing protection on constitutional grounds. Only his South Carolina colleague Stephen Miller, however, went so far as to advocate the remedy of state nullification of congressional legislation.[27] Silence of others on that topic must have given Vice President Calhoun pause.

At last, the disputatious solons confronted the next parliamentary step. Several strategies had adherents and all were combined for submission to the Committee on Manufactures (sidestepping Smith), probably to put Clay, a member and a presidential candidate, on the spot. The panel had instructions to report on abolishing rates for noncompetitive imports and reducing them for others, on cutting all to a uniform low level, on seeking information from the treasury and state departments, and, strange to say, on changing public-land policy, presumably because revenue from that source might affect the tariff. Much to Clay's annoyance, the complex assignment would be impossible to handle in the limited time available and, in any case, appeared to be a political trap.[28]

A week later, on March 30, the committee reported. Chairman Mahlon Dickerson recommended enactment of Clay's recommendations to abolish rates on noncompetitive goods and reduce some others to bring in a revenue of $5.6 million. The report insisted upon retaining the principle of protection, just as the Kentuckian had argued. For fiscal or developmental reasons, the report continued, lowering all rates to a a uniform level, as Hayne had proposed, was undesirable. On its other instructions, the committee advised postponement because information requested from the executive branch had not arrived. Hayne, Smith, and Benton led an assault against the committee, depicting it as completely subservient to manufacturing interests. By a close vote, the Senate delayed action until obtaining more facts. Clay acquiesced.[29]

Meanwhile, the House had been struggling with these issues too. The central figure was Adams, elected to that body after leaving the presidency. It was his misfortune to be selected chairman of the Committee on Manufactures and to be the center of hopes for some amicable compromise. Such a role, of course, seemed out of character for Adams, better known for his rigidity; but his experience and influence were resources that he recruited in an interesting fashion.[30] Soon after the session began in December, he and Clay attended a joint caucus of protectionist legislators to discuss what to do. As the former president sourly noted in his diary, Clay dominated the talk and assumed a "super-presidential" air, unwilling to accommodate other views. To save the American System, according to Adams, Clay vowed he would "defy the South, the President, and the devil."[31]

Worried that contention over the tariff posed great danger to the Union and convinced that any alteration of the schedule had to have Democratic support, Adams decided to collaborate with the administration. So in conferences with Secretary of Treasury Louis McLane, he promised concessions by his committee to reduce rates, but to do it gradually so that there would be enough revenue for the president to achieve his goal of retiring the national debt within the year. National Republican candidate Clay naturally had no interest in that kind of pledge to benefit Jackson in the fall elections. Nevertheless, Adams tried to honor the agreement with McLane while maintaining as much protection in a new tariff as possible.[32] He received a massive report from the secretary on the status of manufactures in late April, as well as a plan to cut the average rate from 45 to 27 percent. The House committee then adjusted some provisions upward, as Adams wished, and secured passage of a bill in that chamber.[33]

A lively debate in the Senate added to July's heat. Though willing to pacify his opponents somewhat, Clay thought the House bill went too far. He sought to rescue the American System from destruction, especially to restore higher levies on woolens and cotton bagging. He had some success, though the votes were quite close, and Vice President Calhoun broke ties to check Clay's rally. Webster heartily supported the protectionist cause, and Hayne again led the opposition. An amended bill went to a conference committee where the Senate's representatives, William Wilkins and others, gave way on every point. The final scene was one of unrestrained anger. Clay verbally lashed Wilkins for his timidity, while from a different perspective Hayne deplored the result as quashing any southern hope for justice. The bill did pass the Senate, however, and Clay repressed his dissatisfaction enough to vote for it.[34]

As his feelings calmed, he could look at the tariff of 1832 more positively.[35] To be sure, it abandoned the system of minimum valuation of woolen imports and abolished duties on cheap wool. But on most grades of textiles, the rate was fairly high—50 percent. And if imposts on cotton bagging, sugar, iron, and glass were a little lower, one would still classify them as protective. Over all, the average went down from 45 to about 33 percent.[36] Even the dedicated protectionists Niles (author of the recent protariff convention's report) and Mathew Carey spoke approvingly of the outcome. Other friends of the senator seemed satisfied.[37] Democrats, many of them southern congressmen and one of them the president, concluded that the threat to the nation's peace had disappeared.[38] Not so the followers of Calhoun and Hayne.

Through summer and autumn 1832 antiprotectionist feeling intensified, especially in South Carolina, where extremists threatened collection of the tariff and strengthened their political structure accordingly. Hayne became governor, and Vice-President Calhoun took over his senate seat. Leading nullifiers sought support from other southern states, among them Georgia, unhappy about the Supreme Court's intervention against its attempt to evict the Cherokees.[39]

Responding to this restiveness, Jackson sought to reassure the country in his annual message of December 4 by saying the government had all the necessary means to enforce the laws and maintain the peace. Nevertheless, he believed widespread complaints about the tariff required legislative relief. The measure he approved in July as a just settlement must now be revised down to a level only for essential revenue and national defense. Besides, expenditures would decline due to imminent retirement of the public debt.[40]

Within a few days news arrived at the capital that a South Carolina convention had adopted an ordinance nullifying the tariff statute as unconstitutional and setting up barriers to its enforcement. It proclaimed that this sovereign state would prohibit state officers from compliance. If the national government did not respect nullification, South Carolina would secede from the Union.

Jackson reacted quickly. In animated conversations he slashed at the miscreant state and its nefarious strategist. The old general vowed he would himself head troops to put down traitors. But characteristically he also assembled a careful if vigorous countermove to nullification. After hurriedly drafting a long statement of his views, he asked Secretary of State Edward Livingston to rework the paper in the context of constitutional law and political principles. Livingston could draw upon his extensive governmental experience and legal scholarship. The final form of Jackson's proclamation to the people of

South Carolina on December 11, 1832, therefore advanced persuasive doctrine, as well as the chief executive's own convictions. It emphasized the perpetuity of the Union, created by
the American people acting through their states. It rejected the
claim of a state's right to nullify a national law or to secede.
And it upheld the role of the Supreme Court in interpreting
the Constitution. As for secession, he warned, it becomes an in-
surrection; and "disunion by armed force is treason."[41]

Clay's reaction to Jackson's proclamation was mixed. He
privately observed that "although there are some good things
in it, especially what relates to the Judiciary, there are some
entirely too ultra for me." The senator objected to passages
pointing toward consolidation of federal power, which would
"irritate instead of allaying any excited feeling." He had in
mind states' righters such as those in Virginia who disapproved both South Carolina's nullification and broad national
authority.[42] General reaction was mixed. Protectionists such
as Niles and Webster applauded, but the president's trusted
lieutenant Van Buren also found features of the paper on national power too ultra. The crisis afflicting the country involved such differences of opinion.[43]

The administration joined conciliation with its show of
strength. To carry out Jackson's recommendation for tariff reduction in his annual message, Secretary McLane's report
outlined specifics: gradually cut rates from the present 33 percent to at least 20 percent, down to the level of 1816 or further, since the public debt would be retired and less revenue
would be needed. A proposed bill went to the House Ways and
Means Committee, chaired by the Democratic, commercially
oriented representative from New York, Gulian Verplanck.
Significantly, it did not go to Adams's Committee on Manufactures, inasmuch as the existing, controversial tariff of 1832
had been Adams's product. Predictably he spiritedly opposed
the bill, designed to upend his tortuous work of the preceding
session. The House discussed it unprofitably through the next
two months as adjournment (March 4, 1833) approached.
Chances for passage dwindled.[44]

Meanwhile in the Senate, instead of addressing the substance of the current issues, the members spent many days
arguing whether to ask McLane for the same kind of infor-

mation given to the lower house. At last they voted not to do so. Clay cared little about McLane's recommendations, even less about Verplanck's formula, destructive to the American System as it could be.[45]

Though Jackson pursued a two-part policy, rejection of nullification and reduction of the tariff, he now emphasized the first more than the second. Following up his proclamation to South Carolina, he selected a number of means to overcome the state's resistance. Some required congressional authorization, which he requested in mid-January 1833: closure or relocation of ports of entry for collecting customs, removal of tariff cases from state to national courts, use of the military where necessary. Incorporating such provisions, a so-called force bill came out of the Senate Judiciary Committee, of which Webster was a key member, and Congress debated it the rest of the session.[46] During that period there were protracted and ponderous speeches on constitutional as well as economic aspects of the controversy, most notably extended disquisitions by Calhoun and Webster on the nature of the federal Union.[47]

Clay took a critical view of all this. Not that he doubted the doctrine of a perpetual Union formed by the American people and immune from state nullification. He disliked the emphasis upon abstract principles inflaming this confrontation and interfering with a practical adjustment. He also disliked the shape of the force bill, giving the president such broad powers. Who the president was probably bothered him more than what his powers were to be. At any rate, he visualized an outcome in which Jackson might destroy the American System with the Verplanck bill and also emerge as a political autocrat.[48]

Ever since the beginning of the crisis, Clay had been searching for a promising plan to end it. In December 1832, following news of the state's nullification ordinance and the president's proclamation, he visited relatives in Philadelphia. Here he discussed possible compromises with friends, including several businessmen, who encouraged him to go forward with a proposal. It would maintain present tariff rates until 1840 and then lower all of them to an equal revenue level without regard to protection. Webster happened to pass through the city, was shown a statement of this approach and vigor-ously disapproved abandoning protection.[49] On the other hand, Clay had received advice from Carey months earlier, suggesting a similar solution. And Niles was now urging him to resolve the controversy with some concessions to the South.[50]

Returning to Washington on January 3, he conferred with colleagues and listened day after day to speeches revealing a wide variety of opinions on what ought to be done. He discovered he would have to modify the plan he drafted at Philadelphia, then somehow recruit support from different sections, parties, and interests. Notwithstanding the difficulty, he believed that compromise was indispensable to preventing a terrible civil war. Yet it was imperative too, in his judgment, to head off passage of the Verplanck tariff bill, which could destroy the principle of protection in the American System either this session or the next. He also wanted to counter what he perceived as Jackson's grasp for power, not merely his determination to pacify South Carolina.[51]

In fashioning his revised proposal, he consulted a number of businessmen and senators, of whom the most important was Calhoun. The Carolinian felt great pressure from fire-eaters at home as he searched for a reconciliation of his state's demands with the value of Union, according to his definition. After conversations with Clay about a new approach, he pledged his cooperation. It seemed more palatable than going for the administration's bill and hoping the hostile president would then extricate him from an uncomfortable position.[52]

Clay explained his compromise to the Senate on February 12, 1833. He would reduce rates gradually. Beginning that year, then at intervals in 1835, 1837, and 1839, he would cut 10 percent off the excess over 20 percent in all rates. From the remaining 60 percent excess he would cut half in 1841 and the other half in 1842. Thereafter, all duties should be "laid for the purpose of raising such revenue as may be necessary to an economical administration of the Government; and, for that purpose, shall be equal upon all articles, subject to duty, according to the value thereof. And until otherwise directed by law, . . . such duties shall be at the rate of twenty per cent ad valorem." He added a few provisions as consolation to American manufacturers: cheap woolens would be levied at the same rate as those of high quality (50 percent), the free list of raw materials would be expanded, and cash payment of customs would replace the existing credit system available to foreign exporters.[53] After saying he wished to avert civil conflict and preserve the American System, he pointed out that both sides in the current crisis would gain much. Northern and western industry would keep most of its protection for a decade, and southern planters would eventually get low rates. It was truly a balanced compromise, he reasoned. But why cave in to nullification, of which he definitely disapproved? He weakly answered that despite his earlier strict response, he now saw South Carolina avoiding any violent tactic and peacefully testing a national policy by legal procedures.[54]

Hugh White, president pro tem of the Senate, appointed a committee to report the bill—Clay as chairman, Felix Grundy, George Dallas, William Rives, John Clayton, Webster, and Calhoun, who had dramatically announced he supported the plan. Though Jackson tried to get a panel more favorable to his views, White resisted, so that Clay had a majority with him.[55] In preliminary debate one of the committee, Webster, attacked the compromise for what he believed to be an abandonment of the protective principle. He would make some concessions for lower rates but do so selectively and not all to the same level.[56] Apart from this and a few other negative reactions, the prospects for accepting the Kentuckian's proposals seemed good.

A week later, Clay reported a measure substantially as he had drafted it. Before much discussion he did move an amendment for home valuation, a requirement that each American custom house fix the value of imports instead of accepting valuation by shippers at foreign ports. An important reform, Clay said, to eliminate extensive fraud in paying tariffs. This section came from John Clayton of the committee, who insisted he would not vote for the bill unless modified. His vote could be pivotal for passage. Still, Calhoun disliked it. And in subsequent debate others did too. They argued that valuation at individual American locations would produce variations in violation of the Constitution's prohibition against preferences to one port over another. No doubt they disliked it because it could result in higher prices of goods, a higher tax they would bear, in their view. Webster proposed specific instead of ad valorem duties as the only way to prevent inaccurate assessments. However true that may have been, it did not generate much enthusiasm, and Clayton's amendment passed. While complaining strongly, Calhoun voted yes, gathering other votes of hesitant senators for a majority of twenty-six to sixteen.[57]

A finespun question bothering many senators involved the constitutional requirement that the House must initiate laws to raise revenue. No matter, said Clay, he was lowering revenue and rescuing the country from bloody strife at that.[58]

As the discussion neared an end, the gulf between Clay and Webster became very clear. Time and again Webster charged that this formula would abandon the very principle of protection, the heart of the American System. How else could one describe the point when after ten years all rates would fall to a flat 20 percent with a commitment never to exceed it? Repeatedly Clay tried to blunt that criticism by saying that after 1842 this good-faith assurance would carry very great weight, yet every Congress would retain the power to do that which was necessary for the safety and well-being of the nation. He also countered the objection that all rates would have to be a flat 20 percent by stipulating that some could go below the 20 percent amount.[59]

Turning on the New Englander, Clay asked, "Would the Senator from Massachusetts send his [force] bill forth alone without this measure of conciliation? . . . The integrity of the Union" is at risk. The reporter of the debate recorded that Webster muttered, "The gentleman has no authority for making that assertion," to which Clay exclaimed that "he would not submit to interruption." As a matter of fact, as Webster emphasized, he had advocated his own reductions but not so low and not at a uniform rate.[60]

Granted that Clay had a strategic reason to pick up support from states-rights senators, one is struck by his steadfast caution, seemingly inconsistent with his opposition to nullification. Nowhere was it more apparent than in his silence during the full-scale debate between Calhoun and Webster on the nature of the Union and the claimed right of state interposition. When the force bill to collect the tariff in South Carolina was voted upon during an evening session, Clay was absent. Though later saying he would have voted for it if present, he had continued to avoid entanglement in a Jacksonian policy he had called too "ultra."[61]

Clay rounded out his advocacy of compromise with one of his best-known speeches. He reviewed the advantages to both northern industry in the next ten years and to antiprotectionists in the long run. Repeating his reasoning in sponsoring the settlement to preserve the American System and to prevent sectional war, he again made some pointed remarks about Webster's opposition. "The difference between the friends and the foes of the compromise, under consideration," he declared, "is, that they would, in the enforcing act, send forth alone a flaming sword. We would send out also, but along with it the olive branch, as a messenger of peace. . . . While we would vindicate the federal government, we are for peace, if possible, union and liberty. We want no war—above all, no civil war; no family strife. We want to see no sacked cities, no desolated fields, no smoking ruins, no streams of American blood shed by American arms!"[62]

The next day, February 26, he learned that the House had passed a bill identical to the one pending in the Senate. No unforeseen coincidence. His fellow Kentuckian, Robert Letcher, had managed to hurry it through the lower chamber, thereby crowding out the administration's Verplanck bill. So ended whatever problem there may have been about the constitutional requirement that only the House originate revenue laws. Southerners, including Calhounites, could find some satisfaction in thwarting Jackson in this way. In any case, Verplanck's measure might not have passed the Senate.[63]

The new tariff and the force bill had been moving concurrently through the two houses. And their relation to one another was important. It seemed certain that Clay's compromise tariff could not win acceptance by some members without an assertion of federal authority over states. And vice versa, some uneasiness about Jackson's display of the sword subsided only with the show of Clay's olive branch. Both bills had passed, and the president signed them on March 2, just before the session ended.

An analysis of House and Senate voting shows strong support for the compromise from the middle Atlantic states, with an overwhelming affirmative from the South. Opposition from New England was solid, together with a significant number of nays from Atlantic and western states. As for parties, Democrats favored the legislation two to one, while National Republicans (Clay's ranks) opposed in about the same ratio. Using House votes as a gauge, one finds 188 representatives voted on both bills, of which 114 voted for only one or the other. The outcome was therefore not a firm consensus on the entire compromise, since only 74 out of 188 accepted both parts. Nevertheless, this may be typical of many parliamentary compromises that would be impossible to attain without such a middle group adding to majorities for parts of a package. On the individual measures, some northerners and westerners would not have voted for the lowered tariff if it had not been coupled with a force bill. And there were many southern votes for the force bill, indicating either dislike of states-rights radicalism or acceptance of this route to tariff relief.[64]

Dissatisfaction with the settlement prevailed in several quarters. As a spokeman of New England, Webster left no doubt of his views. The intensity of his exchanges with Clay over the tariff matched those with Calhoun over nullification. He persisted in charging the Kentuckian with trading off the very principle of protection. Through the next decade whenever his relations with Clay hardened, Webster might recall the history of the compromise. He claimed to have seen Clay's written statement of his first plan in late December 1832, calling for a tariff "without regard for protection." And he authorized publication of his copy of that statement to prove this was the chief characteristic of the ultimate legislation.[65] The cool relations of the two senators fed a widespread belief that Webster would go over to Jackson, perhaps succeed him as a Democrat in the White House. The fact is the situation never got close to that kind of alliance, despite suspicions of contemporaries and many present-day historians.[66] As for Clay, he put the best face he could on the affair. "There is no breach between Webster and me," he said cheerfully. "We had some friendly passes, and there the matter ended."[67] Despite personal rivalry throughout their careers, they usually cooperated with one another politically.

Among those who had previously collaborated with Clay and now found fault with the compromise, Adams stood out. In the House, he spoke unreservedly against this retreat from protection, a ruination of the manufacturing interest, he charged. The flawed policy could not last, he correctly predicted.[68] Undoubtedly the criticism Clay received from his faithful advisers Carey and Niles hurt most. Carey was so upset he gave up his journalistic advocacy of the American System, "I am sick, sick, sick, of the prospects of the country," he moaned.[69] Niles, too, saw the outcome as a disaster. In his *Register* during and after the debates at the Capitol, he deplored the new policy. "We render all possible respect to the motives of our honored friend," the editor declared, "but cannot go with him in a measure, which in our humble opinion, contains the surrender of a power which is vital to the independence of the United States—which is firmly held and daily exerted by every commercial nation in the world."[70]

There was naturally a good deal of praise from others. Madison commended the agreement as strengthening the Union and quieting the unsound nullification movement.[71] Abbott Lawrence, the New England cotton-textile manufacturer, not feeling the need for much help from the tariff, lauded Clay's achievement.[72] And Clay's friend Nicholas Biddle, president of the national bank, perceived the senator's position as "firm and commanding."[73]

A major figure in the story, President Jackson, emerged quite pleased about turning back nullification with the force bill. Dependable followers, such as Silas Wright, John Forsyth, Felix Grundy, even Gulian Verplanck, author of the discarded House bill, voted for passage of the tariff. Not so Thomas Hart Benton, who unceasingly voiced opposition. Jackson himself took pride in the nationalistic exposition of his proclamation to South Carolina, which would have a lasting impact on American politics.[74]

Leaders in that state believed they had triumphed. Calhoun not only escaped an embarrassing squeeze between fire-eaters there and unionists everywhere but also felt more confident of enhanced justice to the South.[75] Governor Hayne happily concluded that "South Carolina by her brave and determined course, had driven the tiger within his den—that the tyrant with his bloody bill had to succumb to the brave and chivalrous spirits of Carolina, and that they never would lay down their arms till congress had repealed the force bill."[76] The last-mentioned goal would be elusive. Of course, some Carolinians worried about a threat to slavery when outsiders pressed for a high tariff. Some of the events and disputes of 1833 were a prelude to subsequent controversy over that peculiar institution.

Clay himself felt proud of his contribution to peace and continuing protection over the next decade. In his opinion, the day the president signed the two parts of the compromise, the tariff and force bills, March 2, 1833, was "perhaps the most important Congressional day that ever occurred." The South's victory, he thought, was only "nominal whilst all the substantial advantages have been secured to the Tariff states."[77] If participants on both sides of the controversy had such positive reactions, then the nation may have fashioned a true compromise.

6

The Bank War

Concurrently with a protective tariff, the issue of a national bank moved to the political foreground. Though the charter of the Bank of the United States would not expire until 1836, the question of congressional renewal was assuming importance as early as 1829, Jackson's first year in office. His annual message then had convinced Clay that the administration seriously threatened the bank. Its constitutionality and expediency were questionable, the president declared, and "it had failed in the great end of establishing a uniform and sound currency." This signaled the beginning of a so-called Bank War, an enormous controversy about financial policy soon inflaming the Capitol and in fact the whole country.[1]

Jackson had several reasons for criticizing this institution, whose president, the talented Nicholas Biddle, conducted operations at its headquarters in Philadelphia. For one thing, Old Hickory had already tangled with banks, including the BUS branch at Nashville, and tended to distrust them all. When he had settled in at the executive mansion, he had concluded that the underlying cause of this bank's misbehavior was political. Disturbing reports came in from several states. In New Hampshire, Webster's intimate friend Jeremiah Mason became president of the branch office, and Jacksonians accused him of partiality in his loan policy. From Kentucky

charges arrived that appointments to boards of directors at the
Lexington and Louisville branches were loyal Clay men. In
other places, it was said that the bank had meddled in the
recent election to help Jackson's opponents. Then at Washington was it not well-known that many pro-bank congressmen
had received overly generous loans? And to widen the abuse,
what of the same sort of laxity favoring newspaper editors
aligned with Clay and Webster? The most notorious example,
the president felt, was a clumsy, indirect loan to Watson Webb
of the New York *Courier and Enquirer*, pulling him over to probank ranks.[2]

Partisanship aside, Jackson thought the BUS, such a
large corporation with such immense capacity to affect the
entire economy, was not only dangerous but also unconstitutional. It could set the prevailing interest rate and regulate the
flow of credit as it discounted loans. It could substantially
control the currency, since its notes were the dominant legal
tender. At the top of the huge pyramid, Biddle could alone
make most decisions. A charter creating this monopoly was
surely not necessary and proper to carry out congressional
powers enumerated in the Constitution.[3]

Jackson's objections to recharter drew upon the current
of anti-BUS opinion that had been building. Radical reformers
pointed to the need to counter the impact of all banks upon a
republican society. Others would at least remove this bank's
grip upon the currency and exchange, probably on other parts
of the financial system.[4] Close to the president's side were advisers urging a bold remedy. Amos Kendall, erstwhile follower
of Clay and now one of the influential "Kitchen Cabinet" at
the White House, emerged from Kentucky's relief struggle
suspicious of banks. Another former Kentuckian estranged
from Clay and now editor of the Jacksonian organ, the Washington *Globe,* Frank Blair expressed the same opinion. In
1831 the new attorney general, Roger B. Taney, joined Kendall and Blair in pressing Jackson to kill the BUS. Some
people thought Martin Van Buren was also a factor, but he
probably was not a large factor, since he was in England as
United States minister during the first battle of the Bank
War. He displayed even more caution than usual about involvement in the question upon his return in mid-1832.[5]

Clay and Webster headed the bank's supporters. Both had been its ablest advocates in Congress whenever legislative action affected it as the federal fiscal agent. They had been well compensated, successful bank attorneys in the courts, working closely with Biddle. And the banker had been helpful to them as they obtained liberal personal loans. By the 1830s Clay had paid off most of his debts, though Webster added much more to his borrowings. Even in a period when such mixture of public and private interests was fairly common, the two senators' connections were noteworthy and would be more so in the mounting controversy.[6]

The Kentuckian recognized the importance of Jackson's views. It was premature, he advised Biddle, to advance the issue of recharter ahead of time. Better to delay and sidestep the general.[7] He did not say so but no doubt thought he might become the chief executive himself before the deadline arrived.

Meanwhile, an extensive effort to enlist public opinion for renewal developed. In a number of places National Republican meetings supported it, which showed it could be an important question in the next election. Biddle recruited veteran financier Gallatin to contribute a long article in the *American Quarterly Review* (November 1830) supporting the bank. Another Jeffersonian elder statesman, former president Madison, wrote a public letter contending that the experience of having no such institution during the War of 1812 demonstrated how essential it was. An unsigned piece in the *North American Review* early the next year fully described the valuable features of the currency provided by the BUS. Even Hezekiah Niles, whose *Register* had long deplored undesirable banking practices, would accept recharter with modifications.[8] While some state-incorporated banks understandably would welcome the elimination of their powerful competitor, many of them in all sections favored renewal because of the advantageous credit and exchange operations of a national network. Because Kentucky was losing its only state facility, the Commonwealth Bank, people there would depend upon the two BUS branches.[9]

By late 1831 Clay shifted his thinking about strategy from opposing to favoring a recharter petition. He reckoned a presidential veto was less likely before than after an election.

Jackson might be more accommodating if he faced a formidable opponent in the coming contest. That person would be
Clay himself. The National Republican convention nominated
him in December, and its address strongly defended the bank.
If Jackson did not come around, Clay would count on victory
to enable him to sweep away the present obstruction to renewal. In any case, he urged Biddle to move ahead with a petition.[10]

What Clay, and Webster too, advised may have had an
effect upon Biddle's decision, but not as much as sometimes
portrayed. Instead, the BUS president depended mainly upon
his own assessment of the congressional situation. Sending his
associate Thomas Cadwalader to Washington to survey possibilities, receiving specific reports on lawmakers' sentiments,
relying especially upon the enthusiastic recommendation of
Calhounite George McDuffie, chairman of the House Ways and
Means Committee, he concluded that the president would
probably veto a recharter bill but that Congress might override. If not, he would hope for Clay's election and an amenable
new Congress. Biddle's prediction of a veto would prove to be
more accurate than Clay's assumption that the president
would not dare to take that risk. At any rate, both of them saw
that the entire question had been thrown into the political
arena.[11]

Biddle also pursued a compromise with Jackson, as he
had from the beginning. He continued to negotiate with Secretary of Treasury McLane, who himself wanted recharter and
sought to persuade Jackson to accept it. Assembling a package
designed to retire the public debt, to secure the bank's help in
selling the government's shares of bank stock to finance it,
and to get the president to take a passive position on the charter problem, the secretary felt he would succeed. A draft of the
annual message in early December 1831 included a passage
leaving the question to Congress. But Taney and Kendall
jumped in to forestall such a neutral statement. Afterward
about all McLane could do was personally recommend recharter but observe the chief executive taking the opposite
course.[12] As late as February 1832, when Congress was de-
bating the subject, Biddle tried to get an understanding with
Jackson by way of Secretary of State Livingston, another pro-

BUS cabinet member. But Livingston had no leverage in this partisan area where the president preferred counsel from the Taney-Kendall-Benton bloc.[13]

In January, George Dallas, a Pennsylvania Democrat, had presented a bank memorial to the Senate, requesting renewal of the charter. A committee of five, including Dallas and Webster, gathered information from the Treasury and the bank, then reported a bill two months later.[14] Recurring debate and roll calls revealed that senators favorable to recharter had a majority of about ten votes. Opponents resorted to a strategy of delay. Their very visible leader, Benton, therefore had a representative, Augustin Clayton, move an investigation by a House committee of alleged bank misconduct.[15]

Meanwhile Benton accelerated his attack against the bank. One of its worst abuses, he charged, involved branch drafts. BUS offices in various places had issued this paper in large quantity to avoid the cumbersome rule that the president and cashier at the main office sign all notes, which made up much of the currency—a difficult task as business increased. So the numerous branches across the land, by arrangement, issued drafts upon the Philadelphia office, which endorsed and circulated them as an important medium of exchange. But the requisite safeguards were inapplicable to branch drafts, Benton contended; and the Senate should forthwith declare them "illegal" in a resolution he offered. How could this body make such a serious charge without getting more information, several members asked. A good question, thought a majority, defeating Benton's precipitate move.[16]

Benton also complained about the projected retirement of the federal government's 3 percent bonds, issued to pay the state Revolutionary War debts, which it had assumed. Biddle, he said, had earlier discouraged the government from buying up these low-interest bonds with its funds at the bank when their market value was low. Later the BUS president obtained an arrangement with bondholders to delay presenting the securities for payment. Otherwise the government would have drawn out a large amount of its funds from the bank, which had been pressed for ready cash. That maneuver had interfered with a fiscal function of the Treasury, the Missouri senator asserted.[17]

Branch drafts and 3 percents were only two of a long list of Benton's indictments possibly amounting to felonies or at least misbehavior. While not making much progress in the Senate, Benton had better results in the House, where he gave his list to Clayton's investigating committee. Its critical report could have an impact upon the public and, of course, upon Andrew Jackson.[18]

The Senate did not seriously discuss Dallas's bill until late May, much to Clay's displeasure. The recommendations were chiefly for minor revisions of the existing charter, with nothing said about constitutionality. As the committee member most experienced in the bank's operations, Webster guided the debate through a series of amendments proposed both by Dallas's report and by the Massachusetts senator himself. After making an impressive case for the bank's benefits to the nation's economy, he moved several reforms, calculated to soothe the opposition. Among those adopted were provisions loosening the restriction on who could sign bank notes (to suppress branch drafts), prohibiting notes of small denomination (to expand hard money), raising the corporation's bonus paid to the government, and regulating the holding of real estate by the bank.[19] Argument became heated over unsuccessful motions from the floor to allow states to exclude the BUS branches and to tax them. Webster and Clay could recall their own participation in the *McCulloch* and *Osborn* cases on the subject before the Supreme Court and were alarmed when several speakers insisted that Congress could override such decisions protecting the bank.[20]

Only a few members delivered full-scale attacks on the policy of incorporating the institution. The tireless Benton did so in many hours of talk, emphasizing abuse of power subversive of democratic government. Ike Hill of New Hampshire, prominent Jacksonian editor-politician and fierce adversary to Webster, developed the theme as well. And Hugh White of Tennessee, a future Whig presidential candidate but now in Jackson's ranks, made a strong impression.[21]

Clay seldom entered the bank debate, leaving it to Webster to guide the bill through. The Kentuckian gave attention in this session primarily to the tariff and land questions. But he was always present and regularly voted—in behalf of the bank, naturally.

The Senate passed the recharter bill on June 11 and sent it to the House. Here McDuffie had been leading the recharter effort, mainly by turning back hostile amendments. So after unproductive orating and maneuvering, the lower chamber adopted the Senate measure with no substantive change.[22] As for sectional opinion, the Northeast was probank, the South decidedly opposed, and the border and western states divided.[23] Neither vote of the two bodies supported renewal by a two-thirds count, spelling trouble if, as expected, the president vetoed.

At the White House Kendall and Taney were at work on a message expressing presidential objections to recharter on grounds of just policy and strict-constructionist constitutionalism. It became a leading statement of Jacksonian Democratic tenets.[24] The veto emphasized undue favors granted to the bank's stockholders, particularly the "gratuity" of a large enhancement of the value of their stock if the charter were renewed. It played upon patriotism too, by a strong attack upon numerous foreign stockholders, declared to be a serious danger to America. A more convincing argument, probably Taney's contribution, found no constitutional warrant for such an institution as this. No matter that the Supreme Court and other sources had pronounced its validity as a necessary and proper execution of the enumerated powers of Congress. This could not bind "coordinate" branches of the government at the stage of making a law. The president therefore, in his "legislative capacity," must determine whether a bill was necessary—it was a question of degree. The obligation to prevent special privilege conferred by government, such as this "monopoly," infused all parts of Jackson's reasoning and would be a durable influence upon politics.[25]

As soon as the chief executive's veto arrived in the Senate, on July 11, Webster fired a mighty blast against it. With the message at hand, he proceeded through it, paragraph by paragraph. He rejected the argument about undue favors and privileges to stockholders as groundless, just as the supposed peril of foreign investors was. His response to the charge of unconstitutionality was not only what one would expect of the nation's renowned lawyer but also quite spirited: "If that which Congress has enacted, and the Supreme Court has sanctioned, be not the law of the land, then the reign of individual opinion has already begun."[26]

Clay, who had hardly spoken during the debate leading up to the bill's passage, rose up as an eloquent spokesman for the bank. His emphasis was a denial of the executive power being flourished. None of Jackson's predecessors had employed the veto to the present degree, he lamented. Indeed, it reminded him of its use by kings of times past, now abandoned. "The veto is hardly reconcilable with the genius of representative Government," he declared. "It is totally irreconcilable with it, if it is frequently employed. . . . Ought the opinion of one man overrule that of a legislative body twice deliberately expressed?" Like Jackson, Clay was establishing a party principle, in his view opposition to excessive presidential authority. On various substantive points of the message, the Kentuckian reinforced Webster's preceding attack.[27]

Inevitably Benton had his say. In addition to his well-known criticism of the bank monster, he gave great weight to Jackson's patriotic character, ever a formidable resource. And when Clay appeared to have sullied the old hero's reputation by recalling Jackson's brawl with Benton in frontier days, the Missourian shouted an angry response, ruled out of order along with Clay's remarks. The skirmish showed that then, as so often in discussions of high policy, emotion could easily crowd out sober colloquy.[28]

Finally, on July 13, 1832, the Senate voted on a motion to override the veto. The tally was twenty-two to nineteen to do so, six less than the required two-thirds.[29] Whether this would be a lasting decision hinged upon the fall elections. With his usual optimism, Clay envisioned a repudiation of King Andrew's pretensions.

Through much of this administration he had believed the principles of the American System would be the critical factor in the coming contest. That reasoning had persuaded him to return to the Senate at the start of the present session and to encourage the movement for his presidential nomination, made by the National Republican convention in December. He had felt assured that the party agreed with him on the tariff and internal improvements as well as the national bank. Now the controversy over the bank had intensified, offering him a definite advantage, he concluded. The Democrats, it seemed to him, were relying solely on the personal popularity of Jackson, for they did not even adopt a platform on the issues; and their national convention in May had met only to nominate Van Buren for Vice President.[30]

Clay had Biddle's active support. The bank president had cast aside any show of detachment from politics. Convinced that the veto was self-destructive, he characterized it as "a manifesto of anarchy," such as Robespierre issued to the mob during the French Revolution.[31] So he spent some of the bank's funds, as much as forty thousand dollars, in the National Republican cause. Part went to printing and circulating copies of the veto message, which would amply demonstrate its obvious weakness. Another part went to getting out copies of the speeches of Clay and Webster against the veto.[32] Benton later recalled that the bank had also orchestrated popular meetings in cities across the land, protesting an economic downturn.[33]

Another source of support came from Niles, whose *Register* published many editorials and documents calling for recharter with modifications. It was even more heartening because the editor had made a reversal from his longstanding hostility toward the institution.[34] Surprisingly, Niles's journalistic adversary, the Philadelphia free-trader Condy Raguet denounced Jackson's despotism, revealed in the veto.[35]

Speculation grew that Clay would form an alliance with Calhoun since both had a common foe and since they shared views on the bank. To tell the truth, the Kentuckian needed the kind of help from the South that Calhoun might give him, because support for the American System in that section was sagging, especially due to passage of the protective tariff this year. But Clay doubted such a coalition was practical, despite giving it some serious thought. Already talk of state nullification of federal legislation was building, a development he could not countenance. The best he could expect from Calhoun was de facto collaboration, hopefully to continue on the bank question.[36]

Then there was the current movement of the Antimasons, a new party developing strength, much of it from National Republican quarters. Could their presidential candidate, William Wirt, be persuaded to bow out in favor of his friend Clay? As the election approached, that appeared unlikely.[37]

In November the outcome was a clear victory for Jackson, who swept the South and large northern states. Though Wirt got 8 percent of the popular vote, Clay had needed more than that in addition to his 37 percent.[38] One must guess whether the president was reelected mainly because of his personal popularity or because he had killed the monster bank and had stood for states' rights instead of economic nationalism. It was a mixture, of course; yet the charisma of a heroic tribune, speaking for a democratic people, was probably the more significant element.

In December 1832, shortly after the election, Jackson followed up his victory. In his annual message to Congress he directed attention to the next phase of the Bank War. The country could now see the corporation's dangerous character, he said. So much so that it was "no longer a safe depository of the money of the people." One proof of that situation, in his judgment, had surfaced when Biddle interfered with retirement of the 3 percent securities, reflecting poor liquidity of BUS assets.

As a first step toward disengagement from the institution, the chief executive recommended legislation for selling the government's extensive holdings of bank stock. To lay a foundation for withdrawing all its deposits as well, he recommended a congressional investigation of the bank's general condition. A House committee with a four-to-three pro-BUS majority did inquire and reported favorably on the safety of deposits. Jackson discounted this finding and a House vote (109 to 46) approving it as misguided partisanship. Nor did he welcome a congressional refusal to authorize sale of governmental bank stock.[39] Pleased with these setbacks of the executive, Clay predicted that Old Hickory could not now venture to remove the deposits.[40]

The senator's confidence turned out to be unjustified. Jackson continued to plan how to do that very thing. He explored opinions of his cabinet, only to find that all except Attorney General Taney did not favor removing deposits, at least for the time being. The member who could cause the most trouble was Secretary of Treasury McLane, who by coincidence or otherwise was now shifted to the State Department as replacement for Livingston, another bank supporter and the new minister to France. William Duane, a Philadelphia Democrat who opposed rechartering the bank, seemed to be a desirable substitute in McLane's vacated spot. Since constitutionally the secretary of the treasury had a degree of autonomy in the executive branch because of special fiscal responsibilities to Congress, one wonders why the president did not inquire about Duane's attitude toward removing deposits. Soon it was evident he was no better than McLane on this subject. He did promise to resign if overruled on removal, a promise he later rescinded on the ground of the Department of Treasury's distinctive role in the cabinet. Despite these difficulties in his official household, Jackson did not retreat. And notwithstanding Vice President Van Buren's characteristic caution about moving ahead, he would not wait.[41]

So in September he followed a course he and his intimate advisers Kendall and Blair had long preferred. He ordered removal of deposits, dismissed an obstinate Secretary Duane in the process, replaced him with Taney, and dispatched Kendall on a mission to eastern cities to select some state-chartered banks for the deposits. In a paper read to his cabinet, he set forth his familiar reasons to shut off Biddle's bank: its political partisanship, its conduct concerning the 3 percents, its exclusion of the governmentally appointed directors from information, its tremendous, monopolistic financial power, and, above all, its corrupting impact upon the morals and democratic principles of this republic.[42] On all these points, Clay disagreed. At stake, he declared, were "the free institutions inherited from our ancestors," under assault by the "will of one man."[43]

By the end of 1833 Kendall and Taney had chosen twenty-two state-bank depositories, otherwise known in opposition circles as the "pets," because the selection in most cases depended upon the bankers' politics. Considering the inevitable confusion of such an operation, the process of gradual transfer went rather well. Except in some unfortunate instances. For example, Taney's friend, the president of the Baltimore Union Bank, unjustifiably drew funds from the BUS that the secretary had made available to depository banks only in pressing circumstances. He applied Taney's rather flexible authorization for his more flexible purposes, for personal investments, it was suspected.[44]

The climax of the Bank War came during the legislative session under way in December 1833. All the economic and constitutional arguments of the past two years reappeared at Washington and echoed through the entire country. As head of the bank forces, Clay tried strenuously to reverse what the administration had done, while Democrats pressed their attack upon the "monster."

In his annual message, Jackson depicted the government's fiscal condition as excellent, with the prospect of retiring the debt as centerpiece. He then reviewed events concerning the national bank: removal of Treasury deposits and transfer to selected state-chartered institutions, due to BUS misconduct. Biddle's corporation, he said, had interfered in politics, had become a veritable "electioneering engine." And now it was sharply curtailing credit and inducing a depression to compel return of the deposits. The president felt confident that Congress would find removal quite proper.[45]

Secretary Taney's report arrived at the same time. Whatever the legality of his earlier removal of deposits, he did comply with a provision of the bank's charter to explain his reasons for doing so. Like Jackson, he enumerated several types of misbehavior—BUS extension of loans to influence legislators and editors, interference in governmental retirement of the 3 percent bonds, and immense financial power amassed in Biddle's office. Most unpleasant to Clay, no doubt, was Taney's conclusion that the people had already approved the antibank policy by reelecting Old Hickory.[46]

Each side blamed the other for hard times. The bank was curtailing its loans and note issue, in fact had begun the previous summer in response to the recharter veto and in anticipation of deposit removal. Biddle justified this contraction as preparation for shutting down operations and blamed Jackson's policy for tight credit and economic suffering. For his part, the president condemned curtailment as unnecessary, only proof of the dangerous power at the bank's disposal. "Biddle's panic" was cruel manipulation.[47]

Throughout the tumultuous session, December 1833 to June 1834, economic distress or at least perceived distress fueled the intense controversy. A flood of petitions poured into the Capitol. Some were descriptions of popular suffering, business paralysis, unemployment, shortage of credit, conditions calling for revival of a proven financial system. Others, equally strident, attacked the bank along lines laid out by the patriotic tribune in the White House. Clay assumed a leading role in the battle. He and Webster presented many memorials, then pled for returning governmental deposits and renewing the charter to relieve an afflicted nation.[48]

As a first step, he moved a resolution asking Jackson to send up a paper read to the cabinet in September, advancing his now familiar reasons for removal. To be sure, Clay said, a copy had appeared in the press. Still, he wanted an authentication. In the document the president had not only criticized the bank but had also assumed full personal responsibility for removal without requiring any cabinet member to take a position. This could help the senator fix Old Hickory as his main target. Benton and other Democrats objected to requesting the paper. The Senate seemed to be gathering evidence for a later impeachment trial, they complained. The House constitutionally must first gather evidence for a trial; and then the Senate must sit as a court, not as a partisan body, the Missourian lectured his colleagues. Though Clay got his resolution through, Jackson relied upon executive privilege, protecting internal presidential discussions, and briskly refused. Beyond a little scouting, the skirmish did not yield much of a tactical advantage to either side in the continuing warfare.[49]

Clay's main attack began with two more resolutions in late December. The first charged the president with assuming power "not granted to him by the constitution and laws, and dangerous to the liberties of the people." The second charged Taney with removing the deposits for "unsatisfactory and insufficient reasons."

As for Jackson, his dismissal of Duane and appointment of Taney were unwarranted, not because he could not replace a cabinet officer but because he did so for an unconstitutional object, taking into his own hands the decision to remove the funds. Only Congress and the secretary (limited by the statute chartering the bank) could decide upon that action, he contended. So as in the case of the recharter veto, the problem, in the Kentuckian's opinion, arose from abuse of executive power. To support his reasoning, Clay pointed to Jackson's letter to his cabinet, saying he took full responsibility for removal and did not require the assent of his subordinates. Furthermore, where did the chief executive find the authority to "preserve the morals of the people, the freedom of the press, and the purity of the elective franchise"?

As for Taney's mistakes, Clay rejected the secretary's reasons for removal of deposits as set out in his recent report to Congress. The senator ticked off a series of flaws in that statement. Taney had condemned the bank's financial and political involvements, but Clay exonerated it completely. He also argued that the deposits had been safe and that, if they were not, the secretary need not have been in such a hurry to act while the legislative branch was not in session but could have waited a few weeks for congressional direction. Of all the criticisms of Jackson and Taney, the last was perhaps the most persuasive.[50]

In the weeks ahead Clay would use his considerable resources to obtain a censure of the president for what he had labeled lawless behavior and to block the confirmation of the Secretary's appointment. In a flourish, he warned that "if Congress do not apply an instantaneous and effective remedy, the fatal collapse will soon come on, and we shall die—ignobly die! base, mean, and abject slaves—the scorn and contempt of mankind—unpitied, unwept, unmourned!"[51]

A three-month debate on his resolutions was one of the longest, most acrimonious discussions of a question in the Senate up to this time. At the end in March 1834, few, if any, opinions had changed; but they had been exhaustively expressed. For about a month there were long, set speeches on both sides, notably by Benton and Silas Wright (Van Buren's ally) for removal,[52] by Calhoun and Samuel Southard against it.[53] Then Webster, chairman of the Finance Committee, reported an ample endorsement of the propositions. Afterward most senators who spoke also presented memorials signed by hundreds and thousands of "respectable" persons from both political parties, it was said. There were mounds of petitions complaining of acute economic distress, caused by the heart-

less president of the bank or by the wild president of the
nation. Two speakers who would later play important roles in
the politics of public finance were John Tyler, the future chief
executive who had not liked a national bank but now did not
like Jackson's high-handed conduct, and Nathaniel Tallmadge,
spokesman of New York's state bank system in competition
with the BUS.[54] Clay monitored progress and added argument,
supported with more memorials.

Anti-BUS senators, again spearheaded by Benton, repeated the familiar charges: Biddle's dangerous command
over credit and currency, subversion of the political process
and of the press by leverage of loans, and presently the current suffering brought on by curtailment. They upheld
Jackson's power, both constitutional and inherent, to control
the secretary of the Treasury and thereby the handling of
governmental deposits. In fact, they tended to focus on this
issue of presidential authority more than upon broad policy
concerning the bank, obviously due to the thrust of Clay's
pending resolutions. Yet they did not exploit available historical evidence on executive status to any extent. As for the way
Taney removed deposits, they relied upon the language of the
congressional statute chartering the bank, providing that if
removal occurred when Congress was not sitting, the secretary must report the action as soon as it assembled. They saw
no need for waiting three months in this instance to get prior
legislative approval. Of course, nearly everyone agreed that
Congress could pass a law reversing removal, but that would
be quite unlikely now when the administration had a majority
in the House. Looking ahead, they praised selection of state-
chartered banks as depositories—otherwise known among
National Republicans as the pets. Not only would they be
safe, insisted the Democrats, but the Treasury might regulate
these institutions more effectively than the nearly autonomous BUS.

Clay's contingent of probank senators was largely unified
in pursuing a well-charted route. The point of departure was
the constitutional necessity and propriety of a national bank,
so unwisely assaulted by Jackson. In a political sense, however, the most interesting comments came from Calhoun. Notwithstanding his sponsorship of the BUS charter in 1816, one

might have expected his conversion to states' rights to have caused him to reverse his opinion. But in the short run, he believed such a bank was desirable. Whether or not some other fiscal agent would eventually replace it depended upon Congress instead of the rapacious chief executive or his ready instrument, Roger B. Taney. The precipitate order to remove funds reminded the Carolinian of Caesar breaking into the Roman treasure house. Calhoun's remarks showed that his thinking on the bank issue had developed from the recent nullification crisis and from his perception of Jackson's arbitrary conduct in brandishing the force bill, which he considered proof of Jackson's domineering character. Here, for the time being, was an unforeseen ally of Clay. Did the alliance promise a permanent connection with the new Whig party?[55]

Webster was a key figure in this story. Very knowledgeable about the law and politics of banking, particularly of this corporation, he had taken the lead in shepherding the recharter bill through Congress two years earlier. Now he served as chairman of the Finance Committee, instructed to report on Clay's resolutions to censure the president and reject Taney's reasons for removal. His major speech made the best case for this bank's survival. As he often did, he reasoned on the basis of mutual interest of all parts of the economy. It was a mistake, he declared, to array the poor against the rich, the farmer against the businessman, the worker against the banker. Webster spoke the Whig creed, to which Clay also subscribed: "Sir, the great interest of this great country, the producing cause of all its prosperity, is labor! labor! labor! We are a laboring community. A vast majority of us all live by industry and actual employment in some of their forms." The person who had the greatest interest in sound currency, such as the BUS supplied, was the laborer, he concluded.[56] In his subsequent committee report, Webster urged condemnation of Jackson's removal of deposits as an invasion of the sphere of congressional power. Indeed, even Congress would have to defer to a judicial hearing on the question. There must be clear proof, lacking in Taney's statement, that the funds were unsafe.[57]

In the last phase of deliberations on removal, Clay took the floor a few times for brief comments but did not introduce any new views, let alone persuade any colleague to shift positions. He himself persisted in his belief that the nation had fallen into the depths of a terrible crisis brought about by an unrestrained partisan. It was imperative that the people's representatives move against the present danger.[58]

On March 28, 1834, after these many weeks of disputation, the Senate voted for Clay's two resolutions: (1) to censure Jackson for assuming "authority and power not conferred by the Constitution and the laws, but in derogation of both" (on a vote of twenty-six to twenty); and (2) to reject "the reasons assigned by the Secretary for the removal [as] unsatisfactory and insufficient" (on a vote of twenty-eight to eighteen).[59]

In mid-April the president returned fire. He sent back a spirited, wide-ranging protest, emphasizing that the Senate, not he, had overstepped the dividing line beween the two branches. Cabinet members, whom he appointed, were subject to his supervision, he contended; and if legislators attempted intervention in the executive sphere such as they had done, they undermined the principle of checks and balances, basic to American government. This principle was double-edged, of course, also used against Jackson in the censure denouncing presidential invasion of congressional ground. Then, like Benton and other supporters, Old Hickory interpreted the present reprimand as amounting to an impeachment, though not brought by procedures the Constitution required. He closed with a stirring appeal to his reputation of patriotic service to the nation, belying these unfair allegations; and he requested that his protest be entered in the senate journal.[60]

Immediately George Poindexter moved not to receive Jackson's offensive statement, a parliamentary tactic providing a substantive question the two sides could address while refusing to record the protest. Naturally, Benton was out front in condemning censure, further worsened, he exclaimed, by this disrespectful motion. He compared it to the case of John Wilkes, a member of the British Parliament in the late eighteenth century, who was harshly deprived of his election several times by that body. Eventually, it reversed its rulings and seated Wilkes. Benton vowed he would work unceasingly for a similar outcome, expunging this censure from the journal. He did just that in the next several years.[61]

Among those repelling Jackson's protest was Webster, who spoke confidently about constitutional implications. The Senate had not impeached the president by a shortcut, he held. Instead, it was perfectly in order for the upper house to point out an executive invasion of its legislative power and to protect popular liberty. It had not charged him with a high crime, an impeachable offense. Nevertheless, Webster was not soothing the president's feelings when he obliquely compared him to the divine-right Stuart kings of the seventeenth century.[62] On that point Calhoun agreed by deploring the chief executive's tyrannical tendencies, fortunately opposed by a gathering coalition known as the Whigs. Where there was threat to liberty, he would act with the new party, he announced.[63]

Clay entered the discussion at several intervals and joined his friends in focusing on these constitutional aspects, giving only slight notice to economic issues. His position suffered a weakness in denying Jackson the right to transmit a message of protest while maintaining Congress could send a message of censure. Both branches of the government, it would seem, ought to have communicated more sensibly on a leading problem of the day. Still, the Kentuckian's greatest difficulty was the barrier of a House majority ready to support the administration regardless of what the distinguished senators thought. With refusal to receive the protest as the only move possible at the moment, he pushed forward for the vote to do so on May seventh. It passed, twenty-seven to sixteen.[64]

As this session moved from one angry phase to another without producing anything more than sharp disagreements over increasingly rigid principles, a growing number of the public understandably asked if the outcome would be stalled efforts to deal with the nation's difficulties. Clay, in Washington, seemed far more interested in castigating the president for an unwise, harmful policy than in coming forward with positive proposals to heal the economy. What else could be done besides censuring Jackson and rejecting his protest?

This was the sort of question Webster had been pondering from an early stage of the Bank War. At first, the New Englander felt handicapped in attempting anything, for Clay and other leaders suspected he was flirting with the administration, possibly with a view toward exchanging support of Jacksonianism for a high Democratic appointment and perhaps succession to the presidency. Such thinking grew out of Webster's help to the chief executive in countering South Carolina's nullification a year before. Clay and Van Buren, from different perspectives of course, both feared he was undergoing some kind of conversion. But Clay was soon convinced that such an unholy alliance would not develop and was pleased that Webster welcomed election as chairman of the critical Finance Committee. Nevertheless, on through this tumultuous Congress, even though the two senators worked harmoniously on censure, Webster was seeking a compromise or, more likely, a short-term approach to the banking problem, a different outlook from Clay's single-minded determination to bring Jackson down.[65]

After many weeks of waiting, the Massachusetts senator reported his interim plan. He would extend the present bank charter six years in order to extricate the country from what was now known as the administration's "experiment" of resort to state-institution depositories. It had an appalling impact upon currency, credit, and business activity, he thought. Governmental deposits should be returned to the BUS. To sweeten the proposal, he would restrict small-note issues, put limitations on the branch offices, and consider what other changes the Senate found desirable. Calhoun also moved into action by putting forward a weird remedy: extend the charter twelve years, increase the value of gold in relation to silver at the mint to bring on a wholly metallic medium of exchange with no paper notes, and ultimately "unbank the banks" to get rid of these exploitative enterprises.[66]

Clay had no interest in either antidote. Discussing them merely delayed action on the censure resolution.[67] Biddle, who was kept informed about movement for compromise, told Webster he believed his plan was good but did nothing to help beyond that polite comment.[68] In a few days after presenting his recommendations, Webster gave up hope and moved to table his own report. So much at the moment for Clay's reputation as a compromiser.

If Whig proposals for settling the national-bank question foundered, there was some Democratic sentiment for going beyond mere negativism in financial policy. Toward the end of the session in spring 1834, Benton made another effort for hard money as replacement for bank notes, both national and state. He had gathered a great deal of information on the history and present status of metallic currency, which he lengthily explained to the Senate. The mint had not coined much gold or silver for many years, he pointed out, so that rank-and-file Americans had to depend upon paper notes, easily manipulated by banks. In answer to critics' characterization of him as the "gold humbug," he admitted he did share the people's preference for money "which would jingle in the pocket." As Secretary Taney and a House committee had urged, Benton pressed for revaluation of gold in relation to silver from a ratio of one ounce to fifteen up to one to sixteen, thereby drawing gold bullion to the mint. Before adjournment, Congress adopted such a measure, which Webster and his Finance Committee approved.

Though cold toward such a recipe, Clay did not speak on the question, in fact did not vote on it. Whether a hard-money system was practical remained uncertain. The country continued to use paper currency much more than specie. Even Benton restricted his call for more gold to small denominations, below twenty-five dollars. This movement gave many Democrats a political argument for years to come.[69]

Another Jacksonian goal looked toward development of the state-bank depositories. Taney sent up recommendations for expanding and monitoring this network with requirements on note issue, amounts of reserves, reports to the treasury, and so forth. Though failing to get effective legislative action, the administration proceeded on its own by executive orders.[70] One ad hoc arrangement involved using an agent of these banks themselves as liaison to Washington, perhaps as supervisor, which Clay and his friends thought contrary to the public interest.[71]

One thing seemed clear. There was little hope of returning governmental deposits to Biddle's bank. Clay's resolution in the Senate on May 28, 1834, for doing so generated more talk and then approval, twenty-nine to sixteen; but predictably the House tabled it forthwith.[72]

The leverage Clay's coalition had was therefore confined to the Senate, where the final scene late in June 1834 consisted of taking up Jackson's long-delayed appointment of Taney to the Treasury. The Whigs were so confident the nomination would fail they sat silent before voting to reject. If the Kentuckian had looked ahead realistically, he would have had to concede this was definitely not the political demise of the president's "pliant instrument." Just as Jackson would continue to combat his own censure in the Bank War, he would be all the more attached to his valued adviser after this offensive treatment.[73]

For the previous five years the bank question had been a solvent of ideas and parties. In large part two persons, the popular president and the magnetic leader of the opposition, had shaped the issues and affected the course of history. Jackson had made a persuasive case against a powerful national corporation that he found incompatible with democratic principles. Clay had strenuously attempted to continue a long-established policy of providing a central institution to promote economic growth. From perspectives of both public and private finance, the chief executive's actions may have been more destructive than constructive, but the senator's response lacked the practical statesmanship for which he was known. So the economic outcome was indecisive and would be for quite a while. Politically, the two protagonists had solidified the two-party system with definable differences about the role of government in the economy: the Democrats for avoidance of special privilege and for dependence upon individual freedom; the Whigs for an active national government to stimulate modernization.

7

Internal
Improvements

During John Quincy Adams's presidency (1825-29) and that of his successor Jackson, the question of internal improvements continued to generate lively discussion, some of it ending in important legislative action. As secretary of state, senator, and party leader, Clay attempted to advance programs developing transportation, which he viewed as an integral part of his American System. If a protective tariff was essential to industrialization and if a central bank was essential to economic growth, he believed a positive policy must also include an active role of the national government in promoting a network of roads and waterways unifying the young nation.[1]

On entering the cabinet, he knew that he and Adams agreed on the fundamentals of internal improvements. Both subscribed to flexible constitutional doctrine, permitting broad scope not only to spend but also to shape projects along with states and private enterprise. In their opinion, Jefferson, Gallatin, Madison, and most recently Monroe had too narrowly interpreted federal authority to act. In the new administration congressional dynamics and precedents from the previous twenty years instead of executive scruples would limit what could be done. During Adams's tenure more than four times as much money would be appropriated for this purpose than in any earlier comparable period.[2]

The president sketched a bold program in his message of December 1825 to Congress. In addition to favorable comment on various plans initiated in surveys by Army engineers, he extended his definition of internal improvements to cultural and moral progress. Would it not invigorate republicanism to establish a national university and an astronomical observatory and to promote scientific knowledge further by an exploratory expedition to the far Northwest? His remarks on these topics worried most of the cabinet, including Secretary Clay, who thought the country would find such forays too radical. To press for their adoption was hopeless, the Kentuckian said. With encouragement only from Secretary of Treasury Richard Rush, Adams did tone down these passages in the message.[3]

Clay would find less common ground with President Jackson. To be sure, when Old Hickory had been in the Senate, he had voted to appropriate funds for roads and canals, justifiable as a military necessity. But as chief executive he moved toward strict constructionism and states' rights, though he did sign many internal improvement measures.[4] The issue roughly separated party ideologies by the early thirties. Yet in some respects the division was sectional—the Middle Atlantic and West for national action, the South against it, other areas divided. Local advantage by pork barreling was a factor, regardless of who was in the White House.[5]

This was a time of much canal digging. The highly successful undertaking that impressed people everywhere was the Erie, connecting the upper Hudson River with Lake Erie. It was a project financed and constructed by New York. In the East too, work began on the Chesapeake-Delaware, the Dismal Swamp, and the Chesapeake and Ohio Canals. The West hoped to link the Ohio and Mississipi Rivers with the Great Lakes. Clay strongly supported Adams's recommendations for federal aid. When adopted, that assistance was substantial: grants of five square miles of public land for every mile of the route, or generous governmental subscription of stock in the mixed public and private corporations developing the waterways.[6]

Clay took the greatest personal interest in the Portland Canal around the falls of the Ohio at Louisville. Ever since he had first attended Congress twenty years ago, he had advocated federal assistance to cut a two-mile bypass at this throat of western navigation. Nothing came of this proposal except adoption of a state law incorporating a canal company, with no financial help. When steamboat traffic increased spectacularly, momentum for action picked up, since boats had to unload cargoes at Louisville, run the falls, and then reload at the expense of money and time. So in 1826 and 1829 during Adams's term, as construction neared completion, Clay's friends got a measure through Congress to subscribe a substantial amount of company stock. Soon the Treasury held all the stock, while the corporation managed operations. Quite an interesting public-private mixture. In 1874 the federal government took the canal over completely and stopped taking tolls. Like the Erie, it contributed significantly to expansion of domestic commerce.[7]

In contrast, Clay criticized the protracted effort to cut the Chesapeake and Ohio Canal, beginning along the Potomac at Washington and aiming toward the upper Ohio. This was probably Adams's favorite project. The president referred to it in his congressional message of 1826, succeeded in getting federal subscription to Chesapeake and Ohio stock, and shoveled the first dirt at Little Falls on July 4, 1828. The secretary of state, however, correctly predicted that construction would be too difficult and too costly, compared to alternatives such as the National Road and the Baltimore and Ohio Railroad. It took years for the canal to reach Cumberland, Maryland, and it never got to the Ohio.[8]

When Clay served in the Senate during the Jackson terms, he consistently supported river and harbor bills, to which that chief executive usually had no objection because, strange to say, he distinguished them from those for roads and canals. In the session of 1832, for example, the Kentuckian voted with the majority in appropriating funds for clearing river channels, including the James and the Cumberland. And he concurred in measures to improve coastal installations, though frequently complaining about the preference of policy toward the East over the West.[9]

Paralleling development of water routes, governments at all levels energetically promoted construction of roads. The most visible example was the National Road, commenced in the Jeffersonian era and now in the twenties and thirties being extended westward from Wheeling, Virginia, at the Ohio River through the Old Northwest. Though there were some horrid gaps, the road reached Vandalia in southern Illinois. Legislation had projected it to the state capital of Missouri, but it never got that far. This lapse was one of Missouri Senator Benton's chronic irritants. Congress appropriated money for the road, in addition to drawing upon a fund from land sales, but did not provide enough for completion, nor enough to keep the highway in adequate repair. Traveling often on the road and remaining one of its most dependable advocates, Clay pushed for a program of federal maintenance, supported by erection of tollgates. But there was the uncomfortable precedent of Monroe's veto of such a measure on constitutional grounds in 1822. Clay remembered it well and bitterly. Many members of Congress still believed they lacked the power, so that state after state from Virginia to Illinois began erecting tollgates to finance essential repairs. As they did so, Congress turned segments of the National Road over to them, a process that continued into the fifties. Altogether, it was an untidy process, one that the Kentuckian found imperfect; but he thought the road had moved the economy ahead significantly.[10]

When Clay traveled from Lexington to the East, he began his trip on a primitive road with wicked twists and turns and forbidding hills to Maysville, sixty-four miles to the northeast on the Ohio, thence up that river to Wheeling and on the National Road to the capital. He shared the frustrations and delays of fellow Kentuckians on the first leg of the journey; and as sentiment for improvement of the Maysville Road mounted, he was very interested on both personal and political grounds.

This sentiment was, in fact, long-standing. As early as 1812 the state unsuccessfully petitioned Congress for support. Off and on, meetings were held and the legislature passed bills to organize turnpike companies. By the late twenties Clay had assumed leadership of these efforts and looked upon the timing as opportune, since the spirit of internal improvement was in the air, he remarked. Though he was not in Congress himself, his associates in the enterprise tried again to get federal help for the Maysville Road company. The Senate did pass a House bill on May 20, 1830, providing a subscription of $150,000 in company stock, now a fairly common means of assisting internal improvement enterprises.[11]

Jackson was poised to kill the measure. Here was a good opportunity, he thought, to make a statement checking the current trend toward consolidated power at the expense of states' rights and of the Treasury. No doubt, another motive was to strike at an adversary by denying Clay's home town its coveted turnpike. The president's principal adviser was Secretary of State Van Buren, who years later in his autobiography recalled how he participated in the decision. Considering himself a latter-day Jeffersonian strict constructionist who had forged the new Democratic party as a North-South alliance, Van Buren had long opposed the idea of national involvement in developing transportation. Now as cabinet member and presidential companion, he had urged the chief executive to take a firm stand. In fact, he prepared a "brief," as he called it, laying out the reasoning. Giving this document, along with his earnest advice, to Jackson, he saw the Maysville bill as an excellent occasion to take the necessary step. Whether one can accept this ex parte recollection as wholly reliable history is a legitimate question, but there is probably something to it.[12]

At any rate, Jackson vetoed the bill. His main objection contended that the project was local, not national. The road would extend only sixty-four miles from Maysville to Lexington, all within one state, whereas congressional power could only apply to national projects, he declared. He could not say that this rule had always been applied previously. Other constitutional considerations also required rejection, he believed. Looking back to Madison's veto of the BUS-bonus bill of 1817, he reasoned that its disapproval of *appropriations* for internal improvements supplied a proper guideline in the present instance. A further defect, in his opinion, was the very process of governmental subscription of a private corporation's stock, a dangerous overlap of two spheres. If government were to help internal improvements, it would be well to add a constitutional amendment permitting federal distribution of funds to states for their selection and administration of programs. Distribution, though not requiring a constitutional amendment in their judgment, would appeal to Clay's National Republican following but not to many Jacksonian Democrats.[13]

Not surprisingly, Clay and his disappointed ranks found much in the veto message to criticize. They had no doubt whatsoever that the Maysville Road had national, not merely local importance. Across the Ohio River it would connect with Zane's Road, which branched off the National Road at Zanesville; it was also intended to continue the route south from Lexington into Tennessee, then on the Natchez Trace to New Orleans. As for the president's reliance on Madison's veto to disapprove appropriations, they pointed out that Madison himself would allow appropriations if related to a delegated power in the Constitution; moreover, Jackson admitted that the practice since 1817 had been quite flexible. They could cite a long list of internal improvement measures, some clearly local and most of them mixing national and state and private elements. Madison's successor Monroe had broadened the scope of appropriations, and so had Congress in its resolutions on the issue.[14]

Putting aside constitutional niceties and Van Buren's brief, supposedly the reference used by Jackson, one must say that two other factors must have influenced the veto. The first, lightly treated by the chief executive but a consideration much on his mind, was his desire to pay off the public debt, which seemed reachable soon. The Treasury should therefore not spend $150,000 in this instance. But that motive did not prevent him from signing other internal improvement bills at this session, amounting to a large sum. The second, in the realm of personalities and politics, was his awareness that the Maysville bill was the pet project of a man he truly hated, Henry Clay.

The Kentuckian responded with scathing denunciations, and yet he predicted the veto would be self-defeating. Jackson had poorer prospects for reelection two years hence, Clay said, because of the damage his action inflicted upon his popularity, not only in the West but also across the land.[15] Soon after news of the veto arrived, Clay urged National Republican leaders in the state to hold meetings and circulate counteracting addresses. This occurred. Following his advice they called for a constitutional amendment to replace the requirement for a two-thirds vote to override a veto with one for a mere majority. Already the main thrust against Jackson was a charge of excessive executive power. Though the proposed amendment did not have a promising prognosis, these meetings also spurred thinking about a presidential nomination, perhaps a surer remedy.[16]

Despite failure to get federal aid, the people in Lexington and other towns did not abandon the idea of a Maysville Road and continued work on the project in the next few years. Concurrently, they promoted construction of a railroad to Louisville by way of Frankfort, one of the first such undertakings west of the mountains. Again Clay was enthusiastic and pledged a handsome sum, more than he could later deliver, it turned out.[17]

As Clay's efforts for federal aid to internal improvements encountered stronger resistance, he sought an approach that might bypass states-rights objections and reconcile diverse economic interests. The formula he settled upon involved linking internal improvements with public lands. Both became critical parts of his American System, in some respects as critical as national banking and protective tariffs.

To understand how this may have been, one has to look at the main characteristics of land policy in those days. The public domain was vast—over a billion acres. Only part of it was available, free of Indian possession and surveyed into rectangular sections of 640 acres, necessary conditions before sale at auction in government land offices or before grants of one kind or another. In the late twenties annual sales totaled about 1 million acres, though in the next few years a land boom brought the total up to 20 million. Even at this rate it would take a long time to divest governmental holdings.

Despite the enormous value of this territory, revenue from sales had never been the only objective. From colonial days until the end of the eighteenth century, land policies had often aimed at extending settlement by large grants on very generous terms. Legislation from the period of the Articles of Confederation to the 1820s gradually shifted toward ever smaller parcels at lower prices, even on credit for a while. By 1832 a purchaser could acquire a mere forty acres at a minimum auction price of $1.25 an acre. The trend had been to accelerate the westward movement by individual settlers of modest means. Nevertheless, the objective of gathering revenue not only to supply the Treasury but also to help the states establish schools and build roads remained a major feature of land policy. The political issue involved the relative importance of revenue for national development and of stimulus to western migration. Realistically, the issue seemed somewhat hypothetical until the surge of land sales in the thirties, because revenue had not equaled the costs of administering the system.[18]

President Adams expressed his views in a congressional message of 1827, warning against undue lowering of terms of land sales. The public domain, he contended, was a national resource, much of it derived from cession in that spirit by states during the Confederation period. To dispose of it now on overly generous terms would be quite unjust to those states and to the Union as a whole. Clay, his secretary of state, wholly agreed, as one might expect of an economic nationalist.[19] The secretary of Treasury, Richard Rush, similarly referred to this topic in his report. He added another dimension, however, in urging cautious disposition of lands so as not to draw off too much industrial labor of the East toward the West. Clay had a better grasp of capital politics than to endorse that inflammatory passage; yet for a long time he did have to downplay it whenever land was discussed.[20]

No one used the Adams-Rush statements as a springboard for advocating the opposite principle more often than Benton, an indefatigable spokesman in behalf of the sturdy pioneer. Throughout his thirty-year career in Congress, the Missourian never ceased working for liberalizing land policy. His chief proposal was graduation, annual reductions of the minimum price of unsold land down to twenty-five cents an acre, indeed outright donation to actual settlers or cession of such tracts to the states at that point. Governor Ninian Edwards of Illinois liked the second option and influenced other westerners to favor it. In Congress, beginning in 1824 and every year afterward for a long while, Benton introduced such a graduation bill. Though failing to get adoption, he recruited much support.[21] During the Webster-Hayne debate of 1830 in the Senate, Benton fought an eastern attempt to slow down land sales, which, he said, reflected a reprehensible bias against the West. Instead, he advanced his formula of cheap land as an ingredient of a sectional alliance with the South. The West would help the South get a low tariff in return for southern acceptance of a generous land policy. Hayne and some others of his section had been converted, but not enough to enact a measure for graduation. A bill did squeak through the Senate, though not the House.[22] Benton's threat, as Clay viewed the problem, was rising, particularly because Jackson was showing an alarming interest in this wild notion of graduation.[23]

The Kentuckian responded with the proposal of distribution. Precedents existed. The transfer of federal funds from land sales or of land itself to states had been employed to develop education and encourage internal improvements. In Congress, beginning in 1824 and recurring each year, members had introduced bills for distribution, just as Benton had done in the cause of graduation.[24]

When Clay took his seat in the Senate in December 1831 after several years' absence from the legislative branch, he wished not only to forestall Benton's campaign for graduating land prices downward but also to shore up the rest of his American System. He might save the beleaguered protective tariff if distribution removed land revenue from the general fund and sustained the need for high customs rates. No matter that his opponents would charge that this linkage of tariff and distribution was underhanded strategy.[25] Perhaps more important to the senator was the way distribution would help his stalled internal improvements effort. Jackson's disturbing veto of the Maysville Road bill seemed to signal much trouble, maybe a national withdrawal from this vital responsibility.

As a member of the Committee on Manufactures, he assumed the task of preparing a report recommending distribution. That it was this committee, usually concerned with matters far removed from land, resulted from a Democratic attempt to put him in an uncomfortable position relating to a sensitive topic just before the fall presidential election in which he was a candidate. Ordinarily the task would have gone to the Public Lands Committee, controlled by his opponents. During the course of his work he repeatedly complained about this anomaly. To make it all the more strange, the committee was instructed to report not on his plan but on that of Benton, graduating prices and ceding land to states. Nevertheless, after a long discussion rejecting these impractical ideas, in his opinion, he had the opportunity of laying out the rationale for distribution.

Shortly, in mid-April 1832, he presented his report—he would look back upon it as one of his best state papers. He ripped into graduation as wholly unjust and undesirable. To reduce land prices from the existing minimum of $1.25 per acre to $.50, then probably to free gift, would surely have the effect of devaluing lands already purchased by settlers or intended for sale by states. Citing figures, he sought to demonstrate that the trend was now for sales to increase, which proved that terms were fair. As for the proposal of ceding land to the states, he predicted that a tangle of disparate terms and procedures would replace the present uniform, quite satisfactory system. The fundamental defect in these Jacksonian concoctions, he argued, lay in departing from the initial character of the public domain. It originated with cessions of western territories by a number of states to the new nation in the 1780s. While agreeing to do this, they stipulated that this would be a common resource of the entire Union. If such notions as graduation or donation were accepted, some states and many people would be deprived of precious rights, he declared.

Turning to his own formula, Clay would distribute land proceeds to all states, according to their apportioned representation in Congress. But to extend special assistance to seven newer states, he would continue to grant them 5 percent of land sales within their borders for roads and aid them by 10 percent more. This concession would precede general distribution in which they and the rest of the states would participate. Obviously the senator wanted to sway these westerners from their current attachment to Benton's scheme. The money granted to all states would be used for education and internal improvements, including debts on old projects. A controversial authorization would be expenditure for colonizing free blacks abroad.[26]

After Clay presented his report, the Senate stalled in parliamentary maneuvers. Benton's side now wished the report of the Committee on Manufactures referred to their sympathetic Committee on Public Lands. If they believed this procedure was correct, Clay wondered, why did they not assign the task to that panel in the first place. After many speeches, the matter was referred to Public Lands by a tie vote broken by Vice President Calhoun. Not a friendly gesture by the Carolinian. Predictably, the chairman of this committee, William King of Alabama, made a report that was almost entirely a refutation of what the Kentuckian had said.[27]

King, Benton, and others, mainly southerners and westerners, argued that distribution would decidedly slow down desirable migration to the frontier, while it unfairly tilted toward the older eastern states. So they adhered to downward graduation of prices and cession of land to newer states. A number of them also seized upon the proposed expenditure of funds for colonizing free blacks as a dangerous attack upon slavery.[28] Clay replied with a set speech in late June 1832, filling some gaps and mixing flights of eloquence with aggressive sarcasm.[29] He shot a round at Governor Ninian Edwards of Illinois. His excellency had succumbed to Benton's siren song from Missouri across the Mississippi for cession of "refuse lands, refuse lands, refuse lands," a vague description for less desirable or at least unsold tracts. Indeed the honorable governor had "joined in chorus, and struck the tune an octave higher" to ask for donation of all the public domain in western states.[30]

Near the close of this session in July, the Senate passed the distribution bill, twenty-six to eighteen; but Clay's satisfaction disappeared when he learned that the House had tabled the measure. If the heated issues of banking and tariff had not occupied so much attention during the session, perhaps it would have passed. Still, the known negative views of the president clouded the question.[31]

In fact, when Jackson's annual message arrived at the Capitol in December 1832, it carried a clear recommendation for reduction of land prices.[32] Nonetheless, Clay announced he would again introduce his proposal; and since it was exactly the same as that already considered, he saw no reason to refer it to a committee. A majority disagreed and voted to send it to the dread Committee on Public Lands, which soon enough reported a substitute in Benton's mode of graduation.[33] Clay quickly rose in opposition. Not only repeating his familiar arguments, the Kentuckian warmly defended the provision for colonization of free blacks, a cause he had long supported as president of the American Colonization Society. It would be the "happiest of all events," he asserted, when all blacks, free and slave, were removed from the country.[34] Calhoun, no longer vice president but now a fiery senator in the midst of nullification, must have groaned when he heard that.

Debate resembled what had already been said repeatedly, with opposition coming from southern and western senators.[35] More attention centered on the connection of tariff and land policies, because concurrently the compromise tariff was developing. Clay emphasized the relationship, saying that his concessions on the tariff ought to be matched by southern acceptance of distribution. He did not persuade very many to that view, however, for Calhoun and a number of his followers foresaw excessive national power beyond constitutional limits in administering Clay's land program. They voted against the bill for that reason. The Kentuckian still hoped that Jackson would view tariff and distribution as parts of a grand compromise.[36] He prevailed in the Senate in January and in the House in early March at the very end of the session. Much to his dismay, the president did not return the bill with his signature. So it was a pocket veto.

When Congress convened in December 1833, Jackson sent up a veto message. He had not been able to consider the legislation adequately, he weakly explained, in the short time before adjournment in March. But now he had found a number of objectionable features. He saw no justification for building up a huge fund from land proceeds, which would benefit some states much more than others. Furthermore, national power would endanger the states' sovereignty by intruding into the basic workings of their governments. Far better, he reasoned, to lower land prices and turn much of the public domain over to the states. In other words, put Benton's plan in motion.[37] Clay was furious. Again presidential power by way of the veto had interfered with the will of the people expressed in their representative legislature.[38] He had wished to resign his Senate seat, he said, but this setback on internal improvements and land required him to persist. He introduced his bill with no changes, yet the effort was hopeless.[39] Besides, this session, running on through early 1834, was a very busy one, concerned with removal of governmental deposits from the national bank, the Senate's censure of Jackson, and the mountain of memorials on financial distress induced by Biddle's panic. In the long run, Clay would make other attempts; but he might have to find alternatives to a land fund for internal improvements, particularly while states-rights Democrats occupied the presidency.

8

Jacksonian
Ascendancy

Despite Jacksonian opposition to many proposals for federal internal improvements, Clay did not wholly abandon his effort. Although stung by the Maysville Road veto, the senator sponsored or supported other measures during the middle thirties.

Completion of the National Road was a recurrent issue. In February 1835 the Senate took up a bill for repairing and extending the road before turning it over to western states. He helped passage but believed that the national interest in this artery of transportation surpassed any state interest. And he continued to disagree with Monroe's veto of 1822 as constitutional precedent prohibiting national administration of a tollgate system to maintain the road.[1] Nevertheless, he later favored reducing appropriations for this and other projects, while complaining that Kentucky was not getting its fair share. His friends wondered why he had lost some enthusiasm for what had been his favorite project, yet on second thought they could recognize that a deep-seated localism affected even an economic nationalist.[2] A majority in Congress seemed also to have tired of federal assistance to this road, for it soon stopped.[3]

Clay demonstrated his basic commitment to federal internal improvements, however, by repeated introduction of distribution bills. At each session the provisions were much the same: annual allocation of proceeds from land sales, an initial bonus to newer states, distribution of the remainder apportioned by population to all states, to be used for internal improvements, education, or black colonization. He had come close to success in March 1833 but suffered Jackson's pocket veto. Available funds were now much larger because of a land boom, which would bring in $25 million of revenue in 1836, an increase from $1 million in earlier years.[4]

In the Senate during Christmas week 1835 he reviewed the background and several benefits of his proposal and then countered objections, especially those to its constitutionality. He based authority on the clause empowering Congress to make rules for United States territories and property, which, he reasoned, allowed full discretion on disposition of public lands. He saw no danger to states' rights, as portrayed by opponents.[5] In later debate he warded off other options: Benton's graduation for lower land prices, Robert Walker's full-scale advocacy for preemption rights to purchase by prior settlement and for preference to actual settlers, even Hugh White's startling amalgamation of distribution and graduation. He also rejected a new option, using land revenue to increase appropriations in the current fortifications bill, a poor idea, in his opinion, since Jackson had foolishly generated a crisis with France.[6]

The Senate passed his bill on May 4, 1836, by a vote of twenty-five to twenty-one. Whigs were solidly for it, Democrats opposed. But Clay was again disappointed, because the House tabled it. He could have predicted that the president would have a veto ready anyway, and that was the case.[7]

Another version of distribution took shape shortly after the failure of this plan. It consisted of joining land and financial policies in an intricate, dubious formula that drew a great deal of attention. Rather unexpectedly, Clay might get distribution from the entire surplus in the treasury, not just from land sales.

The first stage of this development had appeared the previous year, February 1835, with Calhoun the principal figure.

Always suspicious of big government and upset about the so-called spoils system, the South Carolina senator sought some way of reducing what he believed to be the source of these threats to liberty and morality, the huge surplus. He would reduce it by a constitutional amendment allowing distribution to the states. Getting this enabling amendment, however, would be quite difficult. The other part of his reform involved stricter regulation of the state banks holding government deposits, indispensable to eliminate Jacksonian corruption, he reasoned.[8]

Though Calhoun's idea did not receive serious notice that session, it did in spring 1836. The fast growing surplus had attracted numerous interests hungry for capital, but it had also alarmed many persons at the Capitol in addition to the Carolinian.[9] Webster delivered a comprehensive speech on the present undesirable impact of the surplus on the state-bank depositories, whose note issues and loans rapidly mounted along with public funds at their disposal. He argued for distributing the surplus to state governments as a remedy.[10]

Parallel to this unusual collaboration of Calhoun and Webster, Clay was pressing for passage of his perennial bill to distribute land revenue. When that attempt collapsed in May, the Kentuckian supported the move involving the general surplus. The proposal now called for apportioned "deposits" with the states, technically subject to the Treasury's recall but recognized practically as a donation. It was nothing less than a transparent disguise for Henry Clay's faltering land scheme, Benton growled.[11] The measure got through Congress in a few weeks, its path made easier because Calhoun gave up his requirement of a constitutional amendment. And the Jackson administration reluctantly accepted distribution in order to get a much needed means of regulating the depository banks.[12] Perhaps, too, a possible favorable effect upon the approaching presidential election counted for something among Democrats working for their candidate Van Buren.

This deposit act directed quarterly distribution of surplus to states in apportioned amounts for one year only. Congress could, of course, extend the process, or it could supplement or replace it. In the next session, beginning December 1836, many proposals appeared, some involving the surplus and some going to its main source, public-land sales. No one must have been surprised to see the determined senator from Kentucky introduce his distribution bill again. But the initiative came from the administration. Secretary of Treasury Levi Woodbury's recommendations in his annual report would reduce the surplus instead of distributing it and would do so by restricting sale of land to actual settlers, not to entrepreneurs and speculators. The Senate Committee on Public Lands favored a version of this approach. Calhoun urged cession of the public domain to the states, while Benton and his followers renewed calls for graduating prices downward, and a growing number of members favored preemption by "squatters" at minimum price, which would bypass bidding to a higher level at auction. More formidable than any of these formulas was the order Jackson had issued, known as the Specie Circular, requiring payment for land purchases in specie rather than bank notes and therefore cutting revenue. William Rives came up with a more lenient model to accomplish the same purpose by gradual steps toward nonacceptance of bank notes in small denominations.[13]

Clay's prescription of distribution was the only serious proposal to maintain the present level of land revenue, but he lacked the necessary support. He therefore concentrated on defeating measures that would lower receipts. Walker's bill to limit sales to actual settlers and to establish a policy of preemption suited the administration and probably a majority in the Senate. So Clay aimed criticism chiefly against it as well as against several amendments brought forward.

Restricting sales to actual settlers, proponents believed, would forestall excesses by speculators. Here was a favorite target for nearly everyone, the rapacious operator grabbing large tracts at cheap prices to the detriment of honest yeomen. Even Clay did not try to defend speculation and indeed declared he had bought only a quarter section of public land in the last twenty years.[14] In truth, many senators, such as Webster and his colleague John Davis, were active speculators but did not admit it.[15] When accused by Calhoun of speculating, Jackson fiercely denied it in public print.[16] About the only good word for the practice came from Thomas Ewing, who pointed out its substantial contribution to economic development.[17]

Clay had very strong objections to the new provision for general preemption, permitting unauthorized settlers on public land to buy it at the minimum price in quantities up to 1,280 acres for each family member. For one thing, he contended, selling such large parcels was not consistent with its supposed democratic impact. Would not speculators fraudulently swear they met the requirements of such a statute—to place the land under cultivation, for example? Preliminary experience with an earlier limited law showed that would be the inevitable result, especially so in light of inadequate administrative machinery. The waste of a great national resource would be tragic, he insisted. Throughout his career, Clay remained intensely hostile to preemption.[18]

Again the demand for downward graduation of prices of unsold land enlivened legislative debate. Benton, of course, urged it, and many other senators did too. Calhoun now came over to that position, however quixotically. He would adopt graduation quite gradually, indeed would lower prices over thirty-five years until 1862. And he would connect it with cession of all lands to the states, which nevertheless would have to sell at a price set by Congress and would have to share the revenue with Washington. Such a policy would be an even greater plunder of this valuable resource, Clay exclaimed. Besides, he saw no justification for selling already cheap land more cheaply when land offices were crowded with purchasers. Nonetheless, Calhoun stirred a great deal of interest among states' righters, especially westerners, even if the Democratic leadership did not incorporate the Carolinian's complicated scheme in its bill.[19]

The outcome of the solons' colloquy on land policy in relation to public finance was passage of Wright's measure for sales restricted to actual settlers and for preemption, twenty-seven to twenty-three, in the Senate. It was to no avail, however, for the House tabled it.[20]

Now, in March 1837, the last month of the congressional session and of Jackson's administration, proponents of distribution tried to extend payment of installments from the general surplus to the states beyond October, the terminal date of the deposit law. The House had attached a provision to the fortifications bill to do so; but in the Senate, Wright, who had never liked distribution, moved to strike that provision. Others joined him in deploring state dependence upon national largesse. And a number touched upon a subject largely avoided for several years, the protective tariff, which might be lowered as a better means to reduce the surplus. With majority backing, Clay had steadfastly opposed tampering with the compromise of 1833.[21] On the other hand, in his annual message Jackson had suggested that this could be a way to escape the present ill-advised distribution.[22]

Never failing to seize the opportunity, the Kentuckian argued that those who opposed the House provision for extending distribution of the general surplus ought to come over to his formula of drawing only from land proceeds. During an excited exchange with Wright, he erupted, "Take the land bill, like an honest man."[23] Buchanan, ordinarily not an ally, declared he would do just that but chided Clay for also "cherishing and caressing" the House measure as an alternative.[24] Webster and Calhoun, concurring with Clay that there was no possibility of passing anything else, joined him in willingness to accept the House provision.

The Senate voted to follow the insistent Wright, however, in twice refusing to go along with the lower chamber after receiving conference committee reports.[25] The last hours of the session had arrived, so that the question of distribution carried over to the new administration of Van Buren. Meanwhile, by the previous law there would be three more quarterly installments to the states in 1837—unless something unexpected happened to the economy.

Over the period of discussion and legislation on distribution of surplus to states, a related question concerned regulation of state-chartered banks holding federal deposits after their removal from the Bank of the United States in 1833. The deposit law of 1836 addressed both subjects. It built upon previous efforts by the administration and the states, such as specifying reserve requirements for notes and their redeemability in specie. Jacksonians, especially the president himself, tolerated inclusion of distribution in the statute in order to get bank regulations, which now provided for periodic reports to the Treasury, limits on the ratio of deposits and notes to capital stock, restrictions on paper of small denominations, and other controls.[26]

Whether the impact of the new system would be helpful or a cause for later financial troubles of the country remained to be seen. Like most Whigs, Clay favored large scope for banking operations in order to stimulate growth, though he had bad memories of the Kentucky relief episode. He did not share the rising antipathy toward banks in general, voiced by radical Democrats like Kendall and Blair. So he voted for the regulatory provisions in the law but did not believe they were an adequate substitute for the late national bank. Although he did not enter the current debate, he would have much to say as banking and politics remained entwined for a long time to come.

Democratic criticism of banks increasingly favored gold and silver instead of notes for currency. Of course, "Old Bullion" Benton had long advocated that policy; and as the war with the BUS reached a climax, the president himself took this position as a means of protecting the people against unstable paper issues. In pursuit of an enlarged metallic medium, the administration had put through gold revaluation in the law of 1834. The next year Congress considered proposals to add branches to the Philadelphia mint for the same objective. In the Senate Clay jumped into a lively discussion about whether to set them up in New Orleans and other southern locations. He launched an animated attack upon the whole idea. Just a waste of money for an unnecessary operation, he declared. He must have hesitated a bit when he joined other special interests and recommended a branch in Lexington, unsuccessfully, it turned out. And he lost his main argument when Congress did authorize establishing several new branches of the mint, which could increase the hard-money supply.[27]

The movement for bullion, however, made little progress. The hundreds of banks across the land, issuing ever more notes feeding all the insatiable segments of the economy, not to mention the decided trend toward deposit currency, effectively blocked this reform. As a lawyer in the Supreme Court, Clay contributed to the maintenance of bank-note currency. In representing a bank chartered by Kentucky, he secured a ruling affirming the constitutionality of notes issued by this institution entirely owned by the state. The decision in *Briscoe* v. *Bank of the Commonwealth* (1837) held that the state itself had not issued the paper and had therefore not violated the constitutional prohibition of state bills of credit. The finespun distinction cleared away a legal objection of many Jacksonians, the president included, but not their political criticism of this medium. It is interesting to notice, however, that the new chief justice, concurring with the majority, was Roger Taney, Old Hickory's right hand in the Bank War. No doubt he was influenced by a states-rights argument as well as by the undesirability of judicial intervention in this deeply rooted practice of circulating notes.[28]

Jackson had also sought to advance a hard-money policy by his Specie Circular in July 1836, directing collectors to receive only gold and silver, not bank notes, for purchases of public land. The Senate had rejected Benton's bill to this effect, whereupon the Missourian had persuaded the president that an executive order could accomplish the same thing. He offered to supply a a draft, which Jackson accepted and signed.[29] As soon as legislators gathered for a new session in December, Clay's lieutenant Thomas Ewing introduced a resolution to revoke the Specie Circular. An angry discussion ensued over the next two months.

Benton and other supporters of the administration contended that it had been necessary to curb wild land speculation, stimulated by financial excesses of western banks. Conditions would worsen next year, they predicted, when the Treasury would distribute large funds to states under the recently adopted deposit law. Benton added a conspiracy theory. Biddle, he warned, was planning to create another panic in the economy, to find an excuse to retrench credit, and to blame the resulting distress on anti-BUS measures in still another effort to gain a recharter.

These senators justified the executive procedure employed in the Specie Circular. An old joint resolution of 1816 had provided that dues to the government could be paid either in specie or in notes redeemable in specie, intended at the time to require the new national bank and other institutions to issue only convertible paper. Now, they reasoned, the regulation authorized the secretary of treasury at his discretion to select only one medium, either specie or notes, in transactions involving the government. In the present instance, it was specie only. This interpretation might check a Whig objection that the executive had unconstitutionally bypassed Congress in high-handed fashion.[30]

Clay and his partisans attacked each point. To be sure, they deplored destabilizing conduct of land buyers and banks, but they identified the fundamental cause to be the sustained Jacksonian attack upon the BUS. In other words, the Specie Circular was only one more misstep in this conflict over the last eight years. Then they criticized, in good Whig rhetoric, the dangerous, unilateral application of executive power to establish a policy after Congress had refused to do so. Furthermore, the resolution of 1816 did not mean what the Democrats claimed, they persuasively concluded, for it allowed those paying dues to the government, but not the Treasury receiving them, to select either of two media.[31] Actually, Clay believed, the preferable course at present was to blend the proposal of William Rives with that of the Specie Circular: allow reception both of a metallic medium and of bank notes redeemable in specie yet in denominations no less than twenty dollars. It would avoid the undesirable effects of small notes but assure reliable, reasonably available currency.[32]

At last, a bill to reverse the Specie Circular passed by a decisive vote of forty-one to five, then in the House by a large margin. The provisions were just as Clay wished: either specie or notes of at least twenty dollars redeemable in specie could be paid to the government.[33] When the president received it on the last day of his administration, he pocket vetoed; and though he prepared a message of explanation, he filed it. So the question remained for the incoming Van Buren administration and would have a longer, still acrimonious history.[34]

Another episode during the final stage of the Bank War involved a vindication of the chief executive. Finally, Benton, who had been attempting for nearly three years to counteract the Senate's censure of Jackson for removing deposits from the BUS and for dismissing Secretary of Treasury Duane's refusal to do so, had the necessary votes. He introduced his familiar resolution to expunge this censure from the journal. The Missourian delivered an encomium on the president's character and contributions to the nation's well-being that surpassed any previous version.[35] Knowing they were outnumbered, the Whigs nevertheless recorded an opposite assessment, centering on BUS politics. Clay surveyed at length the events of the controversy, the veto of recharter, the removal of deposits, the recent declaration of the Specie Circular. To expunge, that is to blot out the official record totally, violated the constitutional requirement to keep a journal, he said.[36] Webster closed the speechmaking in similar vein. Then in a tense evening session, Benton's side looked on with satisfaction as the clerk drew black lines around the words of censure in the journal and wrote "Expunged" over them.[37] Clay remarked to Benton he should be known as the knight of the black lines.[38]

Notwithstanding this triumph, no legislative roll call could expunge the memory of repeated battles over national-bank issues. Party politics had generated confrontations that neither Democrats nor Whigs were willing to resolve by compromise. A useful, if too powerful, financial institution had fallen victim to the polarization of opinion across the land. The few efforts to make a practical adjustment, such as that of Webster, had made no progress as positions on the bank became hardened articles of faith. Though Jackson and his advisers had initiated the Bank War, Clay had fought back with an unyielding strategy, not consistent with his well-known skill of negotiating a resolution of disparate interests. Now, as Old Hickory turned over the presidential office to his intimate associate Van Buren, who was also recognized for his ability to settle conflict of political elements, future financial policy might be somewhat less channeled than it had been. But a factor about which neither Clay nor Van Buren could be certain was the health of the economy in the next few years.

9

Financial Problems

W hen Jackson handed the presidency over to his valued
friend and chief lieutenant Martin Van Buren in March
1837, he could not have been more pleased. This New Yorker,
principal architect of the Democratic party, prototype of a seasoned politician, experienced in high-level offices, and fully
committed to Jeffersonian ideology, seemed certain to continue the policies of his popular predecessor. Yet almost as
soon as he had been inaugurated, his misfortunes began, not
to end during his four years in the White House. A financial
panic, followed by a protracted depression, afflicted the country and beclouded his unhappy term.

The new president's first problem involved a continued controversy about the Specie Circular, requiring payment of metallic currency for public-land sales. Whigs and some Democrats,
irritated by Jackson's last-minute pocket veto of the bill to
revoke this executive order, now pressed Van Buren to withdraw
it. Merchants and bankers from his state sent a delegation to
Washington, urging revocation in order to correct a growing
shortage of specie, which was being drained to transmontane
land offices, they believed. On the other hand, hard-money advocates emphasized the need to retain the circular and put down

the persistent land boom, which, they complained, had been stimulated by speculators, supplied with western paper currency. Probably more persuasive was the correspondence arriving from Old Hickory, lecturing the besieged chief executive about the importance of standing fast. Whatever the reason, Van Buren decided not to touch the Specie Circular. By communicating his decision to the New York committee in writing instead of by a give-and-take conversation he revealed his uneasiness.[1]

Already the first phase of the panic had appeared. In mid-March, just two weeks into Van Buren's tenure, the bank of I. and L. Joseph in New York City failed because of losses from the collapse of the cotton market in New Orleans. The difficulty at the busy southern port had arisen from an over-production of cotton and a contraction of the large supply of British credit, which had previously absorbed that output. Soon other banks in New York and across the country were also affected, inducing them to suspend specie payment of their notes. A general impairment of confidence throughout the economy developed by early May. Through the following months of 1837 it was clear that the enormous growth in the numbers and operations of banks that had occurred in the Jacksonian period was slowing to a halt, if not signaling something even more serious. Curtailment of credit, weakened agricultural markets, faltering business activity, unemployment, all were worrisome. To be sure, the problem could be mainly deflation and necessary readjustment; and perhaps there would be relief after a short while. But the long-range situation could be a sustained cyclical depression.[2]

Predictably, Whigs blamed the Democrats for their policy on banks and currency. As Clay charged, "The intelligence from the South, as to our commercial embarrassments, is dreadful. The most alarming circumstance is the reduction in the price of Cotton. That, if it continues, must affect every interest and every part of our Country.

"The measures of Government have beyond all doubt contributed largely to produce the present calamitous state of affairs."[3]

Webster agreed. In an extensively reported speech in Manhattan, he reviewed the entire Jacksonian record negatively and forecast more trouble ahead unless the administration promptly applied remedies, particularly assistance to banks by revoking the Specie Circular. Later the institutions in the city, citing the scarcity of specie, suspended redemption of their notes. Webster's critics complained that his speech had encouraged a needless step.[4]

Democrats blamed unsound practices of the banks, principally Biddle's BUS, for causing the panic. Excessive note issues in relation to reserves, manipulation of credit for their political advantage, stimulation of land speculation and of unwise commercial expansion—these and other mistakes and abuses, they insisted, had brought on a dangerous, inflated financial condition leading to a downward plunge. It was therefore the responsibility of those who had created this alarming dislocation to provide remedies, since the national administration was neither culpable nor empowered to intervene.[5]

Although contemporaries divided along party lines in explaining causes of the panic, historians later inclined toward the Whig version. Thus removal of governmental deposits at the national bank and their transfer to state institutions fed an overexpansion of credit to business, to land purchasers, and to unrealistic state internal improvement programs. After 1836, in the absence of desirable control by the BUS, a crash was inevitable. Furthermore, a hard-money antidote was then unproductive, according to much scholarly literature.[6]

Although this interpretation was credible, a modern revisionist view gained ground. Econometricians analyzed monetary and price data, from which they concluded that bank-note issues had more than adequate reserves and that actually the problem was a sharp contraction of excessive British specie and credit before the cotton crisis of 1837. Because of pressures at home, England curtailed this source of American capital, and the impact damaged the general economy, though never as severely as depicted. Institutions in this country, in fact, maintained large reserves for their notes in circulation, both before and after announcement of the Specie Circular. So the international dimension was more important than Jacksonian policy as a cause of panic and depression, these researchers concluded. One must accept this corrective, yet recognize that not everything can be measured quantitatively, that political and psychological elements surely carried much weight as well.[7]

Examination of these elements is revealing. State-chartered banks, some of them depositories of treasury funds, show an interesting relation to Jacksonian politics. As the Bank War progressed in Washington, dissatisfaction with all financial institutions increased. In states across the country, concern about their excessive power and various abuses led to efforts toward stricter regulation. Inflated paper currency precipitated legislation such as higher reserve requirements for notes. Entanglement of banks in overextended state internal improvement programs led to public and private retrenchment. Increasingly the movement for hard money to replace paper strengthened. The next step by an advance guard for reform was to demand abolition of banks altogether. After a decade or so, the force of these thrusts diminished; nevertheless, it left a substantial residue of corporate regulations, particularly affecting banks.

To some extent, the same pattern obtained at the national capital. As Jackson beat down Biddle's bank and put deposits in state banks, the secretary of treasury imposed a number of rules to assure the safety of federal funds. Then Congress passed the distribution act, which set forth further regulations—on the ratio of reserves to deposits and notes, for example. When the panic hit in spring 1837 and banks suspended specie payment, however, disillusionment with banks abounded. Much as on the state level, the demand for hard-money currency was followed by sentiment for separation of all banks from the government's fiscal operations.[8]

Such was the direction of Van Buren's thinking as economic conditions worsened. After the banks suspended specie payment on their notes, the Treasury was prohibited by the existing law of 1836 from making deposits in these institutions. Gradually funds accumulated in the custody of federal officials, thereby increasing the distinction between private and public sectors of finance. With this first step, the administration moved toward a permanent separation, an independent treasury. Through May and June, the executive considered such a plan, which had been floating around for more than three years and had even been debated in the House. A clerk in the Treasury, the antibank radical William Gouge, drafted a measure for the president to send to Congress. Before doing so, Van Buren consulted associates and found that some of his friends were unenthusiastic. Wright, his stalwart leader in the Senate, had to be swayed from a negative reaction. And William Rives, Nathaniel Tallmadge, and even Taney opposed abandoning connection with state banks. By midsummer Wright and some others were brought around, making it possible to give adoption of an independent treasury high priority in the work of the next congressional session.[9]

Van Buren had decided he could not wait until the usual opening date in December. Having called a special session to meet in September, he sent up a message to Capitol Hill, reporting on the country's economic problems and recommending measures to alleviate them. He saw a number of causes of the present crisis: the abrupt curtailment of British credit previously extended too far, undue expansion of loans by American banks, the consequent "overaction in all departments of business," and reckless speculation, yes also the "luxurious habits," of the citizenry. He had nothing good to say about banks, misusing government deposits and now suspending specie payment of their notes. The national bank had been no better. Fortunately, Congress and the electorate had repudiated it. It was therefore imperative for the government to separate its fiscal operations from all banks and rely, as it was necessarily beginning to do, upon its own officers to maintain custody of Treasury funds. His only enthusiasm was the promise he saw in a new policy, soon known as "divorce."

The president asked the legislators to deal with several other matters, such as issuing Treasury notes to carry on public business, granting a delay in payment of import duties by merchants, and discontinuing installments to states under the deposit act, now that the surplus had disappeared.

If his prescription to relieve hard times seemed too cautious to his opponents, almost a retreat by the people's government at a time of their need, the Fox of Kinderhook would answer that the best course must be to adhere to proven Jeffersonian doctrine. National power was strictly limited. It must not intervene in the concerns of commerce and agriculture to favor one interest or class against another. "The less Government interferes with private pursuits," he declared in Adam Smith's mode, "the better for general prosperity." One can visualize Senator Clay grimacing when the clerk read that part of the message.[10]

The bill that Wright, chairman of the Senate Finance Committee, introduced on September 14, 1837, would enact Van Buren's recommendation of an independent treasury, what Clay and fellow Whigs deprecatingly dubbed a "subtreasury" under the thumb of a powerful executive. To check as many objections as possible, the proposal would not add a layer of federal appointees but use existing officers to maintain custody of public funds and disburse them as ordered. Hopefully this would avoid the appearance of party advantage from new patronage. The plan would also bypass the highly controversial question of specie or paper currency receivable by the government. The strategy not to forbid notes of state banks was a concession to these institutions, which would already be deprived of all the federal deposits they presently held.

Then the unpredicted happened. Calhoun announced his strong support of the bill, despite years of antagonism toward the president. That assistance came with a price, however, for the Carolinian offered an amendment gradually requiring specie payment of all dues to the federal treasury. Wright saw that the net effect of Calhoun's new-found support could be negative because of state-bank reaction to rejection of their paper. The problem had been difficult enough, owing to alienation of some states' righters at the hands of Van Buren, high priest of states' rights. Benton, at least, was very pleased that the amended measure could at last put the country on a hard-money basis, free from bankers' manipulation.[11]

The Democratic argument for an independent treasury rested mainly on dissatisfaction with the role of depository banks after transfer of funds to them from the BUS. Senators such as Wright and Buchanan concurred with the chief executive that the result had been overextension of credit and overaction of business generally. It was now necessary to prevent recurrences by detaching the connection with government. In effect, they were conceding a failure of what had been called the

Jacksonian experiment. If this was a sensitive point, the unwelcome Calhoun amendment against reception of state-bank notes was also worrisome. Indeed, these party managers admitted they were accepting the proviso in spite of reservations.[12]

A middle group of conservative states-rights Democrats posed a real threat to the administration. One was the able Virginian William Rives, who sought to rescue state banks from the damaging impact of an independent treasury. Rives had been a regular Jacksonian, but now he was entering a phase of political independence. If he could not preserve the existing state-bank deposit system, which he ardently wished to do, he was determined at least to kill Calhoun's utterly unworkable scheme of exclusive specie payments to the federal treasury. The New York senator, Nathaniel Tallmadge, shared Rives's views. It embarrassed Van Buren, since Tallmadge came from his own county and from a compatible association with him in politics. He represented the interest of powerful New York banks, influencing the financial condition of the nation. During the present debate, he criticized the Specie Circular for driving these banks to suspension of specie payment of notes, currently a very contentious subject.[13] Would the Fox in the Executive Mansion, master party chief that he was, manage to avert a terrible split in the Democracy?

Midway through all the speechmaking, Clay had his turn. For days he had been uncharacteristically silent, realizing that his opponents controlled both houses as well as the executive. Of course, he disliked the proposal. It would establish two media of exchange, he thought: hard money for the government and paper money for the people. "We are all—people, States, Union, banks—bound up and interwoven together, united in fortune and destiny, and all, all entitled to the protecting care of parental government," he declared, and this subtreasury would not provide that care. As for the administration of such a system, he found no assurance that it would be efficient and honest. Federal officials could be influenced to handle funds for personal gain or political advantage and would probably become autonomous, unreliable banks themselves.

Lacking the votes, he conceded that he could not succeed in an attempt to restore the national bank, although such an institution was precisely what was needed for recovery. The sad state of affairs came about, he insisted, because of Jacksonian policies—veto of the BUS recharter, removal of deposits, the Specie Circular, and the pocket veto of the distribution of land proceeds. He urged a common effort to meet the crisis. Indicating a willingness to compromise, he even sympathized with the state banks now under attack and offered support for Rives's attempt to come to their rescue.[14]

All the while, petitions for chartering another national bank continued to arrive, and Wright felt that Clay's speech provided a good opportunity to demonstrate that a contrary opinion prevailed—this despite the Kentuckian's remark he would not then try to get congressional action on the subject. Wright's motion not to grant the petitioners' request produced a series of parliamentary tactics, among them Clay's resolution that it would be expedient to establish a bank only when a majority of the people favored it. As the whole Senate well knew, that body was not minded to set up another such institution. Clay's resolution failed, twenty-six to fourteen; and Wright's motion passed, thirty-one to fourteen.[15]

After this national-bank interlude Webster spoke on the Whig side, focusing on the need to provide a uniform currency, impossible with an independent treasury, he argued. One of his telling points was a blow to Calhoun, now allied with the administration and committed to exclusive specie currency. Webster recalled the circumstances in 1816 when he and the Carolinian collaborated to pass a resolution to accept either specie or notes redeemable in specie in payments to the government. And had not Calhoun managed the bill chartering the national bank? Calhoun weakly replied that he had assumed this responsibility because of pressing problems the country faced after the War of 1812, without regard to constitutional considerations. Webster's rejoinder underscored the southerner's title of nullifier, presently denying essential financial powers. The United States must have a national credit system, available for transactions of business beyond the jurisdiction of a single state or the reach of a single bank. And, he continued, uniformity was needed to support active use of bills of exchange throughout the economy. The government should assure that uniformity, should avoid the proposed negativism. It was a practical viewpoint, to be sure, if unlikely to prevail.[16]

The Senate approved the independent-treasury bill by a narrow margin, 25-23, and Calhoun's specie amendment even more narrowly, by one vote. In the House, there was still greater opposition, because of less effective Democratic leadership and because of speeches moving into the sensitive subject of slavery, so that it failed, 120-107. Whigs solidly opposed and were joined by some conservative Democrats.[17] This dissenting segment of the majority party disliked the threatened impact upon state banks, which would lose government deposits and would find their notes no longer acceptable at the Treasury. The states-rights president had paid a price in undercutting this wing of his party, and Calhoun's connection with the bill was not helpful.

In addition to its effort for an independent treasury, the administration had to address an acute fiscal problem of shrinking revenue and, needless to say, vanished surplus. This was a major reason Van Buren called the special session. As soon as Congress convened, it received a message urging circulation of treasury notes to keep the government operating. The secretary of treasury recommended notes of a twenty-dollar minimum denomination bearing no interest. What an opportunity for the Whigs to jump on the hard-money people! What an about-face to resort to this kind of paper currency, the opposition cried! In the Senate, Webster and the Finance Committee got an amendment raising the minimum to one hundred dollars and providing interest. Benton naturally liked this conservative change, and so did Clay; but the terms of the measure, as passed, compromised at a fifty-dollar minimum, with interest. Whatever the details, the Kentuckian would remember the discussion of this question with more than a little satisfaction.[18]

Another proposal to help the hard-pressed Treasury would postpone the fourth quarterly distribution to the states. Since the government lacked enough surplus, $3 million short of the necessary $9 million to fulfill its scheduled obligation, it only made sense to delay or stop this strange operation. Nevertheless, Clay and other partisan Whigs believed the statute of 1836 had created an obligation to the states, which ought to be honored since they had exisiting commitments based upon receiving the installment. Why not draw upon general funds if the designated surplus was insufficient, he asked? Congress did not find that reasoning convincing and approved mere postponement of distribution, which would become an extension to the present day.[19]

Except for this modest success and the authorization to issue treasury notes, Van Buren's recommendations to alleviate economic difficulties failed adoption. Certainly he got no help from Clay. A proposal to extend credit to importers of foreign goods, he contended, would only hurt American manufacturers and violate the compromise tariff.[20] A bankruptcy bill to apply only to banking corporations would be unfair and unproductive, he thought.[21] Though not speaking much on issues other than the deferred independent treasury, the senator voted consistently with the opposition.

After the congressional adjournment he concluded that the president had been cornered, having abandoned both national-bank and state-bank options with little hope of establishing his substitute, widely recognized as altogether faulty. "I do not see he has any thing left but to hang himself," the senator predicted.[22] But such a diagnosis was premature, for the Fox had three more years to run the race. The president's opponents also had problems, particularly an obvious lack of unity about how they would relieve the troubled country.

When Clay took his seat in the Senate for the new session in December 1837, he listened to a presidential message again urging approval of an independent-treasury system. Though Van Buren was determined to prevail on this issue, he attempted to placate pivotal opponents, particularly conservative states-rights Democrats. His tone was moderate and deferential, inviting compromise. It would be possible, he said, to make exceptions for some federal deposits in state banks by "special arrangement."[23] Whig gains in recent elections and evidence of negative public opinion in New York, Virginia, Pennsylvania, and elsewhere influenced this adjustment of strategy. Insufficient adjustment, thought the senator from Kentucky: "The Message of today adheres to the Sub treasury scheme! Nothing more was needed to consummate the overthrow of the President."[24] Nevertheless, that would have to wait until the next election, three years away; meanwhile Clay's option of rechartering the national bank would also have to be deferred until sentiment for it ripened.

After several weeks of debate, on February 19, 1838, Clay had the floor to make a major speech, one fully reviewing the Democratic record. From his first year in office, the Kentuckian charged, Jackson had attacked the BUS in order to replace it with a government bank under the complete control of the president. Step by step over eight years, he advanced toward that objective, so that when Van Buren entered office, the rationale of an independent treasury had been established. The ingredients included separating government and banks, replacing paper currency with hard money, and curbing privileges of corporations. The new chief executive had declared he was the honored instrument to continue Old Hickory's policy. Instead of an "instrument," Clay snapped, he would be a "tool."[25]

After this long, animated attack upon the administration's bill, the senator struck at Calhoun, who maintained his support of an independent treasury with a provision gradually requiring payment of all dues to the government in specie. That in itself rankled Clay, who had lost the Carolinian's cooperation on banking issues. But worse, Calhoun had recently published a letter in a newspaper in Edgefield, South Carolina, defending his switch back to the Democratic side and proceeding to slash at Clay's entire American System. In fact, Calhoun looked back upon the tariff compromise of 1833 and claimed that his implementation of nullification had put an end to protectionism. Clay categorically denied such had been the case. As for the southerner's present inconsistency about parties, the Kentuckian remarked sarcastically: "He took up his musket, knap sack, and shotpouch, and joined the other party. He went, horse, foot, and dragoon; and he himself composed the whole corps."[26]

When the Senate voted on passage of the independent-treasury bill, Calhoun and others supporting the full specie requirement deserted the administration because that provision had been abandoned during debate. Some, Buchanan for example, opposed the bill in response to opinion back home despite their own favorable views. Of course, Clay voted nay.

Even so, the Senate voted to adopt the independent treasury, 27 to 25; but the House again disappointed Van Buren by rejecting it, 125 to 111. The disapproval of sixteen conservative states-rights Democrats in the lower chamber supplied the margin for defeat there.[27]

In the next session, the short one ending in March 1839, the president made another attempt. The economy had worsened after a brief recovery from the panic, and he put an independent treasury forward as the solution to problems created by banks. Seemingly, if the government were to control behavior of these institutions, then it would hardly be pursuing the earlier goal of separation of public and private finance. Interestingly, he would now accept Calhoun's proposal of exclusive specie payments to the treasury. The Senate did pass the bill by a decided majority, twenty-eight to fifteen, but the House persisted in its role of spoiler and did not even develop a committee report to consider.[28] Addressing large gatherings in eastern cities through the summer, Clay bore down on the danger of vast executive power if the administration eventually succeeded.[29]

The country did not have to wait very long to test the senator's predictions. Several conditions finally allowed enactment of a measure. The deepening depression caused many people to demand at least something be done for recovery. In the next session Rives and Tallmadge, the pesky conservatives, were not present. Still more noticeable was the rapprochement of Calhoun and Van Buren, highlighted by the Carolinian's friendly visit at the White House, the first time in years. Westerners had been courted by the administration's endorsement of favorable public-land proposals. Furthermore, five New Jersey Democrats were awarded contested House seats. The lower chamber had been the main barrier to passage, but it could now join the Senate in delivering a long-delayed present to the chief executive. How satisfying it was to him on the Fourth of July, 1840, when he happily signed the independent-treasury bill. It was the nation's second Declaration of Independence, he truly believed.[30]

For Clay that was far from an accurate assessment. He charged that the destructive Bank War waged by Jacksonians had led to a very unwise decision. It sought the impossible by attempting to abandon paper currency in a modern age relying upon other media as well as bullion. The government itself would have to resort to paper in the form of treasury drafts and notes. It had destroyed an indispensable national bank. It concentrated in the executive an unprecedented degree of power. Just as objectionable was the heartless attitude of the president, who "deliberately wraps around himself the folds of his India-rubber cloak, and lifting his umbrella over his head, tells [the people], drenched and shivering as they are, under the beating rain and hail, and snow, falling upon them, that he means to take care of himself and the official corps, and that they are in the habit of expecting too much from government and must look out for their own shelter, and security, and salvation!"[31] As for himself, Clay eagerly anticipated a glorious revolution when the next election would drive these ineffectual incumbents out.

One of the highest priorities when that day arrived, he thought, would be chartering a national bank. With prospects for congressional approval at this time so poor, indeed nonexistent, it would be fruitless to attempt anything before clear popular approval in a national election. Meanwhile, he interjected comments to this effect during discussions of an independent treasury. Toward the end, more and more petitions for a bank arrived at the Capitol; and as he presented them, he repeated his position.[32] He maintained a friendly correspondence with Nicholas Biddle, who naturally hoped that Clay would manage to revive the BUS. For his part, Biddle lobbied the Pennsylvania legislature to instruct Buchanan to vote against an independent treasury in the Senate.[33]

If Clay could have followed his personal preferences, he would have been pleased to revive the old bank with Biddle at the helm; but that was not the case. However much he condemned the Jacksonian assault upon the institution, the years of bank politics could not be ignored. The Kentuckian knew he would have to make adjustments in light of that history when the opportunity to act arrived. Earlier, in May 1838, while presenting a batch of petitions, he had sketched some possible features of a new institution. The capital stock should be raised to $50 million from $35 million, subscribed by states in addition to the national government and individuals. He mentioned several other departures from the old charter, particularly to regulate credit and exchange functions more strictly and to require a greater degree of disclosure to the public. He dismissed all constitutional objections as no longer open to question.[34]

At present the whole question was abstract. The only banks on the scene were state chartered (even the old BUS), many of them depository pets. Despite his preference for a national bank, Clay had suggested to Tallmadge that he might be willing to "make a full and fair experiment" with these institutions. One has to discount such a remark as political maneuver. He could not have been seriously interested in a state-bank "experiment," a Jacksonian term he had often ridiculed.[35]

Bank problems almost always involved currency, which was true now. After the onset of the panic in spring 1837, all institutions stopped redeeming their notes in specie. Among the first to suspend were the New York banks. By state law they had to resume specie redemption of notes within one year, a deadline of May 1838, and they did so. Other banks followed, but the BUS held back. Biddle decided to use resumption as a lever on the government to revoke the Specie Circular and thus allow bank notes for land purchases. He delayed also in order to block passage of the independent-treasury bill then pending in Congress, obviously to promote a BUS recharter.[36] To assist Biddle as well as to restore the pre-panic system of paper currency on its own merits, Clay introduced a resolution in 1838 to receive paper redeemable in specie as well as specie itself for all dues to the Treasury. Concurrently Webster attempted much the same thing, though he felt that the Kentuckian had unfairly preempted him. In any event, Congress approved Clay's resolution, repealing the Specie Circular by a large margin.[37] The outcome was a recognition of the need for both types of currency, but it did not advance the cause of the old national bank as Biddle had wished.

Although issues of public finance received the greatest attention in the late 1830s, another significant question involved land legislation. It was a time of heavy migration into the Mississippi Valley, of settling a broad territory where land was cheap and plentiful. While liberal terms of purchase had reflected a steady trend of governmental policies since the beginning of the century, political pressures aimed at an ever more generous system. The gathering depression had stopped a land boom and spurred sentiment for helping this economic sector.

In his first message to Congress in 1837, Van Buren made some cautious recommendations, which could also attract western votes on other questions, such as the independent treasury. Like Benton, who had focused on the matter for years, the president endorsed graduation, a scheduled reduction of prices of unsold land, but he wished for it to be based on actual value, not length of time after the first offering for sale. He also favored a permanent preemption law, much broader than previous temporary measures, to give extralegal settlers a prior right of obtaining land at the minimum price.[38] There were additional options, carried over from earlier consideration: federal cession or nominal sale of land to the states (now embraced by Calhoun, courting western support) and, of course, Clay's favorite formula of distributing land proceeds to states for internal improvements or other programs. At each congressional session in the four Van Buren years, these possibilities were extensively explored.

In the Senate Clay fought a defensive battle against lowering prices in graduation bills. Repeatedly he contended that existing terms of sale were eminently fair (a minimum of $1.25 per acre) and need not be reduced to give-away levels. The public domain belonged to the whole Union, to the older states as well as the new, toward which this plan tilted, he insisted. The term "waste land," often applied to unsold tracts, was inaccurate, for sales of these valuable parcels proceeded as rapidly as reasonable development required. If the government reduced the price to as little as $.25 per acre, it would wrongly donate a national treasure. When his arguments seemed hopeless, he tried to postpone action until a new Congress would better register popular opinion. Nevertheless, his opponents made headway in picturing him as hostile to deserving frontiersmen while shielding speculation by well-to-do entrepreneurs. In votes in three consecutive sessions, the Senate approved graduation; yet the House disagreed.[39]

Concurrently, Congress discussed and passed preemption bills. Whereas unauthorized occupancy of public land had been a trespass under an early statute, Congress had condoned, indeed encouraged it in legislation from 1830 onward, covering only previous settlement and in force for only two years. But in the late thirties there were strong efforts to adopt a permanent and not merely retroactive measure. Proponents, particularly Benton, Robert Walker, and Clement Clay, advocated the policy as a constructive strategy to develop new areas, to provide opportunity for people in sore circumstances, and even to prevent speculators from dominating the business at government land offices.[40]

In opposition to these Democratic leaders, many Whigs, Clay included, objected that such a preemption policy encouraged fraud, intimidation, and false paper work. Besides, it deprived the Treasury of badly needed revenue during these hard times. Clay attacked preemption with extraordinary vigor during the session of 1838, citing statistics and specific instances to show flagrant abuses it had allowed. The substance of his argument resembled that against graduation, but his tone had escalated. Naturally the other side responded in kind and later liked to attribute an offensive viciousness to his remarks on the subject.[41]

Notwithstanding a good bit of truth in his emphasis upon wholesale abuses in the administration of preemption, as there would be generally in the history of the public domain, he was in the minority when retroactive laws of two years' duration passed in 1838 and 1840. He was disappointed that his fellow Whig Webster went for preemption and other relaxed policies. More than that, Clay was mortified to see that his own vote was a solitary negative among western senators.[42]

Though making no progress in his adherence to distribution of land proceeds to the states, he felt the times demanded that policy. The depression had badly weakened their financial condition, the more so because many of them were greatly overcommitted after marketing huge bond issues in England for enthusiastic programs of internal improvements. By 1839 Clay's colleague John Crittenden unsuccessfully introduced a measure in the Senate for distributing land revenue to assist them to meet these obligations. Some Whig newspapers supported this idea. And in travel to England late that year, Webster was listening to his long-standing legal clients at the banking House of Barings, as they sought cooperation from the national government for payment of the state debts. Webster did agree to issue a statement assuring creditors that the states must and would honor their obligations, although he did not recommend national assumption of those debts. Neither did Clay nor other congressional Whigs, despite approving indirect help by way of distribution. Democrats made some political capital out of characterizing federal intervention as improper and unconstitutional but never had to cope with an explicit proposal to intervene.[43]

When the senator looked back on Van Buren's presidential term, he could find very little to approve. It seemed a true extension of the Jacksonian precedents that had put this nation on a deplorable economic and political course: wreckage of a working banking system, wild ideas about credit and currency, cramped notions of the scope and responsibilities of government, rejection of positive policies for improved transportation and land use, and an altogether cynical attitude toward the citizenry suffering from a deep depression. Whether this estimate of his opponents was largely biased by partisanship is, of course, a perfectly legitimate question. But at least these were the views that would now influence Clay and his party in the coming election of 1840 and, it seemed likely, in the changing of the guard afterward.

10

Log Cabin

Late in 1839 politicians were thinking seriously about the next presidential election, then only a year away. As a key figure in the coming contest, sure of Democratic renomination, Van Buren still had every reason to worry about the outcome. From the very beginning of his term, he had encountered endless problems, most of them rising out of the troubled economy. The financial panic, spreading across the land soon after his inauguration, had eased in the following year but then had led into a nasty depression. Despite his commitment to states' rights, the chief executive had alienated even fellow Democratic states' righters by his relentless pursuit of an independent treasury and other measures at the expense of state banks. And hard times had alienated many others whose economic plight was apparently beyond the president's power or willingness to relieve. Though known for his political magic, he seemed only to be defending against a mounting siege. Buoyed by victories in recent state elections, including a sweep of the Northeast, Whigs projected unbounded confidence that 1840 would mark the end of Jacksonian dominance in national affairs.[1]

No one felt more certain that would happen than Clay. Architect in his party's formation, skillful legislative strategist, and the voice of Whig tenets, he fully expected the national convention, scheduled for December 1839, to nominate him by acclamation. To ensure party harmony he had moved somewhat toward the center on economic issues. While staunchly opposing an independent treasury, he advocated a national bank, but a substantially modified version of the old BUS to remove objections. A firm believer in a protective tariff, he would not touch the compromise of 1833, at least not for three years, until rates reverted to 20 percent or less. And just as he had long urged, he would finance internal improvements by distributing land proceeds to the states. In a general call to arms, he would emphasize the danger to liberty of executive power at the expense of that held by the people's representatives in Congress.

More than any other potential Whig candidate, Clay could count on support across the South. One reason was his moderation on economic issues, especially adherence to the tariff compromise, but also advocacy of state administration of internal improvements. On slavery, too, he seemed to this section to be safe. Was he not a slaveholder himself, and had he not recently taken a conservative position concerning aspects of slavery during a protracted exchange with Calhoun at the Capitol?[2] The Kentuckian was pleased as well to have an early endorsement by Hugh White, the former Jacksonian who had been the principal southern Whig candidate in the last election. White shared Clay's antipathy toward an independent treasury; he had even resigned his Senate seat to avoid complying with instructions of the Tennessee legislature to vote for it.[3]

Logically, Clay should have had solid approval by the Northeast, the part of the country that stood to benefit so much from his American System. It was not turning out that way. In New York the editor-organizer Thurlow Weed decided Clay had accumulated too many handicaps for vote getting and was backing General Winfield Scott. In Pennsylvania another tactician, Thad Stevens, had come to the same conclusion about Clay's chances and was promoting another general, William Henry Harrison, who had shown a great deal of strength in the campaign of 1836. In New Jersey the senator would lose to Scott, and in Massachusetts there was his rival Webster, who would go for Harrison if he could not get the nomination himself. What the Northeast revealed was a great deal of instability of opinion, vulnerable to noneconomic appeals and a good bit of manipulation by the politicos.[4]

Notwithstanding these uncertainties, Clay seemed to have the votes for nomination by the Whig convention in December 1839. Then Weed and Stevens engineered procedural changes to sidestep straight majority balloting by the delegates. The three-cornered contest ended with a decision for Harrison, victimizing poor Clay. For appearances and for party success, he pledged his support of old Tippecanoe, as he was known because of his encounter with Tecumseh's Indians along Tippecanoe Creek in the Wabash Valley years ago.[5]

At the time and in later historiography, the election of 1840 was seen as one of campaign emotionalism and evasion of substantial issues. Pictured as an honest, rough-hewn hero of the West, the Whigs' version of Andrew Jackson, Harrison would stay in a log cabin at North Bend, Ohio, drink his cider, and remain above partisan politics. It is true that this campaign had these characteristics to some extent. Tippecanoe owed his nomination to a belief that Clay and other prominent figures had accumulated a record on specific matters that were negative factors automatically.[6] And the old soldier did avoid concrete statements, as party leaders directed. When he spoke out, his message was unclear. He hardly sounded like a Whig when, among some remarks at Fort Meigs in June, he emphasized that he had been a strict-constructionist Jeffersonian Republican in his early Virginia days.[7] At Dayton in September he referred cautiously to chartering a national bank. "There is not in the Constitution an express grant of power for such purpose," he declared; and he would not sign a bill for one unless a majority of the people thought it essential to collect revenue.[8] Did popular demand determine constitutionality?

Granted that the candidate, known in some quarters as General Mum, neither discussed problems and plans meaningfully nor made frequent public appearances. Granted there was plenty of hoopla at barbecues and parades. A careful look at activity of other Whig and Democratic leaders, however, can provide a different view of the election. For example, Clay thought it was a mistake for the national convention not to have issued a statement of principles. He did remark that "unless you are fully convinced that what you mean to say is right," it is best to remain silent, "and in this instance I do not wish to depart from the rule."[9] And it is true that he had moderated his positions on economic nationalism to fit current conditions. But it is also a fact that he supplied his own statement of principles, skirted by the convention, in the course of the campaign.[10]

In summer 1839 before the convention met, he had traveled from Buffalo through upper New York into Canada and down the East Coast, speaking at many places along the way about economic policies he would pursue.[11] In June 1840, after a quiet period, he had visited his native Hanover County, Virginia, where he fully discussed these subjects, generally to reiterate what he had very often said in the Senate—he could not conceal the record anyway.[12] Near the close of electioneering, he invaded Jackson's home territory, Nashville, to veer off to personal thrusts at Old Hickory, who characteristically replied in kind.[13]

In the Virginia speech, though conceding that sound state banks might supply the nation's need for a reliable currency, he left no doubt, on both constitutional and political grounds, that a national bank was far preferable. Certainly an independent treasury must be avoided, he contended, particularly because it would be subservient to executive will. "Fellow citizens, there is one divorce urgently demanded by the safety and the highest interests of the country—a divorce of the President from the treasury of the United States."[14] As for the tariff, he adhered to a protective system, obtainable under the compromise of 1833, he believed. On land policy, he stayed with his congressional position for distribution as opposed to graduation or cession to the states, both unfairly discriminating against the older members of the Union. So he neither retreated from established views nor sought to obscure them with hazy generalities.

Admittedly, the Kentuckian was not constantly busy campaigning, perhaps because of wounded feelings about being unfairly denied the nomination. Actually, the other Whig giant, Webster, devoted more time and energy to the cause. He had backed selection of Harrison after being passed over himself

and was quite aroused about defeating Van Buren. He helped
organize an immense gathering in Boston, perhaps as many as
fifty thousand, and reached many of them assembled at Bunker
Hill with his powerful voice. He traveled through New England
and the middle Atlantic states, paying special attention shortly
before the election to the New York area, from Wall Street over
to Long Island. Here he had a sharp exchange with Van Buren's
legislative leader Silas Wright. The two of them did lapse into
some petty byplay, but they confronted the issues, especially financial policy, just as they had on the floor of the Senate.[15]

When electoral votes were counted, Harrison had over-
whelmed Van Buren, 234 to 60. One reason for the victory, to
be sure, was the Whigs' effective use of log cabin tactics, pio-
neered by the Democrats before them. But it is safe to say
that the winners' largest asset was the poor condition of the
economy, naturally blamed on the incumbent administration.
And the skill with which they did it involved substantial argument for alternative policies as well as excitement of the
crowd.

During the three-month meeting of the old Congress, beginning in December 1840 and ending with Harrison's inauguration, Clay returned to center stage. He did not yet have
the newly elected majority in place and so could not move
very far on a program. Perhaps the mere fact of a sweeping
Whig victory might help a little, but he would use this period
mainly to demonstrate things to come. After a dozen frustrat-
ing years of Jacksonian ascendancy, he was in no mood to be
patient and forgiving, so much so that his opponents found
him downright dictatorial.

In this spirit he brought in a resolution to repeal the
fresh independent-treasury law, which had been the centerpiece of the outgoing administration's financial system. The
people had unmistakably spoken, Clay declared, and he was
surprised that the Democrats, for all their popular rhetoric,
had not themselves called for repeal forthwith. Peculiar reasoning, thought Wright, coming from a party that had unfail-
ingly avoided discussion of substantive issues during its log
cabin frolic. Though the Senate soon tabled the resolution for
repeal, Clay was fashioning a strategy to put through a national-bank charter.[16] That it ought to be a prime objective he

had no doubt. "Without a Bank," he believed, "the new vessel of State will be thrown on the same Rock which was fatal to the old one."[17] His first step was to present a resolution by the Kentucky legislature that such an institution was indispensable.[18] Then in a Whig caucus, he got agreement on the necessity of a national bank.[19]

While Democrats were on the defensive against Clay's initiative to kill the Independent Treasury, they countered aggressively with a land preemption bill similar to those often debated but not passed previously. They were making a serious attempt finally to obtain a permanent instead of a temporary, limited measure permitting occupants of public land to buy it at minimum price without regard to auction. In doing so, they portrayed Whigs as insincere friends of log cabin folk. That was the way Benton characterized them when he introduced the bill. Indeed, the Missourian charged, Clay's side was more solicitous of British creditors by favoring national assumption of state debts to them or perhaps retirement of these obligations by distributing land proceeds. As usual, Benton urged attaching a graduation clause to the preemption proposal.[20] Calhoun, too, would add his favorite amendment for ceding public lands to the states and sharing revenue from sales with them.[21]

Clay took the lead in combatting preemption, still a very unattractive, unworkable notion in his view. This was not a time to deprive the empty Treasury of vital revenue, he contended. He was unimpressed by Democratic claims that with land currently going at auction for only a few cents an acre above the minimum of $1.25 (the price under preemption) there would be little reduction in revenue. If you also adopt Benton's graduation, you will lose still more of the national treasure, he warned. But most objectionable were the inevitable frauds committed by preemptioners at the land offices, an inescapable result of a lax system.[22]

He could see, however, that he lacked the votes to reject the bill outright. So he and his reliable colleague John Crittenden resorted to the strategy of moving amendments. One, to prohibit preemption rights to aliens, was disapproved decisively.[23] Another, to bar non-whites, passed nearly unanimously, to his satisfaction.[24] The most important amendment was distribution of land proceeds to the states, which the Democrats condemned with customary zeal on financial and constitutional grounds. Defeated again, distribution retained a central position on his agenda for the new administration. As for preemption itself, the Democrats in the Senate picked up fourteen Whig votes to pass it, thirty-one to nineteen. Though the House tabled the bill on the last day of the session, friends of that policy felt encouraged.[25]

If Clay could get a provision for distribution, he believed that would be all that the national government needed to do about internal improvements. Despite the criticism directed against the short-lived deposit act of 1836, distributing surplus funds for several months, he still seemed satisfied with that formula instead of outright federal expenditures and administration of projects.[26] Now when measures, such as appropriations for extending the National Road, were reported to the floor, he was reluctant to vote for them unless they would be financed by distribution. He wanted internal improvements and had often defended the constitutionality of federal help, but he had concluded that a system benefiting all states equitably was necessary. And he left no doubt that generous support for some states in the past, Ohio for instance, and less for others, Kentucky for instance, affected his opinion.[27]

In looking ahead to the new Whig presidency, Clay felt certain that another leading issue would involve revision of the tariff. Although nothing much could be done about it now, he wished to gather information on the subject for an extensive debate, which was certain to arise. So he presented a resolution, which was approved, asking Secretary of Treasury Levi Woodbury to submit a plan for a "permanent" tariff.[28] The compromise of 1833 had called for a huge reduction to a maximum of 20 percent on all rates over that level. This adjustment was to take place during the coming year, by July 1842. It did not prohibit further legislation, though a widely held view interpreted the compromise as nearly sacrosanct and as essential to preserve harmony in the Union.

Off and on, there had been forays into this hazardous thicket to change the schedule ahead of time. Wright, Benton, and some other Jacksonians did not believe the compromise was untouchable; they had attempted reductions on salt, coal, and woolens. They targeted other items then below 20 percent because, it was argued, the compact allowed adjustments on them. Clay invariably fought off attempts as contrary to its spirit and letter. At first he had the assistance of Calhoun, who, of course, wished to preserve the downward course of rates under the compromise. Beginning in the midthirties, however, the Carolinian advocated lowering some rates immediately.[29]

Clay's ability to translate his thinking about economic policies into action depended, of course, on his relationship to President Harrison after March 4, 1841. For a while following the election he believed there would be no difficulty about that, for he and Tip had been on very good terms over the years, not only in the West but at the Capitol, where Harrison had served in both the House and the Senate. In politics the general had supported the American System, and in personal relations he was a warm friend and admirer of the Kentuckian, who had helped him in political and military situations. Soon after the election, when he started preparing to assume office and was traveling in Kentucky, Harrison spent several days visiting the senator at Lexington. The two had long conversations concerning issues and appointments. Clay had no interest in a cabinet post, and indeed recommended Webster for the State Department. He would later be pleased that some of his friends would also be chosen. Though not his first recommendation, Thomas Ewing, a fellow economic nationalist, would go to the Treasury; John Bell, a dependable Whig, to become secretary of war; and Crittenden, his closest ally, would be attorney general. As for the views of the president-elect on measures, Clay remarked he was "happy to find him coinciding with those which I entertained."[30]

Harrison's inaugural address in March 1841 assured the senator all was well. It rejected an exclusive hard-money currency and pledged to leave questions of public finance to Congress, amounting to approval of a national-bank bill. In general, it affirmed the Whig doctrine of executive deference to the legislative branch, including restraint of the veto power.[31]

Despite all these positive signs, Clay had worried for some time that there could be problems. Soon after their meeting at Ashland, he wrote: "I must observe that, notwithstanding professions of the most ardent attachment to me by Harrison, circumstances have transpired which confirm an opinion I have long since formed, that he is apprehensive that the new Administration may not be regarded as *his* but mine. Artful men for sinister purposes will endeavor to foster this jealousy. And to preserve my utility, I must avoid giving it any countenance."[32] Though most presidential appointments seemed quite satisfactory, he had failed in a strong effort to put his friend John Clayton instead of Ewing in the Treasury. It was a foolish move, for both were party men of Clay's persuasion and well qualified. And he had become very upset when, in face of his repeated complaints, Harrison had adhered to his nomination of Edward Curtis, a prominent opponent of the Kentuckian, as collector of New York port.[33]

Another annoyance developed out of Clay's insistence that a special session of Congress be called immediately to launch the new program. Well before the chief executive had taken his oath, Clay had told a Whig caucus in the Senate that an early meeting was imperative, and the caucus had so voted. When some days passed after Harrison took over without issuing a call, Clay sent him a reminder, with an enclosed draft the president might use. The response was a mild reprimand, saying that the senator was too impetuous, that first other circumstances had to be considered and other persons consulted. This was not a bold declaration of independence or a serious rift, as depicted in historical accounts, and it postponed convoking Congress hardly at all. Four days later, Harrison announced the special session for May 31.[34]

He did not live to see it, for he died on April 4 after a short illness. Unexpectedly, Clay and his triumphant party now had to work with John Tyler, whose willingness to follow their agenda remained to be tested. The former vice president was a well-known states-rights Virginian, an aristocratic conservative Whig. Earlier an anti-BUS Jacksonian, he had left the Democratic party because of what he viewed as Old Hickory's executive high-handedness in removing deposits from the national bank. His ideological position was closer to that of Calhoun than of Clay, as he would soon demonstrate. Withal, he had been friendly toward Clay and had admired him for his defense of the Union by fashioning the compromise of 1833.

After taking the presidential oath, Tyler issued an address in which he said he would approve any constitutional measure passed by Congress. He would "resort to the fathers of the great republican school for advice and instruction," he explained. That could mean he would consult either Madison's opposition to a national bank in 1791 or Madison's approval of one in 1816. In any case, he left no doubt that he wanted the Independent Treasury repealed.[35] At Ashland, not yet having read this statement, Clay was wary of what course Tyler would take: "I believe—I should rather say, hope that he will interpose no obstacle to the success of the Whig measures."[36] As he thought of the possibilities, the Kentuckian speculated that the new president would feel obligated to observe the party's principles because of the circumstances of his succeeding to office. Certainly so, if he expected to be elected later in his own right.[37] But in an exchange of letters with Tyler, he found him negatively inclined on the bank question. "I would not have it urgd prematurely," the chief executive declared. "I have no intention to submit any thing to Congress on this subject to be acted on."[38] Privately, he expressed an interest in a bank with states only as shareholders, an institution much different from the old BUS.[39]

No matter what Tyler's model might be, Clay did not change his own thinking. He had outlined a plan very similar to that which he had set forth in the Senate during the debates on the Independent Treasury.[40] It was a revised version of Biddle's bank. He asked Ewing to draw up such a proposal, and the secretary of treasury hesitantly agreed to do so, saying he thought Tyler would probably concur with a congressional decision.[41]

On other subjects the senator had a well-defined agenda. He would not change the tariff more than revenue needs required and would stay within the terms of the compromise of 1833.[42] As usual, he gave priority to land policy, which should be improved by distribution. Fortunately, Tyler was on record in favor of some such legislation about it.

On the eve of the special session Clay had "strong hopes, not, however, unmixed with fears. If the Executive will cordially co-operate in carrying out the Whig measures, all will be well. Otherwise every thing is at hazard."[43]

11

Veto

When Congress assembled for a critical special session on May 31, 1841, Clay was the most visible figure in the Senate chamber, probably in all of Washington not excepting the "accidental" president, John Tyler. He had a modest majority of followers in both houses and a key position as chairman of both the Finance Committee and a select committee to handle banking and currency affairs. Typically, he had prepared a series of resolutions as a legislative agenda and presented them within a week. Heading his list was abolition of the Independent Treasury, an item of old business he had not completed in the last Congress. As a replacement, he called for a national bank. Then he urged revision of the tariff, if more revenue was needed, and distribution of land proceeds.[1]

Now that he had the votes, he made short work of getting rid of what he called the subtreasury. The matter had been sufficiently discussed, he announced, and senators should be prepared for the yeas and nays. Nevertheless, there were some flourishes, chiefly to justify Van Buren's policy. While the upper house was attending to this matter, it also decided to repeal the Deposit Act of 1836, regulating state banks and, in better times, distributing the short-lived surplus, all of which made a national bank more necessary, as Clay unhesitatingly pointed out.[2]

What did Tyler recommend? In his message to Congress, he had plainly rejected other options, an independent treasury and state-bank depositories, which he declared had such horrible records. Yet he was quite vague about the sort of national bank he wanted. In fact, he referred to a "fiscal agent" mainly to perform services for the Treasury. What he did not want was a copy of the BUS, considering it just as bad as the two recent experiments. And he did not conceal his well-known support of Jackson's veto of recharter years ago. For the time being, he would leave it to Congress to solve the problem, but he would only accept an institution free of constitutional objections (his own, of course).[3]

In another resolution Clay formally requested Secretary of Treasury Ewing to submit a bank plan, which he had already sought personally, and the cabinet officer therefore produced one in a few days, on June 12. His recommendation reflected an accommodation by an economic nationalist to Tyler's strict constructionism, though it appears the two officials did not communicate clearly with each other. This shortcoming in the executive branch would reappear in the following weeks. He proposed locating the bank's headquarters in the District of Columbia, where Congress had undoubted jurisdiction, and authorizing branch offices of deposit and discount only in states consenting to entry.[4]

Clay could not have been surprised when he read Ewing's communication, for he had had warnings of Tyler's dislike of what was called an old-fashioned institution. Commenting on the president's preferences as expressed in the secretary's plan, he exclaimed, "What a Bank would that be!"[5] After several meetings of a cooperative Whig caucus and of the select committee, the senator reported a counterproposal: return to a BUS model, and do not require state approval for locating branches.[6]

William Rives supported his fellow Virginian in the White House by moving to add Ewing's proviso for prior state consent to branching, so that he and the Kentuckian were the principal advocates of two different formulas around which the first phase of debate revolved. Clay pressed ahead by opposing Rives's concession to the president and easily prevailed in this first test of strength.[7] Then one of his committee members, Richard Bayard of Delaware, offered another choice, not widely noticed but later quite important. He favored the Rives amendment, but he would alter it by allowing the bank to establish branches if states did not disapprove during the next meeting of their legislatures. So mere state silence would amount to approval and was more generous toward the bank. The Senate did not act on Bayard's proposal at this point.[8]

By early July, despite his satisfaction with the outcome of his skirmish with Rives, Clay was upset by slow progress. Day after day, his Democratic opponents presented amendments to his bill, all for stricter limits on the institution. His irritation and rigidity caused senators to call him a dictator. When he proposed a rule to expedite discussion, he said, "If the clerk will follow me, I will dictate a modification, though I do not like to be a dictator in any sense." Buchanan interjected, "You do it so well, you ought to like it."[9] No one was more offended by the Kentuckian than Calhoun, who charged him with riding a hobby horse, the worn-out BUS.[10] At one point, Clay lashed Rufus Choate of Massachusetts, Webster's friend and successor in the Senate, for predicting defeat and implying a presidential veto if the present version was adopted. How did the New Englander know this, demanded Clay? Obviously he understood Choate was in close touch with Webster and therefore the president. Like the secretary of state, Choate put aside his Whig orthodoxy in order to make essential concessions and stoutly refused to explain his source of information.[11]

For his part, Clay had not been playing his familiar role of compromiser, voted nay to amendments repeatedly, and in nearly every instance quashed them. His opponents would have required reporting more information on the bank's operations, even concerning individuals' stock holdings and loans. Members of Congress, bank directors, and aliens would be restricted or prohibited in certain relations to the institution. And reflecting recent trouble about redemption of notes, these amendments would have invoked penalties for suspension of specie payment, in extreme circumstances forfeiture of the corporate charter.[12]

Finally on July 27, Clay pushed the bill through with few revisions, twenty-five to twenty-four, far short of the two-thirds necessary to override a veto, which he was convinced would follow passage. The stickler, he thought, was the provision on unlimited branching power, against which Tyler was immovably arrayed. So now the Kentuckian began to explore an alternative, the earlier amendment proposed by Bayard of his committee to allow branching unless a state disapproved at its next legislative session.[13] It had lain dormant with no vote for a while, but now it seemed acceptable to the president according to Virginia congressman John Botts, who had shown Tyler a copy and relayed a mistaken favorable impression.[14] Clay had also been drawing upon the advice of his trusted political friend Peter Porter in searching for some common ground with critics. Porter promoted an adjusted plan in New York and among southern Whigs.[15] Soon Clay got the Senate's acceptance of the Bayard-Botts formula on branching, which also had a probank clause permitting Congress to negate a state's dissent to branching. That stipulation had been debated off and on but could be the most important feature of all for nationalists. The House concurred on August 6.[16]

Tyler took the allowed ten days to consider his decision on signature. Meanwhile Webster, Ewing, Crittenden, and other cabinet members urged him to approve Clay's bill. More influential were several states-rights supporters, notably Representative Henry Wise of Virginia, who had an ugly argument with the Whig leader about a bank at the beginning of the session. Another intimate adviser was Professor Nathaniel Beverley Tucker of William and Mary College, once on quite friendly terms with Clay. These persons helped convince the president that the bank plan was altogether dangerous and that the Kentuckian wanted nothing better than to evict Tyler from power. While the chief executive delayed, his disapproval of Clay's position intensified.[17]

Tyler returned the bill with his objections on August 16. Contrary to what Botts had reported to Clay, yet predictable, his view of the branching provision was negative. He thought the decision whether to admit a branch by a state legislature at its first meeting after the law's passage might not correctly register popular opinion because of the timing of state elections, the bicameral character of the body, and other complicating factors. Though the president's reasoning was rather finespun, the procedure that Clay had offered would probably have been clumsy and ineffective. A more straightforward question that Tyler answered negatively was whether Congress should establish a branch it found to be "necessary and proper," in spite of a state's rejection. This clause would have been a strong centralizing feature. Still another presidential objection pointed to the proposed function of making loans and discounting debtors' notes. Here Clay could reasonably complain that Tyler had not previously made his views clear. While he had focused on branching, he had not addressed the matter of discounting, basic to operations of a bank. He had not asked Secretary Ewing to eliminate his reference to discounting in the original report to Congress, and it had not been seriously challenged afterward but now became a principal issue, more so than branching. Tyler attributed many abuses of the old BUS to the process of discounting in credit operations.[18]

When the clerk read the veto message aloud to the Senate, there was commotion by spectators in the gallery, some of it hissing and groans. As he had done before in such situations, Benton immediately rose and demanded the "ruffians" be evicted. His colleagues thought he was exaggerating the problem and pacified the Missourian without punitive action against the protesters. Would that the broader, long-range political impact might also have been smoothed over.[19]

Reaction of Whigs to the veto was mixed. Many of them complained that after Tyler's unforeseen accession to the presidency he had thwarted the voters' will on a basic party position. To have been honest, he should have declined the vice presidential nomination if he disagreed with the restoration of a national bank.[20] Still, there were exceptions within the party to this opinion. In the cabinet, despite great disappointment, no member decided to resign. Webster wanted a bank as much as anybody, but he had sought accommodation by Congress and the White House and continued to do so. As a major figure, Ewing favored another attempt. Crittenden urged Clay to scale down his model of a bank. Make no provision for discounting, he advised, and limit the institution to exchange operations, which Tyler would accept. Furthermore, this change might encourage him to approve a liberal basis of branching. Maintain harmony now and revise the system later.[21] Surprisingly, William Seward and Thurlow Weed, leaders of the powerful organization in New York, wanted a compromise. So did the young editor of the *Tribune,* Horace Greeley.[22]

First, the Senate discussed the veto and voted whether to override it. On August 19 these animated speeches ran for several hours with an aroused Clay the center of attention. Having had time to organize his thoughts, he made a carefully prepared, vigorous argument against the chief executive's reasoning. The tone was severe.[23]

He recalled recent events and circumstances: Tyler's succession to office, his early commitment to approve any constitutional measure on banking, his intention to follow instruction of the "fathers of the republican school," the congressional concessions to him on location of a bank's headquarters in Washington and especially on state authority over admission of branches, then his wholly unjustified veto and professed adherence to conscience and duty.

As for the constitutional question, Clay saw no truth in the president's assertion that there had been nearly as many negative as positive precedents. Every president from Washington onward had recognized the validity of a national bank, the senator said. Though Jefferson as secretary of state disputed the power to create the first BUS, during his own administration he signed legislation supporting its operation. Madison, too, opposed chartering the institution in 1791 but later recommended chartering the second BUS. Even Jackson thought some kind of bank, if not Biddle's model, was constitutional. Congress and the Supreme Court had repeatedly affirmed it as well.

Commenting on Tyler's objection to the provision on state disapproval of branches, Clay emphasized his effort to accommodate the president's wishes instead of leaving full discretion to the bank or to Congress. All to no effect, for after Tyler had assented to the compromise, he vetoed his own bill. Just as deplorable, he now disliked the section authorizing discounting, despite the fact that his secretary of treasury included that function in his report to the Senate. In short, the Kentuckian contended that the president was not only wrong but also guilty of duplicity.

It is true that he cited past friendly relations with Tyler and expressed great respect for the high office he occupied. Nevertheless, he dismissed the chief executive's pleas of constitutional duty and of self-respect concerning his judgments. There were better courses of action, Clay declared. He could have permitted the bill to become a law by returning it without his signature. It would have been desirable deference to a coordinate, popular branch of government. Or he could have resigned—no doubt, the senator preferred that option. A few years ago, Clay recalled, when Tyler was a senator, he had resigned after refusing to obey his state legislature's instruction to vote for expunging from the senate journal a censure of Jackson's removal of bank deposits. That had been a genuine act of conscience, the Kentuckian felt.

When he sat down, Rives spoke in rebuttal, defending Tyler against unfair criticism of the veto as well as regrettable personal attack. The two opponents indulged in exchanges at a lower level than courtesy prescribed. Clay suspected the president of having a devious purpose, of moving toward a new party. Already, he remarked, a band of counselors composed a "cabal," a latter-day Jacksonian kitchen cabinet. Though denying doing so, he was hinting Rives might be one of them. But the movement had few recruits, amounting only to a "corporal's guard," he exclaimed sarcastically. Rives, alluding to Clay, retorted he had heard of an attempted "dictatorship" to dominate the legislative and executive branches of government. After this skirmish the Senate voted on overriding the veto with a count nowhere near the necessary two-thirds.[24]

What should be the next step? Rives had urged setting the matter aside this session, but Clay scolded him for taking an irresponsible position. Aware of a new attempt, possibly for a bank limited to dealing in exchange and not discounts, he supposed that might be the best that could be done. So he promised not to put up any obstacle, though such an institution could only be a temporary expedient.[25]

He knew whereof he spoke, for at that very time, there were movements for something of the sort. On the day of the veto, August 16, the first of a series of conferences to draft a plan acceptable to both Congress and Tyler occurred in an effort marked by too much vagueness and misunderstanding. Alexander Stuart, a friendly Virginia congressman, began the process by visiting the president and running through the text of the rejected bill with him for revisions. Tyler now insisted upon limiting the bank to handling bills of exchange, not to discounting debtors' notes; but his opinion about state admission of branches was fuzzy. He inserted the proviso that branches could not be established "contrary to state law" but did not specify time or procedure, such as Clay's bill had done. Over the next two days, John Sergeant of the House and John Berrien of the Senate also met with Tyler, who seemed ever more negative. Even Ewing, Webster, and other cabinet members, anxious to arrive at a compromise, had trouble fixing terms. Two events clouded prospects: Clay's hard-hitting speech of August 19, attacking the veto, and then the surfacing of a paper written by Botts, accusing Tyler of attempting to form a coalition with the Democrats. Quite upset, the chief executive appeared unlikely to sign any bank bill, regardless of preceding negotiations. Webster sought to get congressional leaders to postpone further effort that session.[26]

They refused to do that. They introduced a bill to create a "fiscal corporation" (the president disliked the name bank) for financial services to the government and for *interstate* exchange operations in the private sector, using branches operating "not contrary to law," presumably state law. After quick House passage, the Senate set up a select committee to report on the measure. Clay declined serving on this panel but claimed he had an open mind. Convinced that it would be well to accept this substitute as better than nothing, he certainly had a decisive influence on congressional action, more than he pretended. While the Senate discussed a committee report that made no significant changes in the Sergeant-Berrien draft, Clay had nothing important to say. His participation consisted largely of a satirical attack upon leading Democratic solons, who had made a congratulatory visit at the White House after the recent veto, perhaps hoping for a coalition with Tyler. He did not believe, however, that the president and the Jacksonian party were compatible. They disagreed on most issues other than banking, he declared. In fact, he predicted that Tyler would not dare veto the pending plan.[27] If he had been more realistic, he would have thought otherwise. Always a barometer of presidential thinking, Rives spoke against it with reasoning that foreshadowed what would come from the chief executive.[28] The Senate passed it, twenty-seven to twenty-two.

Tyler held the second bank bill, too, several days and then fired off his disapproval near the close of the session. He objected to the provision that authorized dealing in exchange. As a number of persons, Clay included, had pointed out, he realized that bills of exchange could be used much as discounted notes as credit instruments in the course of business. In the president's opinion, this bill therefore would still allow the bank to manipulate the economy. No matter that he was the one who had insisted upon this part of the measure. Also objectionable, he wrote, was the absence of a specific requirement of state consent for branching. Here, too, his own clause, "not contrary to state law," now seemed to him inadequate. Contemporaries and historians, whether favorable or unfavorable to Tyler, concluded that it was not so much these details of legislation that induced the rejection as it was Tyler's rising suspicion of what his political adversaries were doing, stimulated by what he was hearing from his inner states-rights circle.[29]

A breakup of the administration and the rupture of the Whig party followed. In the evening after the veto, the cabinet met to discuss its response. Clay was also present and must have had some influence, though after a while he went into another room. Four of the five officers who attended the gathering decided upon simultaneous resignation. Secretary of State Webster left early and would not concur in this action, believing as he did that unity of the party and establishment of a bank were still possible. Five of the six cabinet members did resign—all except Webster—and soon published their versions of the negotiations between Tyler and Congress. The main reason they gave for their action was the president's reneging on the kind of bank plan he preferred.[30]

This failure to restore a banking system to serve the nation occurred because of a collision of personalities, perhaps as much as differences about economic policy. Buoyed by an exhilirating Whig victory in the election of 1840, Clay was impatient with opposition and delay, which his long experience should have told him to expect. His opponents then, as well as scholars later, charged him with being a dictator.[31] He laid out a very full agenda, which required persistence to be put into effect, and he became irritable when events did not go his way. But Tyler's sensitivity and defensiveness also interfered with progress. He constantly suspected his opponents' motives and interpreted their behavior as dangerously aggressive.

As far as broad policy was concerned, there was little in the protracted congressional speeches having to do with that dimension, but much about details of charter terms. Clay did not effectively expound, as he usually did, the economic rationale for another national bank to help the country to extricate itself from the depression and to regain a desirable rate of economic growth. Still, he made substantial concessions in both bank bills, retreating somewhat from sound constitutional and economic ideas on the subject. It was Tyler who was out of touch with reality in these areas.

As predominant as the issue of banking was, Clay confronted others at the same time. He continued to give priority to distributing land proceeds to states for internal improvements, both for the future and for retiring their large debts on existing projects. Though failing to join distribution to a preemption bill in the preceding session, he believed this approach to be most promising. In addition to the necessity of accepting preemption as the vehicle, however, he found he had to connect distribution to bankruptcy and tariff legislation. So he had to follow several intricate paths of senate business to arrive at a package before adjournment in September 1841. The name of the technique is logrolling. He did have some help from Tyler, who recommended distribution in his opening message, but only, he warned, if it did not push tariff rates above the level prescribed by the compromise of 1833. In any case, the depression had caused a shortage of funds.[32]

The senator fashioned a bill and had a Whig member of the House introduce it there in June. Its familiar provisions would give present and future occupants of public land the right of purchasing 160 acres of it at minimum price before auction. Clay's supplement would distribute land revenue, apportioned by population, to all states. Each of eight so-called "new" states (all except Maine, admitted after Ohio in 1803) would further receive five hundred thousand acres and 10 percent from sales of land within their borders for internal improvements.

It was early August before the Senate took up the bill, long since passed by the lower chamber. Like earlier discussions of land policy, this one was lengthy and lively. Calhoun fought the measure on constitutional and moral grounds, predicting it would violate republican principles and undermine civic virtue. Besides, he argued, much as many others did, that the sad fiscal condition of the nation did not permit distributing funds. A good point. Yet Clay prevailed against repeated efforts to prohibit distribution whenever the existing budget showed a deficit. Benton, as expected, fiercely attacked the proposal, hoping as he did that downward graduation of land prices would ultimately win out.[33] One amendment after another to qualify or defeat the bill failed, with Clay firmly resisting them. At last, he won approval of his plan, uniting policies for administering public lands and for supporting internal improvements.[34]

One factor materially helping passage was adoption of a bankruptcy bill, which recruited some necessary votes for distribution. Presently, there was no national legislation on bankruptcy, and there had not been since the repeal of a short-lived measure almost forty years before. Individual states had acted on the subject, yet the Supreme Court had limited what they could do constitutionally if their statutes impaired contractual obligations retrospectively or involved interstate applications. For years Webster, with advice from Justice Joseph Story, had unsuccessfully sought enactment of a federal law, as recently as the last session of 1840. Clay had not taken the lead but fully supported these attempts. Strangely, although he had much legal experience with bankruptcy extending to a key case in the high court, he misstated the meaning of the decision that he had won. Webster, who had also participated in that case on the losing side, remembered the precedent better, especially the part holding that states could not interfere with *interstate* debtor-creditor relations, important in a developing economy.[35]

Now there were better prospects for legislation. The depression had deepened the despair of bankrupt debtors, heightening pressure for congressional relief. Even Tyler saw the need for it. The Senate passed a bill permitting individuals, but not corporations, to petition for discharge of their debts. Antibank Democrats, such as Benton, opposed the exception because they wished to use bankruptcy proceedings to stop abuses by banks. Clay helped to defeat their amendment to do so.[36] But the greatest barrier to the bankruptcy bill was posed in the House. In an agreement with Democratic leaders interested in the measure, Clay persuaded a number of hesitant Whig representatives in the lower chamber to vote for it. This brought around holdouts on distribution in the Senate, who now got a bankruptcy law in exchange. "It was all bargain and sale," Benton later wrote. Many other opponents also complained of logrolling, but the Kentuckian predicted large benefits to a modern economy.[37]

An even more important prerequisite for distribution had been its reconciliation with the tariff. Primarily to raise revenue for a hard-pressed Treasury, Clay's bill to raise some rates then below 20 percent toward that future ceiling was pending at the same time that the Senate discussed distribution. The connection between the two bills was not lost on many members, especially Democratic opponents who strongly suspected that Clay wanted to siphon off revenue from the land offices as an excuse for replacing it with ever higher protective duties at the custom houses. Though denying the truth of these assertions, the senator concluded that he would have to compromise or else run into presidential vetoes on both subjects. So near the end of debate on distribution, his friend Berrien, with his approval, moved an amendment that would suspend distribution whenever any tariff rate exceeded 20 percent after June 1842, the date when the compromise of 1833 would reduce high rates to that level. This, along with arrival of a message that the bankruptcy bill had made it through the House, opened the way for success on distribution.[38] Afterward the revised tariff within the restriction of the Berrien amendment passed too. They received a solid Whig vote, including southerners and some persons of Tyler's persuasion.[39] The president signed all three parts of Clay's logrolled package, as Benton contemptuously viewed it, shortly before adjournment.

The Kentuckian felt pleased with these successes on distribution, bankruptcy, and tariff, all of which had been items on his agenda back in June. No doubt, Clay had sought to accomplish more than ordinarily possible in a short session. Though failing to get a national bank, he probably could not have succeeded if he had had unlimited time, for a decisive factor was the president's idea of an admissible policy, much different than that of the senator.

On September 13, 1841, this tumultuous session ended. From the perspective of the present day, one can see the outcome as a turning point in political history. It turned out to be the Whigs' last and best opportunity to set in motion the full range of the American System. There would be many attempts in the next decade to do so, all falling short of the optimistic targets Clay and his cohorts had set after a heartening electoral victory in 1840.

They expressed their frustration by an address to the public, laying out Tyler's errors and inconsistencies, essentially causing them to read him out of the party. To this a response appeared in the press from Representative Caleb Cushing of Massachusetts, defending the president in every respect.[40] It was arresting to read Cushing's paper in light of his close relation to Webster, the only cabinet member who had not resigned and one of the two most powerful Whigs in the land. Although Cushing called for party unity, the trend was moving in the opposite direction.[41] Notwithstanding Clay's call for Whigs to stay the course toward economic nationalism, prospects of fully developing his program as well as fulfilling his own presidential aspirations had dimmed.

12

Limited
Success

A fter returning to Lexington in fall 1841, Clay spent many an hour reviewing the disturbing course politics had taken. What had caused a reversal when at last his party had gained an opportunity to launch its economic program? And even though an unforeseen change in the presidency had occurred, why could the Whigs not have prevailed in the deplorable confrontation of two branches of government? He concluded that the principal problem was Tyler's faulty and stubborn position on the fundamental power to relieve the nation from its desperate condition by essential legislation. Always the senator came back to the belief that the policies he had advocated were constitutional and desirable and that another attempt to implement them must be made, just as the congressional Whig address had urged at the close of the special session.

For a few weeks he seemed truly uncertain whether he would return to Washington to lead a second effort toward that goal. His dissatisfaction with the present "mortifying" state of affairs was so great he was tempted to resign. He had no hope of converting the president, who had betrayed the trust confided in him. No hope of Tyler coming up with a reasonable substitute for the old national bank or the pet banks or the ill-conceived Independent Treasury. Though he did not say so, Clay must have believed only he could effectively head the party forces in December when they must address this difficult situation. Whether he could actually succeed or not, it is understandable that he thought this was the best strategy.[1]

If his assessment was correct, he would have to try something besides passing bills destined for veto. In good Whig fashion, executive tyranny must be stopped. Only a constitutional amendment revoking the two-thirds rule for overriding vetoes could remove the existing obstacle and restore the popular will. His many years at the Capitol, however, should have taught him how resistant the complicated amending process had proven to be. Perhaps the mere proposal would at least have psychological effect, both to rally his own ranks and to push Tyler farther back on the defensive.

Not long after the Senate settled into its routine that winter, at his usual place in the chamber the Kentuckian introduced three amendments: empowering only a majority of all members of each house to override a veto; abolishing the so-called pocket veto after the close of a session, whereby the legislators had no way to override; and transferring appointment of the secretary of treasury from the president to Congress. When that body got around to discussing these amendments, it was clear nothing would come of the foray. Clay spoke emphatically but mainly for the record.[2] Calhoun, the best-known advocate of limited government, opposed the resolutions on the ground that fortunately the chief executive, by the veto, had prevented enactment of unwise measures on internal improvements and the tariff. Inconsistency with his earlier indictment of Andrew Jackson's tyranny during nullification days did not bother him.[3]

Tyler clung to the possibility of getting a bank bill he would not have to veto. In his annual message he regretted that he had had the painful duty of disapproving previous measures; nevertheless, he believed his objections had been sound. He welcomed another attempt and had a plan that he briefly described and would be happy to submit upon request.[4] In the short period when Congress was not sitting, he had asked Webster to draft a bill for that purpose. The secretary of state had complied, of course with the president's opinions as guidelines.[5] Caleb Cushing, Tyler's active supporter and Webster's loyal friend in the House, then requested that the recommendation be forwarded to his committee.[6]

At the capital an exchequer, with a board of control composed of three presidential appointees as well as the secretary of treasury and the treasurer, would perform functions of deposit and disbursement for the government. So far, it would be similar to the abortive fiscal corporation. It could also receive deposits of individuals in specie and on that basis issue up to $15 million in treasury notes, which could circulate as currency. It would have agencies in states where their laws did not prohibit, and they could handle short-term exchange in areas not exceeding one hundred miles. But they could not discount notes. To avoid the perennially feared union of the purse and the sword in the executive, Congress would have a substantial regulatory power over the whole operation.

The proposal was dead on arrival. It did not get to the floor in either house, for members of every persuasion found serious flaws. The president's plan had not generated much interest even among Democrats. Numerous Jacksonians disliked the provision for treasury notes, amounting to nothing more than old-style paper currency, they contended. Old Bullion Benton compared them to worthless continentals of the Confederation era and waved some old samples as he orated.[7] Clay did not speak on the subject, though he and fellow Whigs saw all kinds of defects in the plan. They were remarkably quiet, wishing not to stir up Tyler on the exchequer question because he might then be less cooperative on other business, chiefly the tariff soon to be considered.[8]

Despite the fact that Webster drew upon his expertise in banking and skillfully wound his way between two hostile sides of the political issue, the plan had dubious value. Undoubtedly, the $15 million limit on circulation of treasury notes as currency would have been insufficient for ordinary business and for economic growth. On the other hand, it was questionable that even that little amount of specie would have been voluntarily deposited with the exchequer in exchange for this paper. Still more inadequate were the time and space limits placed for bills and drafts of exchange to be handled by the institution and its agencies. The provision would not have served a vast country extending across a continent. If Congress had created the exchequer, state-chartered banks would still have carried on most of the financial activity in public and private sectors.[9]

Another economic issue had higher priority than banking. It was the bankruptcy law previously passed but not to go into effect until the first of February 1842, a date rapidly approaching. It had been and continued to be a highly controversial measure, both because it offered relief to distressed debtors and because it had been a linchpin in the parliamentary vehicle carrying Clay's package of distribution and tariff to adoption. The act had stimulated widespread complaint by creditors and conservatives, notwithstanding its merciful policy toward the thousands who would benefit from it. Opponents in Congress introduced bills to repeal the law or at least postpone the date when it would become effective. In Kentucky, feeling against it ran so high that the legislature instructed Clay to vote for a delay. The state's representatives in the House led the move to do so, and it passed there handily.

In the Senate Clay did not obey his instructions. Furthermore, he spiritedly denied the accusation that he had resorted to the devious tactic of supporting the statute while secretly encouraging his fellow Kentuckians to kill it. He insisted not only that the charges were baseless, as they seem to have been, but that, at any rate, he could not control "the judgment of my State & its whole delegation."[10] In speaking against repeal, he punctuated his plea with an emotional description of imprisoned debtors liberated by national legislation. Just as the jail door is swinging open, he declared, "the Senate is called upon to drive them back to their gloomy and loathsome cells, and to fling back the door upon its grating hinges." He was called upon to unite in this cruelty, he said, but "I have not the heart to do it!"[11]

Whether or not governed by such a humane impulse, the senator pointed to a practical reason for leaving the bankruptcy law alone. As he explained in a personal letter, "The truth is that the Bankrupt law was a part of a system of measures of relief. The Distribution bill could not have been

carried without the Bankrupt bill; and if the latter be repealed, there is *much reason to fear* that the Distribution bill
may also be repealed. And if we thus retrace our steps, amidst
our other difficulties, how will it be possible for the Whigs to
maintain their ascendancy?"[12]

He barely managed to fend off the heavy assault, chiefly
from Benton. The Senate decided against repeal, twenty-three
to twenty-two, and also refused to postpone the activating
date of the first of February. That was only a modest victory,
for Congress did repeal the statute during its next session.
For much of the nineteenth century there was no effective federal bankruptcy system, so that the subject reverted to a cir-
cumscribed state jurisdiction. Nevertheless, during the year
this law was in force, thirty-four thousand debtors invoked its
protection.[13]

Clay was quite right when he warned that his opponents
were aiming at distribution as well as bankruptcy. After enactment in the preceding session of the provision transferring
land revenue to the states, Alabama sought to stop it by a
method that other states might adopt. It would refuse to receive its share of the money, supposedly making the law unen-
forceable on the ground that state benefits would then be
skewed. Resort to the process could be a new-model attempt
at nullification, if the resistant state's portion was retained in
the general fund at the Treasury or if it was distributed to
others. Seeing how flimsy this reasoning was, Clay proposed
apportioning the refused funds to all the other states, and his
resolution to do so passed. Other efforts to sidetrack the program of using land revenue for state internal improvements
came forward too. One would use the money for national defense, and another would devote it to retiring the presently
unredeemable treasury notes. To all these diversions the Kentuckian responded with a restatement of his rationale for federal distribution linked to state internal improvements. It
was, by now, familiar to all his auditors. Measures to improve
the lines of transportation, whether for shipping along the
coast or for roads and canals in the interior, were legitimate
regulations of commerce constitutionally, he still believed. Not
only that, they would also greatly stimulate American economic development.[14]

The connection between distribution and the tariff was obviously close, since both significantly involved fiscal policy; over the years politics had amply demonstrated that fact. In the recent special session, the two had been joined in the Berrien amendment, authorizing distribution of land revenue to the states but requiring cessation when any tariff rate exceeded 20 percent. Clay had to pay that price, reluctantly, in order to get approval of distribution. Now, if he could, he wished to eliminate this proviso. The moment was favorable. One reason was that the tariff compromise of 1833 would probably be amended anyway—its ten-year course toward that 20 percent maximum would be reached in July.

It was all the more likely that a new tariff would have to be framed inasmuch as the depression had severely strained the Treasury, cutting revenue and causing a projected deficit of $12 million in a budget of $26 million. In his annual message of December 1841 Tyler urged some steps to reduce extensive borrowing and to escape the necessity of issuing ever more treasury notes. Though it hurt to say so, he conceded that tariff rates would have to go up; yet true to his principles, he insisted that the 20 percent lid in the compromise remain in place. If that became impossible, he declared, then he wanted to adhere to the Berrien amendment and shut off distribution.[15]

Argument about tariffs in general resumed, both in and out of the Capitol. Amos Kendall, the prominent Jacksonian, charged that protectionism allowed capitalists to draw tribute, like a feudal nobility, from honest farmers and laborers.[16] *Niles' Register* had returned to the dialog after a long period of silence to warn against the perils of moving toward free trade while Britain talked about it but pursued the opposite policy.[17] In the Senate Calhoun and others described the menace of higher rates if extravagant expenditures continued. Though reluctant to enter into such debate this early in the session, Clay had to reply. He sought to calm worries by again endorsing the compromise of 1833 as a statement of the revenue standard of duties. And he promised to propose measures for economy in governmental operations.[18]

Within a month, on February 15, 1842, the senator was more explicit about adhering to the compromise. That commitment did not demand staying under the 20 percent ceiling, he explained, but only to impose rates necessary for the "economical administration of government," to use its language. As a matter of fact, he now conceded that higher rates were needed and could be laid without violating the provision of 1833. He took this risky step in presenting the resolutions he had promised. Furthermore, distribution ought not be suspended if rates went beyond 20 percent. Then he called for reductions in expenditures, seemingly to a greater extent than Calhoun had demanded.[19]

As in times past, Clay's resolutions provided an agenda for legislative discussion. In general, he emphasized the elements of the budget, with details on revenue, elimination of a deficit, and the practicability of a higher tariff—much on governmental fiscal reform and a little on the policy of protection.

He discussed the tariff in this fashion in order to prove that maximum rates of 20 percent could not produce the necessary revenue and might have to be raised to 30 percent or more. And since land sales were very depressed, they would not add the necessary amount, even if they were not distributed to the states and went into the general fund. In putting the case this way, he did deemphasize protectionism almost to the level of a side effect of rate revision. Nevertheless, he reiterated his well-known rationale for the American System to combat the extremely high British imposts, even prohibitive ones such as the corn laws, and to achieve a balanced, developing economy in the United States.[20]

His opponents saw higher rates as an inexcusable breach of faith, as breaking the 20 percent promise he had made during a national crisis. Calhoun led the criticism on this point, for he had long claimed that the compromise of 1833 had demolished the American System, not susceptible to this effort to revive it. Silas Wright and Levi Woodbury attacked Clay's fiscal assumptions as well, which drew him, they maintained, to the erroneous conclusion that it was necessary to break a sacred pledge. They relied here on some optimistic figures of savings by retrenchment in governmental operations.[21]

Inevitably, the discussion turned to the policy of distribution. As for Clay's plea for repeal of the Berrien amendment,

his opponents were on solid ground in emphasizing how foolish it would be to donate money to the states at a time when
the Treasury was so hard pressed. In addition, the strict-
constructionist argument reappeared, denying constitutional
authority for the national government to do such things as to
pay the current state debts on internal improvements indirectly. Rives was the foremost critic of Clay's resolution on
these grounds. Instead, the Virginian urged depositing land
proceeds in the Treasury for general use until fiscal recovery.
In return, he would agree to a tariff maximum of 25 percent.
Rives and Clay had another one of their heated exchanges.[22]
No one knew better than the Kentuckian that Rives continued
to reflect Tyler's views, which made it likely that raising the
tariff while retaining distribution would encounter more
vetoes.

By the end of March the senator delivered the last of a
series of long speeches on the tariff. He had decided to resign
his seat, so that conclusion of debate on his resolutions coincided with his widely noticed farewell and shared its drama.
Not that he would never return to Washington, even at the
other end of Pennsylvania Avenue. In any event, he obtained
a roll call on his tariff resolutions. Interestingly, by only a one-
vote margin the Senate rejected Rives's amendment to suspend distribution until retirement of the government's debt.
Yet it did not repeal the Berrien amendment. Distribution, it
appeared, would end, since a new presidential message concluded that rates would have to go above 20 percent and that
the proviso must stand, as Rives had argued. Clearly, it would
stay in effect unless a two-thirds vote overrode a veto of legislation to the contrary. As for disposition of Clay's resolutions,
the Senate skirted around all those having specific application
by referring them to committees. It did approve two general
statements calling for economy in governmental operations
and avoidance of debt.[23]

The next day, March 31, Clay escorted his good friend,
John Crittenden, into the Senate chamber to introduce him as
his successor and to announce his own resignation. A large
audience squeezed into the room for the senator's moving val-
edictory with highlights of his public career. Besides elegant
expressions of gratitude for past favors and apologies for un-

intended wounded feelings, he defended his conduct against the charge of having been a dictator in congressional proceedings.

Insisting he had no such powers as a dictator possessed, neither military nor financial nor political, he believed he had only sought to redeem Whig pledges to restore the nation's prosperity. "That my nature is warm, my temper ardent, my disposition, especially in relation to the public service, enthusiastic, I am ready to own; and those who suppose that I have been assuming the dictatorship, have only mistaken for arrogance or assumption that ardor and devotion which are natural to my constitution, and which I may have displayed with too little regard to cold, calculating, and cautious prudence, in sustaining and zealously supporting important national measures of policy which I have presented and espoused."[24]

Later that spring he had a better opportunity to review past politics and raise the banner for future reform. At a barbecue in Lexington on June 9, a huge crowd listened as he ranged across major issues in rigorously partisan terms, despite urging Democrats to put aside predilections of party. For himself, he denied an excessive ambition for the presidency, but everyone knew that already there were movements, many in his behalf, looking forward to the election two years in the future. In a little more self-vindication he also claimed a high degree of consistency throughout his long career.

His dominant theme, however, emphasized the nation's economic distress caused by Democratic mistakes. Falling prices, unsound money, loss of confidence, failing business, and suffering of farmers and workers had not occurred inevitably due to impersonal forces. Blame must rest upon faulty public policies, which he proceeded to describe. The heart of the problem, he asserted, lay in Jacksonian errors: the veto of a national-bank recharter, the removal of governmental deposits from the bank (followed by failed experiments with pet state-bank depositories and with an impractical independent treasury), and repeated resistance to distribution of land proceeds to the states. Clay recalled the principal conditions resulting from each of these missteps, all to the great detriment of the country.

He thought the desirable remedies were obvious. Return to a national bank for financial recovery. Enact a protective tariff to nourish industry and raise a revenue for the government. Approve distribution to assist the states. Sad to say, the president had obstinately prevented adoption of these measures. Clay exhorted all good Whigs to shake off their lethargy. Do not despair, he exclaimed, "even though you have been *"shamefully deceived and betrayed."* All that Americans needed was a new pilot to replace Captain Tyler on the helpless ship. Would the popular Kentuckian be the new pilot?[25]

During these June days at Ashland, Clay was carrying on an active correspondence with friends and supporters to strengthen his advantage for the presidential nomination. But much of it also kept him informed about proceedings in Congress. Though having withdrawn as a senator, he maintained his position as leader of Whig policy and strategy. And his strongest link to legislative politics was his successor in the Senate, John Crittenden, who reliably shared his opinions.[26]

The principal issue in Washington through the summer was the tariff, which was pending when Clay resigned.[27] Tyler had sent up a message recommending increased rates even beyond the maximum of 20 percent prescribed by the compromise of 1833 because of an acute shortage of revenue. At any rate, there was a widespread belief, then shared by the president until later advised by the attorney general otherwise, that further legislation would be required because the existing law of 1833 might lapse at the end of June. Tyler insisted upon retaining the present prohibition of distribution if rates in a new act rose above the ceiling to be imposed on July 1.[28]

Congress had been slow to adopt any measure, and it seemed unlikely it could complete work on a bill before that perceived deadline. So it passed a temporary statute for collecting customs under the old schedule for another month. Discussion had centered on the question of distribution. Clay's friends had conceded in an amendment to "postpone" distribution until August 1; yet they explained that the process could then resume if rates did not go above 20 percent, thus reactivating the Berrien amendment. Democrats and Tyler's supporters disagreed. The effect, they thought, would be to abolish that proviso, not for just a month, but to allow an unrestricted, permanent policy of distribution.[29]

As he watched congressional proceedings, Tyler was persuaded by that argument, incorrect though it was. Accordingly, he vetoed this temporary tariff, deepening the serious disagreement of two branches of government. The resulting debate in the House laid out large differences on the relation between tariff and distribution. A present-day reading of the speeches confirms the version of those denying that the measure could or was intended to slip in an unlimited policy of distribution. Besides, if Tyler had interpreted it accurately, he would still have had an undiminished power to decide later upon necessary legislation. The House failed to muster the two-thirds to override the veto, but now the president had accepted advice that the old law would not lapse, eliminating the need for temporary action.[30]

As Congress continued to grapple with the problem during July, Clay received frequent reports from the Capitol by Crittenden and other prominent Whigs. It seemed probable that Tyler would veto almost anything they passed. As defensive strategy, they were inclined to propose rates at 20 percent, preserving distribution of land revenue and home valuation of imports. It was surprising that they would retreat from protectionism that far and more surprising that Clay agreed it could be done to save distribution as more important. His position no doubt stiffened theirs on maintaining distribution in the ensuing debate, and Crittenden then decided to try also for higher rates on the slender chance of success. Whatever the outcome of this second effort, Clay opposed complete submission, in his view, to this miserable chief executive.[31] In fact, he looked with interest at suggestions of impeaching Tyler, a justifiable step, he thought, though not to be taken immediately.[32]

The bill that Crittenden managed through the Senate not only raised rates above 20 percent but went beyond the Berrien amendment. It would repeal outright this proviso, which had made distribution conditional on tariff rates staying at that level. Perhaps it was because he thought Tyler would veto the bill in any case that he went for unrestricted distribution and higher rates. A number of senators warned that a veto was certain. Furthermore, there was opposition to an increase of the impost on cotton bagging to five cents per square yard (welcome to Clay and the hemp interest), as well as upward adjustments on iron, salt, coffee, and tea. And Benton, Calhoun, Buchanan, and Wright attacked the general protectionist character of the measure with familiar arguments. In almost every instance Crittenden killed amendments if only by the thinnest margin, usually two or three votes. After passage on August 6, the president hurled back his predicted veto, primarily because of the section on distribution.[33]

Learning that the veto was on the way, Clay sent off his advice about the next phase of struggle. Though a protective tariff was important, he said, Whigs "ought at all hazards to insist upon the distribution of the Land fund." If Congress could not pass such a bill this session, it ought to pass the same bill the next one and let Tyler's Democratic friends take the criticism.[34] Meanwhile, Clay's lieutenant was also less hopeful of getting a protective measure and suggested approving one at the level of 20 percent, thus denying the president his badly needed revenue. Though both men were wavering almost daily between a hard line and some unpalatable concession, it was Crittenden, at the center of the tangle, who had to make the final decision after frequent meetings of the party caucus. And ultimately, Clay would have to bend more than he would have liked. "So much depends upon local circumstances, upon the temper of the two houses &c.," he wrote, "That no person at a distance can judge of what is best to propose." A sensible outlook, although he had already done all he could to influence the course of policy.[35]

In late August the Senate took up a new tariff bill passed by the House, generally for decidedly protective rates but with no provision for distribution. Debate consisted largely of arguments about particular rates as viewed by local interests arrayed against substantial antiprotectionist opposition. Iron, cottons, woolens, hemp, coal, and glass were items receiving much higher rates. Clay's prized provision for home valuation of imports at customs houses was not carried over from the compromise of 1833. The average for all goods amounted to about 35 percent, though individual categories rose to 65 percent or more.[36] Somewhat surprisingly Buchanan, spokesman for Pennsylvania iron masters despite his Democratic opinions, supported the bill not only for that specific interest but also for raising revenue sought by the administration. Similarly, another Jacksonian leader, Wright of New York, voted for it not only for wool and woolen interests but for the hardhit Treasury. The average level of imposts therefore nearly equaled that of the law of 1832, the target of nullification of that day. Calhoun reacted against the present legislation with a great deal of fire, as one might imagine. The absence of a provision for distribution caused a number of southern senators to vote nay—Berrien for one. On the other hand, Rufus Choate, Webster's cohort, thought the legislative strategy of separating distribution from the tariff bill was necessary for passage and spoke persuasively in behalf of the industrialists who would benefit from it. In the end this tariff passed as narrowly as possible, by one vote. The margin in the House had been that thin too.[37]

Although Tyler gave Congress no trouble on protection and quickly signed this version, he would not do the same for a separate provision for distribution, which went to him immediately afterward. By a pocket veto he again rejected a policy of sending money to the states when the national government sorely needed it.[38] In this position he made a credible case, despite Clay's sustained commitment to stimulate economic development and to assist states to pay their large debts. For his part, the Kentuckian would not quit his advocacy of distribution, notwithstanding the dwindling possibility of success.[39]

One might expect him to be unhappy about the outcome of this duel with "Captain" Tyler, yet that was not true. His correspondence assumed a philosophical tone: "We are all perfectly satisfied in this quarter with the passage of the Tariff," he remarked, and "there is no disposition felt to censure those of our friends who voted against it upon high motives by which they were actuated. It was a case of extreme embarrassment; and acquiescence, if not praise, is due to the course of both sections of our friends." As for the suspension of distribution, it would "only be temporary, if the Whigs retain power, and if they lose it, the other party will repeal the law."

All things considered, "I must say that I am not sure how I should have voted, if I had been in Congress."[40]

His generous and calm reaction can be accepted at face value, especially since he did get just the kind of protective tariff he wanted. Still, one can suspect his reaction assumed this cast, in part, to heal partisan wounds, to unify the Whig campaign two years ahead, and, not least, to solidify his own prospects for the presidency. Indeed he was already taking active steps toward that goal.

13

Disappointments

Soon after Congress ended its long, acrimonious session in late August 1842, attention shifted to the coming fall elections, which would be influenced by the disrupted relations between legislative and executive branches of government in Washington. As the acknowleged front runner for the Whig presidential nomination, Clay was unusually active in a day when there was a lingering belief that a candidate for the high office ought to avoid open electioneering. In addition to an extensive correspondence and statements appearing in the press, his widely reported speeches through the next several months addressed leading issues, most of them economic.

A highlight was his appearance on September 29 in Dayton, Ohio. Before a huge crowd, questionably estimated as more than a hundred thousand, he expressed gratitude for resolutions supporting his candidacy together with that of others in his party. In response to opponents' charges that the Whig party had no basic principles, he restated those that he himself had long embraced under the rubric of the American System. His two-hour discussion was comprehensive and explicit. Despite the recent tangle about banking, the nation must have a national institution to supply a sound currency, he declared, not the visionary hard-money medium favored by Locofoco radicals. Nor would the country approve Tyler's version, which the president first agreed to and then abandoned by his treacherous vetoes. Indeed, underlying all measures must be a severe limitation of the kind of executive power the president had claimed. And of course he endorsed a protective tariff, similar to the law just enacted but joined again to distribution of land revenue.[1] During the following week Clay also spoke to gatherings at Cincinnati and Indianapolis, where he advanced similar arguments.[2]

Notwithstanding his optimistic forecast that the Whig cause would prevail, the fall elections were disappointing.[3] The Democrats regained control of the House with a new majority of 142 to 79 and left the Whigs with a narrow margin in the Senate. No doubt the setback reflected dissatisfaction with deadlock at the capital and persistent ills of the depression. Were there fatal flaws in the party system? Probably not, for both parties had held together in Congress quite well except for the small band of Tyler's apostates. Party-line voting on all substantive questions was steady. As the Kentuckian saw it, the problem lay mostly with the undemocratic use of an arbitrary veto power, which he still hoped to eliminate by constitutional amendment.[4]

For the present, he continued speechmaking and other efforts to strengthen his position in the critical election two years ahead. Spending the winter of 1842-43 in New Orleans, he combined politics and personal business there while visiting relatives and friends. On the way down and during his return home he stopped frequently to confer with party leaders. Invariably he met warm receptions and addressed admiring crowds. Back in Lexington at an enthusiastic meeting in April he repeated his well-settled prescription for what must be done to put the nation on a correct course.[5]

Heartened by the response he had been receiving, he decided upon a broader tour of the South, which would begin at New Orleans in February 1844, proceed through the Gulf states into the Carolinas, and end at Washington in April. It would cover a section where his economic nationalism had often encountered much resistance but where he felt it was becoming more attractive, as apparent during his recent travel there.[6]

Clay emphasized the tariff more than any other subject at each stop along the way, just as he did in his ongoing cor-

respondence. His main goal was to reconcile extremes, to promote harmony rather than inflame opposition. Reviewing his
record on the tariff from 1816 and 1824 on to 1832 and 1833,
he contended that he had consistently balanced the need for
reasonable protection of domestic industry with the interests
of agriculture and labor. His particular focus was on the compromise of 1833, quieting the crisis of nullification. As he had
done earlier in the Senate, he defended the present higher
rates as necessary to provide for the economical administration of the government. According to his interpretation of
that compromise, duties did not have to be lower than 20 percent. The determinant was the requirement of revenue in the
federal treasury; and in these difficult days, rates had to be so
adjusted. A desirable policy must be to supply "incidental"
protection within the limits of that requirement. The adjective
and its hazy concept were becoming fashionable among politicos of every stripe.[7]

Although he held out an olive branch to southern advocates of low rates, he would not abandon essentials of the
American System. He deplored the notions of free-traders, especially when Britain clung to duties that, as in the case of the
corn laws, were prohibitive toward American imports. Farmers
and planters, in addition to manufacturers, were hurt badly.
So far as possible, national self-sufficiency was the true object
for the United States. The old doctrine of a home market, of
mutual interest of all parts of the economy, was valid yet compatible with only incidental protection.[8]

To be specific, he endorsed the tariff of 1842, adopted
after the duel of congressional Whigs and Tyler. Its schedule,
he thought, fit the terms of a revenue standard while discriminating in favor of industrial development in this country.
Though saying this, he well knew that Democrats were
already striving to repeal the measure with a different application of incidental protection. One fault he did see in the statute was its abandonment of home valuation of imports by
officers at custom houses, thereby reviving unreliable declaration of value by foreign exporters. This key element of the compromise of 1833, upon which he had then insisted, had
regrettably been dropped, he said.[9]

Another fault in the present tariff, he admitted, was that it lacked a provision for distribution of land revenue to states, one more casualty of Tyler's stubbornness. During speeches in Georgia and Virginia especially, pointing out their loss of proceeds from lands they had ceded to the national government, he urged the justice of compensating them with distribution. In other states too, distribution would be helpful in retirement of debts incurred by their internal improvement expenditures. Clay had lost none of his strong commitment to distribution as a central economic policy. The commitment was so firm that he renewed his willingness to accept preemption in land sales to squatters, objectionable though it was, if connected with distribution.[10]

He dealt with the banking issue cautiously, despite its recent prominence on the political battlefield. On every occasion he called for the restoration of an old-style national bank, but only if a popular mandate clearly favored it. This is what he had been saying ever since Jackson killed the BUS. Probably he would have been less reserved if a popular mandate had brought him into the presidency. Another guarded aspect of handling the issue was his total concentration on the value of a national bank in supplying a uniform currency, as if there were not many other important functions of such an institution in the economy. As a further defensive tactic he explained at length his own shift from opposing a national bank in 1811 to approving one in 1816, a recognition of changed circumstances after the War of 1812, he said. To be sure, since then he had asserted the constitutionality of such a corporation created by Congress. Furthermore, he did not hesitate to attack Tyler for his inconsistency and states-rights rigidity on the question.[11]

From the beginning of his southern tour in February 1844 until its finish in April, Clay felt he enjoyed strong support in that section. His initial confidence showed in a letter, exulting that "There is scarcely a speck in the whole horizon."[12] Aside from whatever number of Democrats might come over to him, Whigs in the South were decidedly favorable, as became obvious in place after place he visited along his route. This was so partly because they had nowhere else to go. He was the certain party nominee, Whigs would not readily join the Democrats, and voting for Tyler was out of the question. Nevertheless, he believed they were attracted to his positions on tariff and banking as the basis of a desirable economic program.[13]

Other developments encouraged him. Webster, one of the Whig founders and a leading economic nationalist, had left Tyler's cabinet and thereby detached himself from that aberrant wing, though for a while he kept his distance from Clay. But he had reaffirmed his orthodoxy and eventually campaigned for the party effectively in the Northeast.[14] And there was the welcome rapprochement of William Rives with the Kentuckian. He spoke in the Senate for a protective policy and could strengthen prospects in Virginia.[15] Of course, Whig pamphlets went out to voters in quantity. One that Clay highly praised was John P. Kennedy's *Defense of the Whigs*, describing the evolution of their nationalist principles from Madison's program of 1815, while old Federalists gravitated to the Jacksonian states-rights camp.[16]

Alas, a very dark cloud was forming. Tyler had grown interested in annexing the former Mexican state of Texas in response to territorial expansionists and southern slaveholders, often the same people. By late 1843, about the time Clay had decided upon his southern tour, negotiations to annex were under way, and from the first he thought the idea undesirable and impractical.[17] A spur to the project soon appeared when Calhoun became secretary of state, rounded out a draft treaty, and prepared to submit it to the Senate for ratification as Clay was finishing his trip in April 1844.

On the thirteenth at Raleigh, North Carolina, he gave one of his best speeches. Widely reported and well received, it ranged over his familiar economic topics but did not mention Texas, just as he had done ever since he had set out. Though believing that he was on the right track and that southern opinion paid little attention to the question of annexation, he now concluded he must issue a statement. He felt confident he could reconcile various viewpoints in a way different from anything he had yet seen.[18] So a few days later, he completed a letter and sent it on to his friends in Washington for publication. He opposed bringing in Texas, he wrote, because it would precipitate a war with Mexico and might break up the Union.[19]

Clinging to the belief that the matter had not attracted "a general expression of public opinion," he resolved to say nothing more about it. At his next stop in Petersburg, Virginia, he followed that strategy, recurring to tariff, banking, and the coming election.[20] His Raleigh letter appeared in newspapers everywhere, but the platform adopted by the national Whig convention on May 1 contained not a word about Texas.[21] Nevertheless, the issue did not go away and in fact crowded out those on economic policy, contrary to the new presidential nominee's assessment. Reluctantly, he later released two letters addressed to supporters in Alabama, explaining and then softening his opposition to annexation. The effect was failure to calm an excitement that had broken through old boundaries of political argument.[22]

Even on a staple of the contest, the tariff, Clay suffered a blow during the summer. His Democratic opponent, James K. Polk, an all-out expansionist nominated instead of Van Buren, gained in the race by an ambiguous letter to John Kane of Pennsylvania about his views on protection versus revenue. Polk, a faithful Jacksonian, freely admitted he had always favored low rates; but in communicating with this person in a manufacturing state, he straddled with language Clay was also using. "I am in favor of a tariff for revenue," he wrote, "such a one as will yield a sufficient amount to the Treasury to defray the expenses of the government economically administered. In adjusting the details of a revenue tariff I have heretofore sanctioned such moderate duties as would produce the amount of revenue needed, and at the same time afford reasonable incidental protection to our home industry." He closed by emphasizing government's duty to protect all economic interests. It is true that Polk opposed publishing the letter, but its eventual appearance damaged Clay's weakening campaign.[23] The Kentuckian recognized that if the Kane letter attracted even a modest number of popular votes in this large state, it might deliver enough electoral votes for Polk's victory.[24]

There was slippage in New York, too. Silas Wright, the stalwart Democrat, had abandoned altogether his moderate approval of protective rates, particularly on wool and woolens. It meant more trouble in this pivotal state on the tariff issue, for Wright would unsparingly attack the American System.[25]

And a further worry for Clay people here was the presence of the new Liberty party, nominating James G. Birney for the antislavery cause, directed against extension of the institution into Texas. It was thought Birney would draw away more Whig than Democratic votes.[26]

After return from the southern tour and nomination by the Whig convention in early May, Clay spent most of his time at Ashland without much electioneering. He made no important speeches and answered less incoming correspondence. He did send off the two Alabama letters in July, attempting to clarify his position on Texas, but otherwise left that issue alone. More than other topics, the revived charge of his corrupt bargain involving Adams's election in 1824 caused him to comment on it often.[27]

Election results in November were bad news. He had lost, though by an incredibly narrow margin. Polk got 170 electoral votes to his 105, seemingly a decisive outcome. But the popular count was 1,337,000 to 1,299,000. Particularly irritating were the 62,000 votes received by the antiannexationist Birney, perhaps the larger part of it at Clay's expense. The two populous industrial states of Pennsylvania and New York and the lower South, both areas about which he had strong hopes, went to Polk.

To explain why an election turned out the way it did is always problematic, and this is especially true for the historian's explanation many years after the event, when some kinds of helpful evidence one has on present-day electoral behavior are lacking.[28] Besides, then as now, contemporaries themselves viewed the event through various filters, personal and external. Such was the case with Clay's interpretation of what happened in the election of 1844. His early reaction was that the foreign vote went against him, owing to lax franchise requirements permitting, in some cases, noncitizens to vote. A rising nativist movement complained about this; and though Clay was not an extremist on the subject, he did believe stricter rules were needed. So he felt his false image as a nativist hurt him among the foreign-born electorate. Another reason he offered was prevalence of fraud at election places— by Democrats, of course. During these years, this was a common complaint by losers.[29]

Clearly, he thought the opposition had misled the people on economic issues, mainly on the principal issue of the tariff. He could cite Polk's Kane letter, deceptive as he saw it, as having a pivotal impact in Pennsylvania and other industrial quarters. The Kentuckian had focused on the tariff in his arduous southern circuit and felt the results were excellent, only to see a regrettable diversion of attention away from it. This had occurred despite his concession of only incidental protection by moderate rates. Anyway, he never forgot the perceived setback to desirable policy the victorious Democrats had inflicted.[30] The only remarkable thing about his view of what happened was that in the immediate aftermath of the election, he did not emphasize its contribution to his defeat.

The same was true of Texas annexation. Beyond the Raleigh and Alabama letters, he had avoided paying attention to that question throughout the campaign. After the election he either ignored it or referred to it cryptically. One reason for the outcome, he once observed, originated with the "abolitionists." Undoubtedly, he had in mind damage from the Liberty party or from a wider array of opinions on adding a new state of Texas, for and against it. His own cautious disapproval and even his subsequent deference to public sentiment in his second Alabama letter did not suit many people who had definite views on either side of the issue. Had he been so occupied with the well-known subjects of tariff and banking, so arrogant and inflexible that he did not respond to a new situation adequately? Difficult to say. Polk had preempted expansionism, and Clay could not have endorsed it with much benefit to his own candidacy even if he had been willing. Yet perhaps in 1844 only an expansionist could have been elected. Then there is the virtue of being faithful to one's convictions; and Clay's worries about the dangers posed by stirring up the question of extending slavery are understandable in light of later events leading to the Civil War.[31]

Over the next five years, in retirement from the Senate and, to some extent, from involvement in politics, he observed events with more than a little discouragement. Tyler carried annexation of Texas through an outgoing Congress by the dubious procedure of joint resolution. In a bellicose, lucky approach, his successor Polk gained a favorable treaty with

Britain on the disputed Oregon boundary. But his bellicose policy toward Mexico pushed the country into war. To fulfill his pledges during the election of 1844 still further, he restored an independent treasury after a hiatus during the Tyler administration.

That left the tariff. Despite Polk's amorphous Kane letter, as president he now wanted a sizeable reduction of rates. His secretary of treasury, Robert Walker, built upon prior work of Democratic congressmen to fashion a detailed schedule of the lowest rates to produce the necessary revenue. The average levy would be 26 percent, several points below the existing tariff of 1842.[32] Adopted by the thinnest margin in the Senate, this measure was linked to a rapprochement with Britain, an exporting country that itself was lowering rates, indeed repealing the hated corn laws. The actions of the two countries on commerce with one another were facilitated by a British concession on the Oregon boundary, warding off possible conflict.

Clay's opinion of the Walker tariff of 1846 and of the British reform was predictably negative. He deplored "the visionary promises of an alien policy of free trade, fostering the industry of foreign people and the interests of foreign countries, which has brought in its train disaster and ruin to every nation that has had the temerity to try it."[33] In fact, neither country had adopted free trade, whatever the claims or criticisms. There was still a measure of protection in the American law, not drastically different from the superseded measure of 1842, which the Kentuckian wanted restored. Besides, he was thrown on the defensive when the statistics on trade for 1847 revealed a favorable balance for the United States. He explained it as the result of the current European famine's stimulus to American export of foodstuffs, a temporary condition.[34]

Hope for long-range improvement, he believed, depended upon a reversal of policy by a Whig victory in the next presidential election. During the campaign of 1848, he advised, the party must look to the old issues, the tariff and internal improvements especially.[35] But he soon found that different factors diverted attention from these economic essentials: the progress of the Mexican War and the gathering interest in a popular general, Zachary Taylor. As for the war itself, he contended that it was unnecessarily and unconstitutionally provoked by Polk. As for Old Rough and Ready, who had sought a warm relationship with him, Clay had long since had enough of military heroes as presidents. At any rate, he himself was the most eligible candidate to handle political affairs. But given the new situation, as well as a growing feeling across the land that he and his positions were becoming rather out of date, his chances for the nomination seemed poor. Even his steadfast friend Crittenden was not steadfast about his making another run for the prize. Indeed, Crittenden headed a strong movement for the more attractive Taylor, even though most people, including the general himself, were not sure whether he was a Whig or a Democrat.[36] Still, when the national convention met in the summer, it selected him. That fall, Taylor won election. Taking the outcome hard, Clay complained that his party had rejected his American System, not just its advocate, merely to gain power. In the early months of the new administration, he found that the president neither invited his advice nor shared his priorities.[37]

Circumstances pressed Taylor toward priorities related to slavery, primarily to its status in the newly acquired Mexican cession, a subject intensifying sectionalism. Clay himself became a major actor in Congress, beginning in December 1849, when he returned to the Senate and took the lead in fashioning a compromise between North and South.

Nevertheless, between then and adjournment in autumn 1850, he had a few opportunities to address economic questions. In debate during this crisis, he occasionally called attention to the tariff. If Democrats and Whigs could cooperate on issues of slavery, he thought, they might find opportunities to remove some problems of commercial regulation. Clay was attempting to connect action on them to legislation within the great compromise. Nothing came of it.[38] He also submitted petitions from particular interests, such as iron manufacturers of Pittsburgh, for adjustments of rates upward, with no effect.[39] In the next congressional session, beginning in December 1850, now that the compromise had been adopted, he made an unsuccessful effort to amend the tariff of 1846 by eliminating fraudulent declarations of value at custom houses. Low-tariff Democrats had a majority in both houses and were not minded to tamper with the status quo.[40]

One important advance in federal internal improvements was a huge land grant for construction of the Illinois Central Railroad. Stephen A. Douglas, the rising Democratic senator from the state that would initially benefit most from the measure, introduced a bill to donate six square miles of the public domain for each mile of the road's right-of-way. Though given to states, the land would then go to private companies. Approved by only one house of Congress earlier, it passed both easily in April 1850, though it generated a full discussion of its terms and of the general policy. There were some predictable constitutional objections; but they were markedly restrained, compared to the fiery speeches of an earlier day. The principal issue involved the relative advantages to be gained by individual states, for the project was to link Chicago with Mobile. It was therefore more than a little interesting to Mississippi and Alabama, which managed to get lands along with Illinois.[41]

Clay strongly supported the bill on the grounds of western development and significant national benefits. He remarked he was familiar with the prairie through which the line would run, presently "utterly worthless" because wood and water were scarce on its flat, treeless terrain.[42] How surprised even he would have been to see the rich agricultural region it became, well beyond his progressive forecast! During discussion on the Senate floor he heard scattered advocacy of his favorite idea of distributing land proceeds to all states yet did not actively help its proponents.[43] By the Illinois Central law Congress added a precedent to earlier measures subsidizing internal improvements, a policy significant during the era of railroad building over the next half century.[44]

A few months later, Clay took a negative position on a modest proposal to appropriate $230,000 for a railroad in Missouri intended to feed a transcontinental line toward the Pacific. The sponsor was Clay's inveterate adversary Benton, who claimed this was justifiable by the old program to assist building the National Road with a percentage of revenue from federal land sales in states from Ohio to Missouri. In a spirited exchange with Old Bullion, Clay argued that the fund for that purpose had long since been overdrawn. It appears he was still rankled by the fact that Kentucky had not shared in this benefit as states north of the Ohio River had in the past fifty years. It was hardly a good reason to take the stand he did. Furthermore, he seemed to oppose Benton's project because it was Benton who advanced it. At any rate, his selectivity found plenty of company, and the bill failed decisively.[45]

The shoe was on the other foot when the Kentuckian's own interest was at stake. He supported a bill a few days later to supply funds for work on interior rivers and harbors. One section particularly important to him would provide for the removal of snags from western waterways. Throughout his long career, he had been a spokesman for this commercial network in which his state had a fundamental interest. In the present instance and in some others related to development of transportation, he apparently had a local as much as a national objective, his denials to the contrary notwithstanding. The bill stalled. So he had to leave such matters to his successors on the political scene.[46]

Increasingly, his opponents charged him with adhering to stale views on time-worn topics, not keeping current with more important questions of the present, therefore not being alive to opportunities for human improvement. Rather than dwelling upon tariff, banking, and land policies, he ought to have confronted more relevant challenges to America, they contended. One line of historical interpretation concurs with this criticism. During a brush in the Senate with Lewis Cass, who called for a sympathetic stance toward the Hungarian revolution against an old, oppressive Austrian empire, Clay categorically denied he was one of those alleged stationary politicians, oblivious to progress. After all, he scolded, he was not like Democrats who favored progress toward a war. Instead, he was committed to the nation's growth and prosperity, to a government supportive of the economic welfare of all citizens. This was his vision of progress, he declared.[47] A fitting statement on this day, March 3, 1851, in the last congressional speech of his long career.

Henry Clay, c. 1848. Engraving of a daguerreotype by Marcus Root. Courtesy of the University of Kentucky Library, Special Collections.

14

Retrospect

In an overview of Clay's political career, a theme that stands out is his economic nationalism, his advocacy of governmental encouragement of growth in all sectors of the economy. He sought a balance of agriculture, commerce, and manufacturing so that the United States would have a home market, not largely dependent upon imports from abroad. The country must industrialize to supply manufactured goods, he believed, while agriculture provided food and raw materials. Improved transportation and financial institutions rounded out an economic program, known as the American System.

An important influence upon his thinking was his own experience as a young man in Kentucky, where individual enterprise and public policies joined to exploit the resources of a new land. Soon, when he was sent to Congress, he enthusiastically supported laying out roads and canals through federal as well as state legislation. He also displayed a keen interest in stimulating manufacturing as it was entering a phase of modernization. Then his nationalism intensified in urging a declaration of war in 1812 to uphold maritime rights and afterward in striving to achieve American self-sufficiency.

In his day a new field of study was political economy, the relationship of government and economic matters. On the Anglo-American scene the point of departure was Adam

Smith's *Wealth of Nations* (1776), which had a decided effect upon many of Clay's contemporaries. Smith had called for an end to mercantilism, a system long employed by England and other nations to control foreign and colonial commerce by numerous regulations to assure a favorable balance of trade. Instead, Smith advised, depend upon individualism without intervention by government. This was termed laissez-faire, which translated into free trade with no commercial barriers. Clay often battled those adhering to Smith's text, but he apparently did not read much in the field of political economy/ He probably did have a significant influence upon the school of writers who endorsed his own economic nationalism. Foremost was Hezekiah Niles's friend Daniel Raymond, a lawyer and professor of Baltimore, whose *Thoughts on Political Economy* (1820) went through several editions, stating the case for the American System with ability. There was also Friedrich List, a German-American, who contributed his theoretical arguments to protariff conventions, organized by Clay's friends. The Kentuckian used political economists occasionally as auxiliaries, but more often as targets.[1]

He began his service in government as a firm Jeffersonian Republican and always insisted he subscribed entirely to the strict-constructionist principles Madison set forth in opposing the Federalist Sedition Act of 1798. Yet, contrary to a common opinion, these Republicans were not rigid on practical questions. They favored agriculture, it is true, but recognized the importance of commerce in marketing products of planters and farmers. They moved toward war with Britain over the cutoff of American maritime rights in this trade. And they came to accept tariffs, protecting new industry and pursuing national economic independence. Secretary of Treasury Gallatin came out with broad recommendations for advancing manufacturing and even broader ones for establishing a network of roads and canals. Clay was this kind of Republican.[2]

Whatever the uses of ideology, he depended chiefly upon the vehicle of a political party to achieve his purposes. With the demise of the Federalist organization in the twenties, there was a unique interlude of one-party or no-party government, to be swept away by the rise of Andrew Jackson, who headed the Democratic party. Clay and Webster led the National Republican opposition to Jackson's adminstration. As the Bank War intensified because of the recharter veto and the executive order to remove the government's deposits from the institution, the coalition of Old Hickory's adversaries assumed the name of Whigs. Although it was often said that the only common ground of the party's elements was disapproval of President Jackson's authority, its core was National Republican, and its leader was Henry Clay. Internal differences of opinion notwithstanding, the articles of faith became the American System.

Democrats held to the objectives of equal rights, no special privileges to corporations or individuals, and a relatively passive government checked by narrow constitutional interpretation. Most Whigs preferred active programs of protective tariffs, a national bank, and federal aid to internal improvements. They had little difficulty in finding appropriate authority to implement them. Intellectual historians have characterized Whigs as modernizers and Democrats as traditionalists. In legislative voting, studies have found a high degree of party solidarity. But in a general sense, counting state as well as national situations, there were similarities between the parties concerning the ends, if not the means, of policy.[3]

A clear difference between parties persisted on the tariff issue. As a protectionist spokesman, Clay emphasized the necessity of attaining national self-sufficiency within a well-balanced economy. There were benefits for all interests and all sections. The plantation South would find a market for its staples in the North, the West for its foodstuffs in the East, and the North for its industrial products throughout the nation. Labor would greatly benefit by employment at higher wages. Harmony, mutual advantages, and prosperity would follow adoption of a truly protective system, he reasoned. Do not be diverted by the siren song of free trade, he warned, for no other country had, in fact, adopted it. Do not be diverted by the false assertion that such a tariff would hurt consumers by higher prices. On the contrary, the stimulus to business would lead to more competition and lower prices, once growth was achieved. And do not believe the charge that Congress lacked the power to establish protective rates, because it did have unqualified authority to lay imposts on imports and to regulate commerce.

After a very modest start toward this sort of policy in the first tariff of 1789, in which the object of protection was mentioned but not achieved beyond a low revenue level, legislation moved slowly upward—by a moderate amount in 1816, further by the tariff of 1824, which the Kentuckian sponsored as the beginning of true protection, and then by the so-called abominations of 1828, the highest until the Civil War. Reaction set in and brought reduced rates in 1832 and 1833 as concessions to a ruffled South. A higher tariff of 1842 finally survived vetoes by Tyler but was lowered four years later.

Antiprotectionists maintained a strong attack upon the American System. It began with the agrarian branch of Jeffersonianism, arguing that it was quite undesirable to nurse industrialization, which would unfairly subsidize some capitalists while bringing to this country all the social ills then besetting English cities. They liked to quote Adam Smith, who had advised nations to buy goods at home or abroad, depending upon where they were more efficiently and cheaply produced. In the United States, they also insisted that the tariff raised consumer prices and amounted to an oppressive tax. It was Calhoun who made the most of this point, since, he said, the South suffered northern exploitation as a result. For a remedy, he assembled his dubious theory of state nullification against the tariff of 1832. Clay responded by a ten-year gradual reduction, which he felt forestalled secession and war. Be that as it may, he hesitated to repeat his well-known constitutional view of a popularly based, inseparable Union to counter nullification.

In assessing the tariff controversy, one can begin by looking at British-American commerce. England was the largest supplier and customer of the United States, with about 40 percent of American trade both ways involving that country. In nine of the years 1821 to 1833, imports from Britain exceeded exports there. Fine cottons and woolens as well as iron led the list of imports, while cotton fiber was the largest export by a great margin.[4]

Aside from the imbalance of this trade, there were other problems. One was evasion of American customs regulations.

Invoices on British imports often declared lower than actual values. Until the thirties, officers at ports in the United States did not have authority to value this merchandise; and even when so-called home valuation went into effect, there were mistakes and frauds and differences from one place to another. Furthermore, there were notorious practices in consigning goods to agents for sale at auction, often a strategy of selling at cutthroat prices to unload surpluses, even consciously to take a loss or to deceive customs. Eventually rules and taxes reduced the use of auctions, yet the whole system was full of defects.[5] Statistics, which are not very reliable, show no substantial impact by new tariffs upon price levels, but they may reflect dumping with low profits or the widespread laxity of customs administration.[6] Clay frequently tried to get congressional reforms to check fraud and improve efficiency, but never successfully.

On the other hand, British commercial policy controlled imports strictly. On many products its rates were higher than those of the United States, and some goods were prohibited altogether. Cotton came in with only a nominal levy, of course, for it was a vital industrial raw material. Overall, the balance of trade was very favorable to that country.[7] The greatest American complaint involved the corn laws, which laid an escalating scale of duties on imported wheat and flour as the British products' prices declined; indeed, importation was prohibited if prices fell to a certain minimum.[8] This sore grievance lasted until repeal in 1846. Moreover, the navigation acts of American pre-Revolution memory still preserved a large share of the carrying trade to British or colonial vessels and crews.[9]

So it seemed to Clay that British political economists and politicians warmly commended free trade but clung to the reverse, the old mercantilism. True enough, a reform movement was trying to discontinue it by the twenties, with leaders such as William Huskisson making quite an effort; and to a limited extent he obtained revisions. Yet he had to deny that he aimed at complete abandonment of the system, and in fact, he left much in place. How different was Huskisson's position from his own, Clay asked?

Historians have found it difficult to evaluate the impact of protective tariffs from that day to this. Since it has been one of the most partisan questions in politics, an impartial interpretation is rare. Recovery and accuracy of sufficient information about the effects of that policy have posed serious problems, even for the best equipped investigator. Besides, many factors determined these effects, so that weighting them has been nearly impossible. It is uncertain whether the effects were actually slight or substantial.

On the wide range of interpretations, Edward Stanwood's thoroughly researched, two-volume work presented the most convincing protectionist view years ago (1903). After investigating political aspects especially, he believed tariffs were quite effective in stimulating the economy and that they had the opposite effect when rates were reduced. About the same time, on the other end of the interpretive spectrum, the classic volume of Frank Taussig conceded a possible impact, particularly in an early stage of an industry's development, but very little in the long run. Victor Clark's full *History of Manufactures* (three volumes, 1916) resembled Taussig's position. It recognized that tariffs might have offered some economic help, yet much less than contemporaries supposed. Between these opposing views are a number of good studies of individual industries—hemp, iron, textiles, for example. All find some impact, but how much in comparison with other factors, it turns out, is not clear.[10]

Unsatisfying though this may be, there seems to be no definite answer. There were numerous elements affecting changes, as all these authors point out: freight and insurance in shipping, cyclical movements of depression and prosperity, many features of supply and demand, financial and labor conditions, and so forth. Econometricians have recently addressed the problem and cannot move their mathematical models very far toward clarification.[11] An inspection of statistics on imports and exports, on volume and value of many goods, does not reveal a close congruity of movement with particular tariff laws.[12] As a number of experienced observers say, the chief effect may have been psychological, either to encourage entrepreneurial expansion or to cause retrenchment, depending on various circumstances.[13] Even after a sober study of hard figures, it is clear that politics also supplied a significant force. Clay's speeches, though laced with numbers and a good deal of information, were no exception.

Another pillar of the American System was a national bank to provide adequate credit and currency for the growing economy. Hamilton's first Bank of the United States (1791-1811), performed these functions well, on the whole, despite continuing criticism by some Republicans.[14] Many Jeffersonians did become reconciled to it, and Secretary of Treasury Gallatin recommended renewing the bank's charter. Slower to move away from his constitutional scruples was Clay, but he became an adherent by 1816, when the second BUS was chartered. He now had much business with the institution's branches in Kentucky and Ohio as lawyer and entrepreneur. He was on intimate terms with its presidents at the central office. As standing counsel his cases in federal circuit and supreme courts were mutually rewarding.

The period when he was most involved with the BUS was, of course, that of the Bank War, 1832-37, when Jackson vetoed the recharter bill and removed the government's deposits. Clay's adversaries thought he was merely forwarding his presidential bid and protecting his personal financial connections instead of taking a dispassionate stand on policy. Actually, his motives were mixed. He accepted proposed revisions of the charter in the bill, but the president vetoed it. When, in the congressional session of 1833-34, he attacked Jackson's order to remove deposits and pressed for censuring him by the Senate, his emotions got the better of him. He would have taken better ground if he had sought a practical compromise, possibly Webster's proposals for short-term extension, and thereby had been true to his reputation as a peacemaker. In general, he could have more effectively addressed the tilt of the BUS toward particular interests and individuals, its broad powers over terms of credit and volume of currency, and the inflated authority of its president.

Opposing opinions on finance hardened during the depression beginning in 1837, when the unlucky new president, Van Buren, relentlessly pushed his independent-treasury prescription. It was not a useful idea as far as an acceptable banking system was concerned because it was essentially a retreat, a divorce as Clay and other opponents dubbed it, from constructive action by government in order to guard its own funds. It turned out that when the Independent Treasury was permanently established (1846-1913), it did not deliver on Democratic promises.[15] Clay had the better argument here.

An unfortunate episode concerning banking occurred during the Harrison-Tyler administration in 1841-42. Clay now had a Whig majority in both houses and insisted upon another national bank. He made concessions to meet Tyler's states-rights sensitivity, but both the senator and the chief executive failed to communicate well and took rigid stands, again notwithstanding Webster's plea for more attempts to reconcile differences. Regardless of whether Clay's demands were better than Tyler's objections, his last opportunity to put this and the rest of his American System into operation slipped away.

In addition to a protective tariff and a national bank, improvement of transportation was a prime component of Clay's program. During this early phase of developing a modern economy, new forms and a better quality of transportation contributed so much to growth that historians have called the process a revolution.[16] As a westerner, the Kentuckian understood the importance of linking his section to East and South. It required a National Road, on which he traveled to and from Washington. It also depended upon improved waterways, the cleared channels of the Ohio-Mississippi river system as well as projects such as the Louisville and Portland Canal at the falls where hundreds of the newly developed steamboats passed. They accommodated him for frequent trips eastward or down to New Orleans and carried his hemp to market. Soon an extensive railroad network handled freight and passengers faster, farther, and more cheaply than ever thought possible. This dramatic transition involved not only vigorous efforts by private enterprise but huge governmental support at several levels. Throughout his career he played a major role in this internal improvement policy making.

When he arrived at the capital as a young senator in 1806, the Jefferson administration had already set a plan in motion for the National Road, to be financed by federal receipts of land sales in Ohio and to connect that new state and the territory as far as the Mississippi Valley with Maryland. He strongly approved the commitment as one of Gallatin's ambitious proposals for a national grid of improvements. During the decade of 1815-25 he fought many a battle to advance work on the National Road and to broaden policy for other undertakings. He sometimes encountered stiff resistance. On constitutional grounds, President Madison vetoed a bill to use the bonus received for chartering the bank as a fund for internal improvements. Over the next several years Clay responded to Madisonian objections and those of other strict constructionists, even President Monroe. His cogent argument was that the postal, military, and commerce powers of Congress justified federal action. He fared well enough on the National Road, which ultimately reached western Illinois in the 1830s, but less so on other proposals for monetary grants. Indeed, he himself opposed some bills with the complaint, widely heard in other quarters, that his state was not getting a just share.

A low point of his efforts appeared in 1830 when Jackson vetoed the Maysville Road bill, an improvement from Kentucky's northern boundary on the Ohio River to Lexington, hopefully to link the National Road with New Orleans in the future. Jackson, with Van Buren's urging, selected the measure as a test case to stop what he felt was undue expansion of federal authority, no doubt also to deliver a blow to his foremost political adversary. Clay had a good argument in rejecting the president's reason that this was a local not an interstate project and therefore beyond constitutional limits. Segments of major routes had been previously approved. Furthermore, contrary to Jackson's position, there were many precedents for the government to mix its funds with private capital by subscription to this turnpike company's stock, as the bill provided.[17] Though large appropriations were made for internal improvements throughout Old Hickory's administration, the veto was a signal to Clay that he had better look for some other strategy in order to bypass Jackson's constitutional inconsistencies.

The option he found was distribution of the federal revenue from sale of public lands to states for internal improvements. The idea was not new when he proposed it in 1832.

The congressional law for the admission of Ohio as a state in 1802 had provided for granting 5 percent of this revenue to construct the National Road to and through the state. And later the same provision was attached to admission of others. In the twenties senators presented bills for distributing such funds to all states, old or new. A competing proposal would have ceded the public lands themselves to the states in which they lay. Clay assembled his own formula as part of a committee report in 1833, which would distribute not only for internal improvements but also education and colonization of emancipated slaves to Africa. It passed Congress, but Jackson vetoed. Clay was furious, contending that the distribution measure was considered part of the tariff compromise relating to nullification.

Time and again, he strenuously attempted to obtain adoption of distribution, just as strenuously as for a national bank or a protective tariff. During the Whig confrontation with Tyler in 1841-42, he managed to get legislation, only to have to stipulate that it would not operate if tariff rates exceeded 20 percent. His opponents always charged that distribution was his effort to draw off funds from the Treasury to make it necessary to keep tariff rates high. Not true. He sought this policy mainly to facilitate internal improvements, as he declared he did. After he left the Senate in 1842, his successor Crittenden tried his best to get an unrestricted provision in the new tariff but had to yield to the president's unshakable opposition. During the Jacksonian era, there were only two brief periods of distribution before repeal. It was one of Clay's greatest disappointments.

Toward the end of his life, he witnessed the spectacular rise of the railroad as an immensely important form of transportation. Many of the arguments of previous years in behalf of governmental aid now applied to it. And that aid was forthcoming in huge amounts for decades. Land grants and loans were often voted, though monetary distribution was not. The Senate extended a very generous donation of land to the Illinois Central, sponsored by the Jacksonian Democrat Stephen Douglas and heartily approved by the venerable Whig Henry Clay.

In the winter of 1852 as the desperate
year-old senator sat in his Washington h(
much to remember from his long politic
though he had enjoyed most of the honors
public man could hope to gain, he had no
prize he thought was his due, the presidency. But he had exer-
cised strong leadership in the cause of economic nationalism,
of his American System. At a time when the economy had an
encouraging rate of growth and had already crossed the
threshold of an industrial revolution, he had some success in
defining a positive governmental role. In the thirties his party
followers made a good run against the prevailing Democratic
opinion, which called for a limited national government, equal
rights, and individualism. But after the stalemate of 1841, the
Whigs had a long period ahead as a minority party. Furthermore, the crucial question of slavery obscured objectives Clay
might have implemented.

During the Civil War, a decade after the Kentuckian's
death, however, Lincoln and the Republican party implemented much of the American System.[18] From the beginning
of his political career, the president had been a confirmed
Whig and follower of Clay. When he had served in the Illinois
legislature in the thirties, he was a leader in promoting an
ambitious internal improvement program of roads and canals
for the state. He had also urged distribution of national land
proceeds. Despite little help from that direction, the state em-
barked on an extensive, if financially disastrous, effort on its
own.[19] Nonetheless, Lincoln never abandoned the underlying
rationale. His party put important measures through Congress for transcontinental railroads, subsidized generously by
federal land grants and loans directly to private companies,
such as the Union Pacific. To be sure, the formula was somewhat different than Clay's proposals to distribute funds from
land sales to states for developing transportation, but the
basic idea was the same: a modern economy in peace or war
required a good infrastructure, whose development government ought to assist.[20]

Another wartime policy persisting in the years ahead
was a much higher tariff than those of the preceding fifteen

years or earlier. The thrust came from the boundless need for ever larger revenue, still primarily derived from customs receipts. But the president and his party in Congress also justified this trend as desirable protection for industry, as Clay and other Whigs had previously.

Equally noteworthy is the impact of the war and Whiggish ideology upon banking. The disarray of hundreds of state-chartered banks and the consequent confusion of their note issues as well as other operations posed a serious problem in financing the Union cause. So a remedy was establishment of national banks with fiscal and monetary functions that Clay and Nicholas Biddle would have approved.

It is incorrect to attribute these changes entirely to a supposed presidential dominance of Congress or to a neo-Whig-Republican majority there. They came about when they did, in large part, because of conditions during the conflict. But that is not to say that they would have assumed the same shape if a Jacksonian Democratic administration had been in power. In the White House Lincoln would recall his long attachment to Clay's American System. He still remembered the Kentuckian as "the beau ideal of a statesman."[21]

Appendix

Tariff and Prices at New York

Year	Textiles	Metals
1824 R	191	242
1825	198	279
1828 R	190	234
1829	182	229
1832 L	161	212
1833 L	162	205
1841	140	204
1842 R	132	183
1843	114	172
1846 L	122	191
1847	117	186

Prices are based upon an index of 100 for the years 1910-14. R = raised tariff rates. L = lowered rates. Source: *Historical Statistics,* part 1 (Washington, D.C., 1975), 201.

Tariff and Volume of Imports

In a comprehensive study of annual tariff rates and the volume of imported textiles and metal products, 1823-43, Victor S. Clark, *History of Manufactures in the United States, 1607-1860* (Washington, D.C., 1929), 1: 604-10, concludes, "Any analysis that we may make of these figures brings us at least to the negative conclusion that rates of duty had little effect upon the fluctuation of *quantity* of imports from year to year, and therefore upon the evenness of foreign competition."

Notes

1. Jeffersonian Nationalist

1. Thomas D. Clark, *Kentucky: Land of Contrast* (New York, 1968), 55-68.

2. Reliable older biographies, with information on Clay's early life, include Bernard Mayo, *Henry Clay: Spokesman of the New West* (Boston, 1937), and Glyndon G. Van Deusen, *The Life of Henry Clay* (Boston, 1937). Valuable recent studies are Merrill D. Peterson, *The Great Triumvirate: Webster, Clay, and Calhoun* (New York, 1987), and Robert V. Remini, *Henry Clay: Statesman for the Union* (New York, 1991).

3. Dale M. Royalty, "Banking, Politics, and the Commonwealth: Kentucky, 1800-1825" (Ph.D. diss., University of Kentucky, 1972), 7-38; Mayo, *Clay,* 158-77. See the editorial note in James F. Hopkins et al., eds., *The Papers of Henry Clay,* 11 vols. (Lexington, 1959-1992), 1:161 (hereafter cited as *CP*).

4. Royalty, "Banking and Kentucky," 54-65, 87-111; Clay's reports to the bank's directors, May 10 and Oct. 28, 1808, June 2, 1809, *CP,* 1:325-28, 382, 412. Hereafter the Notes will cite Clay as HC.

5. Emory R. Johnson et al., *History of Domestic and Foreign Commerce of the United States,* 2 vols. (Washington, D.C., 1915-22), 1:206-9.

6. Robert W. Binkley Jr., "The American System: An Example of American Nineteenth-Century Economic Thinking" (Ph.D. diss., Columbia University, 1949), 128-31; editorial note, *CP,* 1:162.

7. James F. Hopkins, *A History of the Hemp Industry in Kentucky* (Lexington, 1951), 117-18; editorial note, *CP,* 1:315-16; HC and James Maccoon to William Macbean, [June 17, 1808], HC and Maccoon to Macbean, [June 18, 1808], *CP,* 1:345-46.

8. HC, resolution and editorial note, [Jan. 3, 1809], *CP,* 1:396-97; Mayo, *Clay,* 334, 337-42.

9. Van Deusen, *Clay,* 45; Binkley, "American System," 69.

10. Joseph H. Harrison, Jr., "The Internal Improvement Issue in the Politics of the Union, 1783-1825" (Ph.D. diss., University of Virginia, 1954), 136-61, 171-74; Philip D. Jordan, *The National Road* (Indianapolis, 1948), 72-75; *Annals of Congress,* 9th Cong., 2d sess., 14-15.

11. *Annals of Congress,* 9th Cong., 2d sess., 25, 29; Mayo, *Clay,* 273-75.

12. HC, resolution, Jan. 12, 1807, *Annals of Congress,* 9th Cong., 2d sess., 30; HC, committee report, Feb. 24, 1807, *Annals of Congress,* 9th Cong., 2d sess., 92-93, 96.

13. *Annals of Congress,* 9th Cong., 2d sess., 33-36, 55-60, 77-88; Carter Goodrich, *Government Promotion of American Canals and Railroads, 1800-1890* (New York, 1960), 26-27; Mayo, *Clay,* 277-79.

14. *Annals of Congress,* 9th Cong., 2d sess., 95, 98.

15. Text of report, *American State Papers; Miscellaneous* 1:724-41. See the evaluation in Goodrich, *Government Promotion,* 28-37.

16. Harrison, "Internal Improvement," 251-58.

17. Binkley, "American System," 153-54; Harrison, "Internal Improvement," 265-97.

18. Jefferson to Thomas Leiper, Jan. 21, 1809, Paul L. Ford, ed., *The Writings of Thomas Jefferson,* 10 vols. (New York, 1892-99), 9:238-39; James L. Bishop, *A History of American Manufactures from 1608 to 1860* (Philadelphia, 1864), 2:138.

19. Bishop, *American Manufactures,* 2 vols., 2:130, 140-42, 165, 174.

20. *Annals of Congress,* 10th Cong., 1st sess., 363-65.

21. Bishop, *American Manufactures,* 2:138-59.

22. Ibid., 159-63, 183-91.

23. *Annals of Congress,* 11th Cong., 2d sess., 626-30; Hopkins, *Hemp Industry,* 153-54.

24. HC to Adam Beatty, Apr. 23, 1810, *CP,* 1:470.

25. Davis R. Dewey, *Financial History of the United States* (New York, 1968), 130, 142.

26. *CP,* 1:467.

27. *CP,* 1:532; for the text of whole speech, see *CP,* 1:527-39.

28. *CP,* 1:543-44; Mayo, *Clay,* 376-78. The question whether Clay participated in writing Clinton's statement depends upon Clay's memory of the point years later.

29. Samuel F. Bemis, *John Quincy Adams and the Foundations of American Foreign Policy* (New York, 1949), 212-14, 495-509. In 1822 Adams defended his record in a protracted public controversy, which he thought had been generated by Clay to hurt his reputation in the West in the next presidential election. Bemis concludes that Clay was probably behind the affair.

30. Ibid., 225-27; Johnson, *Commerce,* 2:296-97. For HC's report to President Monroe, see *CP,* 2:30-37. For communications

between American and British commissioners and text of treaty, see *CP,* 2:44-59.

31. *Annals of Congress,* 14th Cong., 1st sess., 419-20, 455-57, 462-94, 546-57, 564-616, 639-51, 674.

2. American System

1. Thomas C. Cochran, *Frontiers of Change: Early Industrialism in America* (New York, 1981).

2. Robert F. Dalzell, *Enterprising Elite: The Boston Associates and the World They Made* (Cambridge, 1987); Stanley Lebergott, *The Americans: An Economic Record* (New York, 1984), 127-30.

3. Douglass C. North, *The Economic Growth of the United States, 1790-1860* (New York, 1966), 234.

4. Timothy Pitkin, *A Statistical View of the Commerce of the United States of America* (New Haven, Conn., 1835), 474. Pitkin's first edition came out in 1817 and reflects American reaction to this British view. The emphasized words were those of Pitkin.

5. Edward Stanwood, *American Tariff Controversies in the Nineteenth Century,* 2 vols. (New York, 1967), 1:39-71.

6. Jacob E. Cooke, *Tench Coxe and the Early Republic* (Chapel Hill, N.C., 1978), 134-503. Comparison of the several drafts of Hamilton's report on manufactures shows Coxe's initial work and subsequent drafts by Hamilton, who did subscribe to the protective idea and did not wish to give overriding weight to British-American commerce. Harold C. Syrett, ed., *Papers of Alexander Hamilton* (New York, 1966) 10:1-341.

7. Texts of HC's speeches of Jan. 20 and 29, 1816 may be found in *CP,* 2:134-36, 140-58. He favored an enlarged military establishment and extensive internal improvements.

8. Bishop, *American Manufactures*, 2:210. Madison's comment was in the message on submitting the peace treaty to the Senate, Feb. 10, 1815.

9. *Annals of Congress,* 14th Cong., 1st sess., 960-67.

10. Ibid., appendix, 1678-87.

11. Ibid., 1257-72, 1313-52. On hemp, see *CP,* 2:180.

12. Webster's autobiography, Charles M. Wiltse, ed., *The Papers of Daniel Webster: Correspondence,* 7 vols. (Hanover, N.H. 1974-1986) 1:23. He explained his interest in providing more protection for textiles in his letter to James W. Paige, [March-April 1816], Paige Papers (Mass. Hist. Soc., Boston).

13. Frank W. Taussig, *The Tariff History of the United States* (New York, 1899), 30.

14. *Annals of Congress,* 14th Cong., 1st sess., 1329-36; Charles M. Wiltse, *John C. Calhoun: Nationalist* (Indianapolis, 1944), 120-24. Webster would use the expression of liberty and union in his debate in the Senate with Robert Hayne on nullification in 1830.

15. Victor S. Clark, *History of Manufactures in the United States, 1607-1860,* 3 vols. (Washington, D.C., 1893-1929) 1:239-41. Stanwood, *Tariff Controversies,* 1:140-59, is informative on the debate, provisions, and voting breakdown. As a protectionist himself, he is critical of the final form of the measure.

16. Bishop, *American Manufactures,* 2:230-38.

17. *Annals of Congress,* 15th Cong., 1st sess., 18.

18. Stanwood, *Tariff Controversies,* 1:176-78.

19. Bishop, *American Manufactures,* 2:256-58, 261; Taussig, *Tariff History,* 19-24; *American State Papers: Finance* 3:415.

20. *Annals of Congress,* 16th Cong., 1st sess., 1663-69, 1914-15.

21. Ibid., 1915-46, 1952-63, 2093-2115.

22. Ibid., 2034-52.

23. Stanwood, *Tariff Controversies,* 1:192-94. William Lowndes of South Carolina, a leading proponent of protection in passage of the law of 1816, opposed the present bill on the ground that no further help to manufacturing was justifiable (*Annals of Congress,* 16th Cong., 1st sess. 2115-35). Related tariff bills to require cash payment and to tax auction sales—both to eliminate alleged unfair trade practices by foreign merchants—also failed at this session. Ibid., 2173-85, 2193-2202.

24. *CP,* 3:81.

25. Mathew Carey, *Essays on Political Economy* (New York, 1968, reprint), 77-79, 146-54, 188, 236, 262, 383-408, 511-46; Kenneth W. Rowe, *Mathew Carey: A Study in American Economic Development* (Baltimore, 1933).

26. *Niles' Register,* vol. 20, Aug. 11, 1821, 370-74; vol. 24, Apr. 19, 1823, 99-103; vol. 26, Mar. 3, 1824, 65-68.

27. HC to Carey, May 2, 1824, *CP,* 3:745; HC's speech on tariff, Mar. 30, 1824, *CP,* 3:716; Richard G. Stone, *Hezekiah Niles as an Economist* (Baltimore, 1933).

28. Bishop, *American Manufactures,* 2:247, 263-64.

29. Chase C. Mooney, *William H. Crawford, 1772-1834* (Lexington, 1974), 152, 161-67.

30. *Annals of Congress,* 18th Cong., 1st sess., 20.

31. Ibid., 1471-80.

32. Ibid., 1916-45.

33. For the full and annotated text of the speech, see *CP,* 3:683-727.

34. *CP,* 3:684-85.

35. *CP,* 3:692.

36. Hamilton in *Federalist,* no. 11 (New York, Modern Library edition, 1937), 69; Jefferson to American Society for Promoting Manufactures, June 26, 1817, in *Niles' Register,* vol. 38, June 12, 1830, 294; HC, in speech of May 10, 1820, *Annals of Congress,* 16th Cong., 1st sess., 2228.

37. *U.S. v. The William*, 28 Federal Cases 614 (1808), a federal district court decision.

38. *CP*, 3:716-17, 720-22.

39. *Annals of Congress,* 18th Cong., 1st sess., 2068-82, 2271-87.

40. Maurice G. Baxter, *One and Inseparable: Daniel Webster and the Union* (Cambridge, Mass., 1984), 104-7.

41. *Annals of Congress,* 18th Cong., 1st sess., 2177-2209, 2232-35, 2400-26.

42. Ibid., 2357-81.

43. Arthur H. Cole, *The American Wool Manufacture* (Cambridge, Mass., 1926), 1:164-67, concludes that the new rates did not hurt woolen manufacturers much, despite lessened protection of the tariff. Problems of the industry, he finds, arose from general conditions of the economy, but manufacturers would soon blame the tariff.

44. *Annals of Congress,* 18th Cong., 1st sess., 1705-12, 2258-88.

45. Ibid., 1488-1512.

46. *CP*, 3:677-81.

47. *CP*, 3:642-44, 658-61.

48. *Annals of Congress,* 18th Cong., 1st sess., 1519-1679.

49. Hopkins, *Hemp Industry,* 90.

50. *Annals of Congress,* 18th Cong., 1st sess., 1880-93; *CP,* 3:676.

51. *Annals of Congress,* 18th Cong., 1st sess., 2429-32, 2674-75.

52. Frederick J. Turner, *Rise of the New West, 1819-1829* (New York, 1962), 172-73.

53. Wiltse, *Calhoun: Nationalist,* 286-93.

54. Jackson to L.H. Coleman, Apr. 26, 1824, John S. Bassett, ed., *Correspondence of Andrew Jackson* (New York, 1935), 3:249.

55. HC to Francis Brooke, [Feb. 29, 1824], *CP,* 3:666-67.

3. Postwar Issues

1. Murray N. Rothbard, *The Panic of 1819: Reactions and Policies* (New York, 1962), 6-23; Samuel Rezneck, "The Depression of 1819-1822, A Social History," *American Historical Review* 39 (Oct. 1933): 28-47.

2. Curtis P. Nettels, *The Emergence of a National Economy, 1775-1815* (New York, 1962), 332–35; Paul Studenski and Herman E. Kroos, *Financial History of the United States* (New York, 1952), 78-81.

3. Ralph C.H. Catterall, *The Second Bank of the United States* (Chicago, 1903), 7-17 (title abbreviated hereafter as *Second BUS*).

4. *Annals of Congress,* 14th Cong., 1st sess., 494-514, 1060-66, 1091-1122, 1136-58, 1189-95, 1202-20, 1337-44; Wiltse, *Calhoun: Nationalist,* 108-11.

5. Baxter, *Webster,* 58-59, 64-65.

6. Clay's speech of Mar. 9, 1816, was not reported in the *Annals of Congress.* But he spoke on the subject at Lexington on June 3, apparently repeating the substance of what he had said in Congress. It is published in *CP,* 2:199-204. The provisions in the Constitution that could be applied to uniformity of currency are Art. I, sec. 8, par. 1, requiring all duties and excises to be uniform, and par. 5, empowering Congress to regulate the value of money.

7. *Annals of Congress,* 14th Cong., 2d sess., 1219, 1337-44.

8. Ibid., 1345-46, 1382-1401, 1415-18, 1428-31, appendix, 1919.

9. Walter B. Smith, *Economic Aspects of the Second Bank of the United States* (Cambridge, Mass., 1953), 102-4 (title abbreviated hereafter as *Second BUS*).

10. Catterall, *Second BUS,* 22-50; Thomas P. Govan, *Nicholas Biddle: Nationalist and Public Banker, 1786-1844* (Chicago, 1959), 55-59; HC to Caesar Rodney, Jan. 19, 1817, *CP,* 2:287-88. *Niles' Register* severely criticized Jones's management of the bank through this period. For example, see issues in vol. 14 (Feb.-Apr 1818).

11. HC to William Jones, Dec. 17, 1816, *CP,* 2:262; Jan. 12, 1817, *CP,* 2:283; Mar. 7, 1817, *CP,* 2:323; Dec. 12, 1817, *CP,* 2:410; Feb. 4, 1818, *CP,* 2:433-35.

12. HC to Jones, Oct. 6, 1816, *CP,* 2:235; Aug. 2, 1817, *CP,* 2:369.

13. HC to Thomas Bodley, Jan. 4, 1817, *CP,* 2:277; HC to William Jones, Jan. 8, 1817, *CP,* 2:281.

14. Catterall, *Second BUS,* 70-81; Smith, *Second BUS,* 119-24; Mooney, *Crawford,* 141–46.

15. HC to Langdon Cheves, Nov. 14, 1819, *CP,* 2:721-22; Dec. 13, 1819, *CP,* 2:728-31; Nov. 20, 1820, *CP,* 2:902-4.

16. Govan, *Biddle,* 84-85; Bray Hammond, *Banks and Politics in America: From the Revolution to the Civil War* (Princeton, 1957), 296-98, 304-5, 323.

17. Van Deusen, *Clay,* 152-53; statement of property in Kentucky Hotel as security for HC's note of $22,000 to the BUS, [July 8, 1820], and statement of J. Harper, cashier, that he had paid debt in full, Dec. 8, 1830, *CP,* 2:876-77.

18. HC to Langdon Cheves, Mar. 10, 1821, *CP,* 3:63-66; Feb. 10, 1821, *CP,* 3:24-26; Feb. 23, 1821, *CP,* 3:47-48; Feb. 27, 1821, *CP,* 3:50-51; Mar. 3, 1821, *CP,* 3:57-58; June 23, 1822, *CP,* 3:238. For his resignation, see HC to Nicholas Biddle, Mar. 8, 1825, and Biddle to HC, Mar. 11, 1825, *CP,* 4:93, 103.

19. HC to Langdon Cheves, Nov. 21, 1821, *CP,* 3:139-41. HC also handled collection of a huge debt to the bank by the Kentucky senator and future vice president Richard M. Johnson, apparently on generous terms. HC to Cheves, July 21, 1821, *CP,* 3:102-3.

20. This case, won by Clay, *BUS v. Roberts and Norvell,* had to do with the jurisdictional question central to *Osborn* v. *BUS,* con-

cerning an Ohio tax. See below for Clay's role in *Osborn*. Royalty, "Banking and Kentucky," 235.

21. Royalty, "Banking and Kentucky," 218-24, 230-31; Arndt M. Stickles, *The Critical Court Struggle in Kentucky, 1819-1829* (Bloomington, Ind., 1929), 18-19; HC to William Jones, Mar. 3, 1818, *CP,* 2:442-43; HC to Martin Hardin, Jan. 4, 1819, *CP,* 2:623-24.

22. Royalty, "Banking and Kentucky," 193-203.

23. HC to John J. Crittenden, Jan. 29, 1820, *CP,* 2:769-70.

24. Royalty, "Banking and Kentucky," 186-89, 257-68, 277-95, 306-14, 324-25.

25. The brief description here draws from a very full literature on this highlight of the state's history. Among these references are Rothbard, *Panic of 1819,* 32-56; E. Merton Coulter in *History of Kentucky,* edited by Charles Kerr (Chicago, 1922), 2:595-649; Stickles, *Court Struggle,* 16-110. For a well-researched, interesting view of John Crittenden's role in the relief struggle, see Albert D. Kirwan, *John J. Crittenden: The Struggle for the Union* (Lexington, 1962), 50-63. Though president of the Commonwealth Bank, Crittenden, like his friend Clay, sought to stay clear of the partisan aspects of the relief episode.

26. HC to John J. Crittenden, Jan. 29, 1820, *CP,* 2:769-70.

27. HC to Crittenden, Aug. 22, 1825, Ann Mary Coleman, *The Life of John J. Crittenden with Selections from His Correspondence and Speeches* (Philadelphia, 1873), 62. On Mar. 3, 1826, he told Crittenden he intended to "abjure" Kentucky politics. Coleman, *Crittenden,* 65.

28. Kendall to HC, June 20, 1822, *CP,* 3:237; Oct. 4, 1825, *CP,* 4:719; HC to Kendall, Oct. 18, 1825, *CP,* 4:746-48.

29. Blair to HC, Aug. 30, 1825, *CP,* 4:603-5.

30. Robert V. Remini, *Andrew Jackson and the Course of American Freedom, 1822-1832* (New York, 1981), 27-28.

31. HC to Langdon Cheves, Jan. 22, 1821, *CP,* 3:11-13.

32. HC to Cheves, Sept. 13, 1822, *CP,* 3:286-87.

33. Smith, *Second BUS,* 112; R. Carlyle Buley, *The Old Northwest: Pioneer Period, 1815-1840* (Bloomington, Ind., 1951), 1:588-94; *Niles' Register,* vol. 16, Oct. 9, 1819, 85-87; see later issues for events in Ohio.

34. HC to Thomas Scott, June 22, 1820, *CP,* 2:873-75; HC to Langdon Cheves, Nov. 5, 1820, *CP,* 2:900-901.

35. HC to Langdon Cheves, Jan. 22, 1821, *CP,* 3:13; Jan. 31, 1821, *CP,* 3:21; Feb. 15, 1821, *CP,* 3:41.

36. HC to Nicholas Biddle, Jan. 28, 1823, *CP,* 3:354-55.

37. The report of counsel's argument and Marshall's opinion is in 9 Wheaton 738 (1824). The case of *Roberts,* which Clay had won in the federal circuit court in Kentucky, is discussed above. The Constitution, Art. III, sec. 2, par. 1, extends federal jurisdiction to cases involving laws of the United States.

38. Harry R. Stevens, "Henry Clay, the Bank, and the West in 1824," *American Historical Review* 60 (July 1955): 843-48.

39. Coulter in *Kentucky,* edited by Kerr, 2:650-73; Paul W. Gates, "Tenants of the Log Cabin," *Mississippi Valley Historical Review* 49 (June 1962): 3-31.

40. 8 Wheaton 3-18.

41. HC's speech before Virginia legislature, [Feb. 7, 1822], *CP,* 3:161-70. For documents and correspondence concerning his role as commissioner for Kentucky, see Dec. 1821-Nov. 1823, ibid., passim.

42. 8 Wheaton 39-58. The Constitution, Art. I, sec. 10, par. 3, requires congressional assent to agreements between states.

43. Benjamin W. Leigh to HC, Feb. 12, 1823, *CP,* 3:377-78.

44. 8 Wheaton 69-108.

45. This decision was one of several, spurring attacks upon the Supreme Court at the time. In a debate in the House on a proposal to require a majority of the whole Court in constitutional cases, Clay spoke in support of it with a warning against glorifying the intellect and virtue of the justices. Remarks on May 14, 1824, *Annals of Congress,* 18th Cong., 1st sess., 2618-20.

46. *Hawkins v. Barney's Lessees,* 5 Peters 457 (1831).

47. Harrison, "Internal Improvement," 300-333; James B. Swain, pub., *The Life and Speeches of Henry Clay* (New York, 1842-43), 1:116.

48. Wiltse, *Calhoun: Nationalist,* 132-36 (the quotation is from page 134). Harrison, "Internal Improvement," 333-78, is a useful legislative history of the measure and draws from *Annals of Congress,* 14th Cong., 2d sess., 851-934, 1051-63.

49. HC, speech, Feb. 4, 1817, CP, 2:308-11.

50. Harrison, "Internal Improvement," 375-78.

51. HC to Madison, Mar. 3, 1817, *CP,* 2:322. Clay had a weak argument about allowing an incoming president to sign a bill that Congress had passed before inauguration. The Constitution, art. 1, sec. 7, par. 2, says that an unsigned bill, if not returned to Congress before adjournment, "shall not be a law."

52. Harrison, "Internal Improvement," 389-90.

53. *Annals of Congress,* 15th Cong., 1st sess., 17-18.

54. Ibid., 451-60.

55. Ibid., 1116-80, 1185-1249, 1268-1353. 1359-80.

56. Ibid., 1381-89. Clay did not vote; but if state consent had been stipulated, he would have approved the resolutions with that concession.

57. *CP,* 2:625-32.

58. Harrison, "Internal Improvement," 462-66; the text of the report is in *Niles' Register,* vol. 16, May 8, 1819, 186-89.

59. Archer B. Hulbert, *The Cumberland Road* (Cleveland, 1904), 54-57; Jeremiah S. Young, *A Political and Constitutional Study of the Cumberland Road* (Chicago, 1902), 23; HC, speech on congressional

appropriation, [April 1, 1816], *CP,* 2:187-88. There is a monument at Wheeling with an inscription honoring Clay for promoting construction of the road, which benefited the town and the nation.

60. Stanislaus Hamilton, ed., *The Writings of James Monroe* (New York, 1898-1903), 6:216-83; Harrison, "Internal Improvement," 515-36.

61. Goodrich, *Government Promotion.* John Lauritz Larson, "'Bind the Republic Together': The National Union and the Struggle for a System of Internal Improvements," *Journal of American History* 74 (Sept. 1987): 363-86, concludes that the principal reason for the failure of a comprehensive national program was the conflict of local interests, fear of undue advantages of some parts of the Union over others. One should not underestimate constitutional and political factors, so prominent in the sources, as also very important.

62. Congressional opinion and action are revealed in *Register of Debates,* 18th Cong., 2nd sess., 189-261. Clay's speech on extending the road is in *CP,* 4:19-32.

63. Philip D. Jordan, *National Road.* A table on p. 94 shows expenditures on the road.

64. Harrison, "Internal Improvement," 552-640 and appendix B; *Annals of Congress,* 18th Cong., 1st sess., 990-99, 1005-63, 1233-1469. HC, speeches, *CP,* 3:568-69, 572-92.

65. Forest G. Hill, *Roads, Rails & Waterways: The Army Engineers and Early Transportation* (Norman, Oklahoma, 1957), 21-26, 54-55, 58-59, 78, 222-26.

66. Harrison, "Internal Improvement," 640-50; *Register of Debates,* 18th Cong., 2d sess., 216-24, 285-303, 319-34, 487-518, 681-83, 687.

67. An example is his speech at Lexington, [June 17, 1824], *CP,* 3:779-80.

68. Daniel Feller, *The Public Lands in Jacksonian Politics* (Madison, Wis., 1984), 40-47, 72-73; Merrill D. Peterson, *Olive Branch and Sword—The Compromise of 1833* (Baton Rouge, 1982), 12. An early proposal for distribution in Congress was a resolution in the House by Andrew Stewart of Pennsylvania, Jan. 15, 1824, *Annals of Congress,* 18th Cong., 1st sess., 1042-43.

69. Feller, *Public Lands,* 68-69.

70. Mary W.M. Hargreaves, *The Presidency of John Quincy Adams* (Lawrence, Kansas, 1985), 19-33.

4. Secretary of State

1. Remini, *Clay,* 234-72.

2. Hargreaves, *Presidency of Adams,* 62, 65.

3. Text of speech, Mar. 24, 25, 1818, *CP,* 2:522-25; Randolph B. Campbell, "Henry Clay and the Emerging Nations of Spanish America, 1815-1829" (Ph.D. diss., University of Virginia, 1966), 68-94.

4. *Annals of Congress,* 16th Cong., 1st sess., 2223-29.

5. Ibid., 2d sess., 1071, 1088-89, 1091-92.

6. *CP,* 4:292-99.

7. Campbell, "Clay and Spanish America," 287, 297-304; Baxter, *Webster,* 120-24.

8. *CP,* 5:326-36. Clay showed much interest in an interoceanic canal in Central America and hoped the meetings would consider it.

9. Campbell, "Clay and Spanish America," 200, 354-55; Bemis, *Adams and Foreign Policy,* 448-49.

10. Hunter Miller, ed., *Treaties and Other International Acts* (Washington, D.C., 1931-48), 3:209-33; Vernon G. Setser, *The Commercial Policy of the United States, 1774-1829* (Philadelphia, 1937). Clay wrote an editorial for the Washington (D.C.) *National Journal,* Nov. 2, 1826, reprinted in *CP,* 5:839-40, on the treaty.

11. HC to Condy Raguet, Apr. 14, 1825, *CP,* 4:251-53; HC to William Tudor, Mar. 29, 1828, *CP,* 7:200-203; Mar. 31, 1828, *CP,* 7:205-6.

12. HC to Joel Poinsett, Nov. 9, 1825, *CP,* 4:802-5; Dec. 29, 1825, *CP,* 4:887-88; Theodore Burton, "Henry Clay, Secretary of State," in *The American Secretaries of State and Their Diplomacy,* edited by Samuel F. Bemis (New York, 1928), 4:131-32.

13. HC to James Cooley, Nov. 6, 1826, Apr. 18, 1828, *CP,* 5:865-70, 7:227-30; HC to John M. Forbes, Apr. 14, 1825, *CP,* 4:246-50.

14. *Historical Statistics of the United States,* part 2, (Washington, D.C., 1975), 904-5, 907.

15. Hargreaves, *Presidency of Adams,* 84-90. A typical treaty was concluded with Sweden in Jan. 1828 (HC to John J. Appleton, Jan. 12, 1827, *CP,* 6:48-52; Miller, *Treaties,* 3:283-52). Clay commented on the general situation of reciprocal agreements in a note to Levi Woodbury, Dec. 29, 1827, *CP,* 6:1397.

16. William Smart, *Economic Annals of the Nineteenth Century, 1821-1830* (London, 1917), 101-12, 160-68, 264-90; editorial written by Clay for the Washington (D.C.) *National Journal,* June 10, 1826, reprinted in *CP,* 5:423.

17. The measure of 1818 had been debated and tabled in 1817 (*Annals of Congress,* 14th Cong., 2d sess., 772-78, 816-40). It passed in 1818, when Clay spoke again (*CP,* 2:565. On the whole subject of the West Indies trade, see F. Lee Benns, *The American Struggle for the British West India Carrying-Trade, 1815-1830* (Bloomington, Ind., 1923). For the American legislation of 1818-20, see Benns, *West India Carrying-Trade,* 50-80.

18. Benns, *West India Carrying-Trade,* 81-107.

19. HC to Samuel Smith, May 9, 1825, *CP,* 4:337-38; Smith to HC, June 25, 1825, *CP,* 4:468-75; James Lloyd to HC, June 27, 1825, *CP,* 4:437-85; HC to Lloyd, Aug. 30, 1825, *CP,* 4:601-3; John Holmes to HC, June 8, 1825, *CP,* 4:421-25; HC to Holmes, Aug. 31, 1825, *CP,* 4:607-8; Daniel Webster to HC, Sept. 27, 1825, *CP,* 4:695-98.

20. HC to Mathew Carey, June 6, 1825, *CP,* 4:416-17.
21. The text of the instructions, June 19, 1826, *CP,* 5:440-75.
22. George Dangerfield, *The Awakening of American National- ism, 1815-1828* (New York, 1965), 261-65.
23. Benns, *West India Carrying-Trade,* 108-33, 144-46. Corre- spondence concerning Gallatin's mission is in *CP,* vols. 5, 6, passim.
24. See the statistical table in Hargreaves, *Presidency of Adams,* 111.
25. HC to Robert M. Harrison, May 14, 1827, *CP,* 6:552-54; Harrison to HC, Mar. 2, May 27, 1828, *CP,* 7:138, 302.
26. Stanwood, *Tariff Controversies,* 1:253-59; Wiltse, *Calhoun: Nationalist,* 350-51. Van Buren did not vote, perhaps with the inten- tion of setting up the tie.
27. Malcolm R. Eiselen, *The Rise of Pennsylvania Protectionism* (Philadelphia, 1932), 74-76. Clay spoke at Pittsburgh on June 20, at Washington in Pennsylvania the next day, and at Steubenville in Ohio on June 23. The texts of his speeches are in *CP,* 6:700-701, 705-6, 712.
28. Stanwood, *Tariff Controversies,* 1:264-68; Stone, *Niles,* 75- 77. Issues of *Niles' Register* during October and November carried much information and opinion on the convention. The address, writ- ten by Niles, is in the issue of Oct. 13, 1827.
29. Charles F. Adams, ed., *Memoirs of John Quincy Adams,* 12 vols. (Philadelphia, 1874), 7:355-56.
30. Peter B. Porter to HC, Nov. 22, 1827, *CP,* 6:1303-4; Thomas McGiffin to HC, Jan. 29, 1828, *CP,* 7:64; HC to Allen Trimble, Dec. 27, 1827, *CP,* 6:1384-85.
31. Stanwood, *Tariff Controversies,* 1:268-90; Remini, *Clay,* 328-30. Despite his negative criticism of the tariff bill during this session, Clay was silent about it after passage. He seemed to con- clude that it was the best that could be made out of the political ma- neuvers.
32. Hargreaves, *Presidency of Adams,* 262-63, 287-88; Feller, *Public Lands,* 101-10; Robert V. Remini, *The Life of Andrew Jack- son* (New York, 1988), 168-69.
33. Wiltse, *Calhoun: Nationalist,* 375-98; John Niven, *John C. Calhoun and the Price of Union: A Biography* (Baton Rouge, 1988), 133-37, 158-64; Clyde Wilson and W.E. Hemphill, eds., *The Papers of John C. Calhoun* (Columbia, South Carolina, 1977), x, 442-539.

5. Nullification

1. Stanwood, *Tariff Controversies,* 1:360-61; Remini, *Life of Jackson,* 176.
2. HC to Hezekiah Niles, Oct. 4, 1829, *CP,* 8:108-9; HC to John W. Taylor, Nov. 13, 1829, *CP,* 8:125.
3. Stanwood, *Tariff Controversies,* 1: 363-67.

4. Baxter, *Webster,* 180-88.

5. Wiltse, *Calhoun: Nullifier,* 17; Peterson, *Olive Branch,* 19-21; C. Wilson and Hemphill, *Papers of Calhoun,* 11:413-39.

6. Stanwood, *Tariff Controversies,* 1:298-301; texts of memorials by Raguet and by Gallatin in George R. Taylor, ed., *The Great Tariff Debate, 1820-1830* (Boston, 1953), 50-52, 58-64.

7. Editorial note, *CP,* 8:282-83.

8. Kerr, *Kentucky,* 2:693-94; HC to Josiah S. Johnston, Feb. 27, Mar. 11, 1830, William C. Duralde to HC, Mar. 18, 1830, Calvin Colton, ed., *Private Correspondence of Henry Clay* (Cincinnati, 1856), 254-55, 256.

9. *Niles' Register,* vol. 40, Nov. 5, 12, 1831, 177, 190-92, 202-16; vol. 41, passim; memorial to Congress, Taylor, *Tariff Debate,* 52-58.

10. *CP,* 8:237-39; Calvin Colton, ed., *The Life, Correspondence, and Speeches of Henry Clay,* 6 vols. (New York, 1857), 5:396-401.

11. Van Deusen, *Clay,* 238-39.

12. Speech at Cincinnati, Aug. 3, 1830, Colton, *Life and Speeches,* 5:401-6. On Oct. 9, 1830, Madison answered Clay's inquiry about the meaning of the Virginia Resolutions by agreeing that the nullifiers could not now rely upon them. Colton, *Private Correspondence of Clay,* 284.

13. HC to Thomas Speed, May 1, 1831, *CP,* 5:344.

14. HC to Josiah Johnston, July 23, 1831, *CP,* 8:375; HC to Francis Brooke, Oct. 4, 1831, *CP,* 8:412-13.

15. Text of convention's address, *Niles' Register,* vol. 41, Dec. 24, 1831, 307-12.

16. Bishop, *American Manufactures,* 2:365; Richard E. Ellis, *The Union at Risk: Jacksonian Democracy, States' Rights, and the Nullification Crisis* (New York, 1987), 41-46.

17. *Register of Debates,* 22d Cong., 1st sess., 5-41.

18. Ibid., 66-77. Clay may have reasoned that the use of revenue gained from customs was limited to operations of the federal government, not applicable to those of states, although states did have a stake in revenue from the public domain. But his reasoning was weak and variable.

19. Ibid., 77-104.

20. Ibid., 296-97.

21. Ibid., 257-95.

22. Colton, *Life and Speeches,* 5:447-48.

23. *Register of Debates,* 22d Cong., 1st sess., 416-38, 462-86.

24. Ibid., 227-53, 302-28, 393-412.

25. Ibid., 335-67.

26. Ibid., 556-90.

27. Ibid., 438-61.

28. Ibid., 607-10, 614-20, 624-35, 638-39.

29. Ibid., 647-78.

30. For an informative description of Adams's role concerning the tariff in the House, see John D. Macoll, "Congressman John Quincy Adams, 1831-33" (Ph.D. diss., Indiana University, 1973), 28-112.

31. Adams, *Memoirs,* 8:443-49. To the disappointment of many researchers, there is a gap in the Adams diary from Mar. 22 to Dec. 1, 1832, an important time in Jacksonian politics. Adams, *Memoirs,* 8:502.

32. John A. Munroe, *Louis McLane: Federalist and Jacksonian* (New Brunswick, N.J., 1973), 312, 342-43.

33. Ibid., 344-47; *Documents Relative to Manufactures in the United States,* House Executive Doc. 308, 22d Cong., 1st sess., 2 vols. Timothy Pitkin, *A Statistical View of the Commerce of the United States of America* (New Haven, Conn., 1835), 482, an able, if anti-Jacksonian compilation, says McLane's report was so incomplete as to be very defective. *Niles' Register,* vol 42, May 5, 1832, 182-85, predictably found McLane's draft bill entirely unacceptable. Clay wrote Peter Porter that some provisions were "utterly destructive" (May 1, 1832, *CP,* 8:504). Adams's report to the House, modifying McLane's recommended rate changes upward, is in *Register of Debates,* 22d Cong., 1st sess., appendix, 69-92.

34. *Register of Debates,* 22d Cong., 1st sess., 1174-80, 1188-1221, 1274-93.

35. HC to Associates of Mechanics, July 4, 1832, quoted in editorial summary, *CP, Supplement,* 239.

36. Taussig, *Tariff History,* 102-5; Sidney Ratner, *The Tariff in American History* (New York, 1972), 18-19.

37. *Niles' Register,* vol. 42, Apr. 14, July 21, 1832, 105-10, 369. For support of compromise by prominent New Yorkers, see Allan Nevins, ed., *The Diary of Philip Hone* (New York, 1936), 65. There are numerous supporting letters in *CP,* vol. 8 and *Supplement,* passim.

38. Remini, *Life of Jackson* (1988 ed.), 228.

39. Ellis, *Union at Risk,* 25-32, 102-22, relates the Cherokee controversy to the nullification crisis.

40. *Register of Debates,* 22d Cong., 2d sess., 4-5.

41. Remini, *Jackson,* 3:13-23; Ellis, *Union at Risk,* 83-91. One of Livingston's clerks in the State Department was the Virginia Jeffersonian Nicholas Trist, who reflected ex-President Madison's view on the nature of the Union. But Livingston himself had expressed that view as a senator in the Webster-Hayne debates of 1830.

42. HC to Francis Brooke, Dec. 12, 1832, *CP,* 8:603; Brooke to HC, Dec. 25, 1832, *CP,* 8:605.

43. *Niles' Register,* vol. 43, Dec. 15, 29, 1832, Jan. 12, 1833, 255-60, 314; Baxter, *Webster,* 210-11; John C. Fitzpatrick, ed., *The Autobiography of Martin Van Buren* (Washington, D.C., 1920), 541-65; Donald B. Cole, *Martin Van Buren and the American Political System* (Princeton, N.J., 1984), 237-44.

44. Munroe, *McLane,* 368-69; Macoll, "Congressman Adams," 155-65; Stanwood, *Tariff Controversies,* 1:390-97.

45. *Register of Debates,* 22d Cong., 2d sess., 6-8, 13-27, 49-60. Clay was willing to ask McLane for information but not for a draft bill.

46. Ibid., 174-78, 187, 510, 518-19, 595, 601, 638; Peterson, *Olive Branch,* 56-57, 60-61.

47. Baxter, *Webster,* 212-19.

48. HC to Frederick Rapp, Jan. 27, 1833, *CP,* Supplement, 249; HC to Francis Brooke, Jan. 28, 1833, *CP,* 8:616.

49. Peterson, *Olive Branch,* 51-55. Whether Clay would have permanently abandoned the principle of protection is doubtful. This early plan was not adopted. Even if giving up protection had been its purpose, did it show the intent of the revised plan, which was adopted? It seems to be a moot point in the later part of the story. See Webster to Hiram Ketchum, Jan. 15, 1838, and enclosure, Charles M. Wiltse, ed., *Papers of Daniel Webster: Correspondence,* 7 vols. (Hanover, N.H., 1980), 4:263-65. See also the discussion of the revised plan below.

50. Kenneth Rowe, *Mathew Carey: A Study in American Economic Development* (Baltimore, 1933), 103-4; Niles to HC, [Dec. 1832], *CP,* 8:602-3.

51. HC to Thomas Helm, Jan. 5, 1833, *CP,* 8:609; HC to Roswell L. Colt, Jan. 11, 1833, *CP,* 8:610; HC to Francis Brooke, Jan. 17, 1833, *CP,* 8:613-14.

52. Peterson, *Olive Branch,* 64-69; Peterson, *Triumvirate,* 224-28; William W. Freehling, *The Road to Disunion,* vol. 1, *Secessionists at Bay, 1776-1854* (New York, 1990), 282-84.

53. Text of Clay's manuscript draft of the bill, c. Feb. 11, 1833, *CP,* 8:619-20, which with minor exceptions became the terms of a statute. Notice that though it provided for an equal rate of 20 percent on all dutiable imports after 1842, there was the proviso "until otherwise directed by law." If a later law so directed, there could be differences of rates on different goods below 20 percent, and there could be rates higher than 20 percent. This would be a situation contrary to what Webster later said Clay's first plan written at Philadelphia would provide, a permanent abandonment of the protective principle.

54. *Register of Debates,* 22d Cong., 2d sess., 462-73. In the possible confrontation of the South Carolina courts and the federal Supreme Court, he saw similarities to the *Osborn* case, involving Ohio's conflict with the national bank, for which he had served as counsel. The state had accepted a national rule without forcible resistance, he pointed out. It was a dubious parallel.

55. Remini, *Jackson,* 3:39-40.

56. *Register of Debates,* 22d Cong., 2d sess., 478-79, 483-84.

57. Ibid., 694-717.

58. Ibid., 478, 719-20, 722; Constitution, Article I, sec. 7.

59. *Register of Debates,* 22d Cong., 2d sess., 727-42.

60. Ibid., 723-24.

61. HC to Philip R. Fendall, Aug. 8, 1836, *CP,* 8:862-63.

62. Colton, *Life and Speeches,* 5:552-67.

63. Peterson, *Olive Branch,* 80-81; *Register of Debates,* 22d Cong., 2d sess., 785-86.

64. Peterson, *Olive Branch,* 80-87, has a valuable analysis of the voting.

65. Wiltse, *Webster: Correspondence,* 4:263-65. See comment in above notes.

66. Remini, *Clay,* 421-22; Baxter, *Webster,* 220-22. Much of the basis for believing a Jackson-Webster alliance was possible rests on the partisan narrative of Van Buren. Fitzpatrick, *Autobiography of Van Buren,* 549-65.

67. HC to Francis Brooke, Mar. 11, 1833, *CP,* 8:352.

68. Macoll, "Congressman Adams," 173-80.

69. Peterson, *Olive Branch,* 94.

70. Stone, *Niles,* 86.

71. Madison to HC, Apr. 2, 1833, *CP,* 8:635-36.

72. Lawrence to HC, Mar. 26, 1833, *CP,* 8:635.

73. Biddle to HC, Feb. 28, 1833, *CP,* 8:627.

74. Remini, *Life of Jackson* (1988 ed.), 249, though praising the president for his firm stand against disruption of the Union, says he was caught off guard when Clay's tariff bill was suddenly substituted for the Verplanck bill in the House. "He was so preoccupied with winning passage of the Force Bill that he let everything else, including the tariff, go by the board." After studying the situation in the Senate through this session, one would have to doubt that even an alert Jackson could have pushed the Verplanck bill through that body at this time.

75. Peterson, *Olive Branch,* 88-90.

76. *Niles' Register,* vol. 45, Oct. 26, 1833, 129.

77. HC to James Barbour, Mar. 2, 1833, *CP,* 8:629; HC to Nicholas Biddle, Apr. 10, 1833, Reginald C. McGrane, ed., *The Correspondence of Nicholas Biddle Dealing with National Affairs, 1807-1844* (Boston, 1919), 202-4.

6. Bank War

1. Remini, *Jackson,* 2:222-24.

2. Catterall, *Second BUS,* 174-82, 245-84; Govan, *Biddle,* 112-13, 118-19, 146-58, 165-66.

3. Smith, *Second BUS,* 155; Govan, *Biddle,* 78-79, 96-97, 107; Fitzpatrick, *Autobiography of Van Buren,* 641-43.

4. Arthur M. Schlesinger Jr., *The Age of Jackson* (Boston, 1945), 78-79 and passim; [George Bancroft], "Bank of the United States," *North American Review* 32 (1831): 21-64.

5. Schlesinger, *Age of Jackson,* 65, 67-73; D. B. Cole, *Van Buren,* 233-34.

6. HC to Nicholas Biddle, May 28, 1828, *CP,* 7:303-4; Biddle to HC, May 31, 1828, *CP,* 7:313; HC, speech in Senate, denying undue financial connection with the bank, Apr. 28, 1834, *Register of Debates,* 23d Cong., 1st sess., 1530-31; Baxter, *Webster,* 203-4 and passim.

7. Speech at Cincinnati, Aug. 3, 1830, *CP,* 8:242-43; HC to Biddle, Sept. 11, 1830, *CP,* 8:263-64.

8. Samuel R. Gammon, *Presidential Campaign of 1832* (Baltimore, 1922), 119-20; Gallatin's article on banking, *American Quarterly Review* 7 (Nov. 1830), cited in Catterall, *Second BUS,* 199-200 and n. 1; Madison to C.J. Ingersoll, in *Niles' Register,* vol. 40, June 25, 1831, 332; [William B. Lawrence], "Bank of the United States," *North American Review,* 32 (1831): 524-63.

9. John M. McFaul, *The Politics of Jacksonian Finance* (Ithaca, N.Y., 1972), 16-29; Coulter in *Kentucky,* edited by Kerr, 2: 694-95.

10. HC to Biddle, Dec. 15, 1831, *CP,* 8:433.

11. Catterall, *Second BUS,* 189-224; Govan, *Biddle,* 171-73; Peterson, *Triumvirate,* 206-8. Unlike these authors, Remini, *Clay,* 379, attributes Biddle's decision to deference to Clay's presidential ambitions.

12. Munroe, *McLane,* 296-97, 308-14, 319-21, 339.

13. Catterall, *Second BUS,* 225-29.

14. *Register of Debates,* 22d Cong., 1st sess., 53-55.

15. Thomas H. Benton, *Thirty Years' View,* 2 vols. (New York, 1856), 1:235-41.

16. *Register of Debates,* 22d Cong., 1st sess., 113-54.

17. *Thirty Years' View,* 1:242-43.

18. Ibid., 237-38. Benton later recalled that Clayton read off the list of abuses he gave the congressman on a narrow slip of paper, wrapped around his finger for concealment. Whatever the effect of Clayton's speech, it is doubtful anyone was uncertain about the identity of the director of the attack upon the bank.

19. *Register of Debates,* 22d Cong., 1st sess., 954-65, 977, 1007; Baxter, *Webster,* 198-99.

20. *Register of Debates,* 22d Cong., 1st sess., 981-1005.

21. Ibid., 1008-13, 1034, 1045-68.

22. Ibid., 3851-52, and passim.

23. Frederick J. Turner, *The United States, 1830-1850: The Nation and Its Sections* (New York, 1935), 407-8, map and analysis of voting. On the southern vote being decidedly against recharter, see William J. Cooper, *Liberty and Slavery: Southern Politics to 1860* (New York, 1983), 171.

24. Carl B. Swisher, *Roger B. Taney* (New York, 1935), 190-97; Carl B. Swisher, ed., "Roger B. Taney's 'Bank War Manuscript,'" *Maryland Historical Magazine* 53 (June-Sept. 1958); 103-31, 215-37.

25. *Register of Debates,* 22d Cong., 1st sess., appendix, 73-77.

26. Ibid., 1221-40.

27. Ibid., 1265-74; Remini, *Clay,* 397-401.

28. Benton, *Thirty Years' View,* 1:257-64.

29. *Register of Debates,* 22d Cong., 1st sess., 1296. Seven senators did not vote. If six of them had voted to override, the Senate would have had the two-thirds necessary to do so. But, of course, the House stood in the way of success for the bank forces, since a larger proportion would have to have voted to override than earlier to recharter.

30. Remini, *Clay,* 403-9, discusses the election of 1832 very informatively.

31. Biddle to HC, Aug. 1, 1832, *CP,* 8:556.

32. Gammon, *Campaign of 1832,* 150-51; HC to Biddle, Aug. 27, 1832, *CP,* 8:562; HC to Webster, Aug. 27, 1832, *CP,* 8:565-66.

33. Benton, *Thirty Years' View,* 1:280-81.

34. Stone, *Niles,* 87-105; *Niles' Register,* vol. 42, Aug. 18, 1832, 433-36.

35. Joseph Dorfman, *The Economic Mind in American Civilization* (New York, 1949), 2:505.

36. HC to Thomas Speed, May 1, 1831, *CP,* 8:344; HC to Francis Brooke, Apr. 1, 1832, *CP,* 8:485-86; Cooper, *Liberty and Slavery,* 172-73.

37. HC to John Bailhache, Nov. 24, 1830, *CP,* 8:289-90.

38. Remini, *Clay,* 409-11.

39. Benton, *Thirty Years' View,* 1:286-91, 294-96; Remini, *Jackson,* 3:52-53.

40. HC to Biddle, Feb. 16, 1833, *CP,* 8:623.

41. Swisher, *Taney,* 210-34; D. B. Cole, *Van Buren,* 244-50.

42. Remini, *Jackson,* 2:112-25.

43. *Philadelphia Gazette,* Oct. 14, 1833, quoted in Dorfman, *Economic Mind,* 2:606.

44. Frank O. Gatell, "Spoils of the Bank War: Political Bias in the Selection of Pet Banks," *American Historical Review* 70 (Oct. 1964): 35-58; McFaul, *Jacksonian Finance,* 29-57.

45. *Register of Debates,* 23d Cong., 1st sess., appendix, 4-6.

46. Ibid., 59-69.

47. Smith, *Second BUS,* 160-67; Govan, *Biddle,* 250-60.

48. *Register of Debates,* 23d Cong., 1st sess., passim. Clay actively encouraged organizing local committees to memorialize Congress. For example, in his letter to Biddle, Dec. 21, 1833, he urged that this be done in Philadelphia, setting an example for similar meetings elsewhere. McGrane, *Correspondence of Nicholas Biddle,* 218-19.

49. *Congressional Globe,* 23d Cong., 1st sess., 20-21. The text of Jackson's paper is in *Register of Debates,* 23d Cong., 1st sess., appendix, 284-89.

50. The texts of Clay's resolutions and his three-day speech of Dec. 26-28, 1833, are in *Register of Debates,* 23d Cong., 1st sess., 58-94.

51. Colton, *Life and Speeches,* 2:118.
52. *Register of Debates,* 23d Cong., 1st sess., 97-139, 397-405.
53. Ibid., 143-98, 206-23.
54. Ibid., 663-79, 892-942.
55. The condensed description of positions of the two sides in the debate is based upon the lengthy texts in the *Register of Debates*. Calhoun's speech is reported in it, pp. 206-23.
56. Ibid., 405-10.
57. Ibid., appendix, 146-56.
58. Ibid., 1172-77.
59. Ibid., 1187.
60. Ibid., 1317-36.
61. Benton, *Thirty Years' View,* 1:423-33.
62. *Register of Debates,* 23d Cong., 1st sess., 1662-90.
63. Ibid., 1640-50.
64. Ibid., 1482-83, 1485-86, 1546-47, 1564-81, 1711-12.
65. Baxter, *Webster,* 227-28, 232-33.
66. See *Register of Debates,* 23d Cong., 1st sess., 984-1005, for Webster's speech and the text of his bill. The debate on it from March 18 to March 25, when it was tabled, is reported on pp. 1019-1145. Calhoun's presentation of his plan is reported on pp. 1057-73.
67. On March 24 Clay told Joseph Gales, an editor of the *Washington (D.C.) National Intelligencer,* "It is idle to think of any thing being done towards a recharter of the Bank, until it is called for by popular demonstrations or the exercise of the elective franchise." *CP,* 8:707.
68. On an earlier idea of recharter for only three years, Biddle wrote to Webster that he was on the "right track." Wiltse, *Webster: Correspondence,* 3:321.
69. House documents and report on coinage, Feb. 19, 1834, *Register of Debates,* 23d Cong., 1st sess., Part 4, appendix, 242-84; Benton's speech, May 26, Part 1, 1073-1107; Senate consideration and passage of bill, June 28, ibid., 2121-22.
70. McFaul, *Jacksonian Finance,* 71-81.
71. The agent of the pets was Reuben Whitney, former BUS director, viewed by Whigs as a freewheeler. Ibid., 64-69.
72. *Register of Debates,* 23d Cong., 1st sess., 1817-24, 1848-60, 1871-74, 1879-96; *CP,* 8:728.
73. Swisher, *Taney,* 287-89, 300-301. Webster later used the term "pliant instrument," and in response Taney said Webster was the bank's pliant instrument. Baxter, *Webster,* 238.

7. Internal Improvements

1. HC to Webster, June 7, 1827, *CP,* 6:654.
2. Dewey, *Financial History,* 216.
3. Adams, *Memoirs,* 7:58-65; James D. Richardson, ed., *A*

Compilation of the Messages and Papers of the Presidents, 10 vols. (Washington, D.C., 1896-99), 2:299-317.

4. Ellis, *Union at Risk,* 19-25; Remini, *Jackson,* 2:168. Interesting in light of his changing views after a period in the presidency was his initial inclination toward federal distribution of funds to the states for internal improvements, perhaps authorized by a constitutional amendment.

5. Feller, *Public Lands,* 82-85, 96-101, 222 nn. 28 and 29.

6. Hargreaves, *Presidency of Adams,* 177-78; Goodrich, *Government Promotion,* 40-41; Adams, *Memoirs,* 8:6-7, 24, 32-33, 38, 45, 49-50; Ronald E. Shaw, *Canals for a Nation: The Canal Era in the United States, 1790-1860* (Lexington, 1990), 201-36.

7. Paul B. Trescott, "The Louisville and Portland Canal Company, 1825-1874," *Mississippi Valley Historical Review* 44 (1958): 686-708.

8. Adams, *Memoirs,* 7:190-91, 195, 198-99; Shaw, *Canals,* 226.

9. *Register of Debates,* 22d Cong., 1st sess., 1120-23, 1181-84, 1296-98.

10. Adams, *Memoirs,* 7:442; *Niles' Register,* vol. 36, April 18, 1829, 115-16; editorial summary of speech at Wheeling, Mar. 31, 1829, *CP,* 8:20, taken from *Lexington Kentucky Reporter,* Apr. 22, 1829; Jordan, *National Road,* 159-75.

11. Thomas D. Clark, *A History of Kentucky* (New York, 1937), 219-20, 257-60; Coulter in *Kentucky,* edited by Kerr, 2:695-99; HC to Henry Clay Jr., Dec. 2, 1829, *CP,* 8:204.

12. Fitzpatrick, *Autobiography of Van Buren,* 312-38; D.B. Cole, *Van Buren,* 211-13, accepts Van Buren's version of his role and takes a generous view of Jackson's position in the veto message.

13. Richardson, *Messages and Papers,* 2:483-91.

14. HC, speech at Cincinnati, Aug. 3, 1830, Colton, *Life and Speeches,* 5:409-15; Feller, *Public Lands,* 137-40.

15. HC to Peter B. Porter, June 13, 1830, *CP,* 8:223.

16. HC to Adam Beatty, June 8, 1839, *CP,* 8:220-21; address of Fayette County meeting, June 21, 1830, *Niles' Register,* vol. 38, July 31, 1830, 406-12.

17. T.D. Clark, *History of Kentucky,* 262-67.

18. Roy M. Robbins, *Our Landed Heritage: The Public Domain, 1776-1970* (Lincoln, Nebr., 1976), 13-55; Benjamin H. Hibbard, *A History of the Public Land Policies* (New York, 1924), 100.

19. Hargreaves, *Presidency of Adams,* 197-99.

20. Feller, *Public Lands,* 93-94.

21. Raynor G. Wellington, *The Political and Sectional Influence of the Public Lands, 1828-1842* (Cambridge, 1914), 6-10, 13-22; Feller, Public Lands, 93-96.

22. Feller, *Public Lands,* 131-33.

23. Jackson's annual message to Congress, Dec. 1832, *Register of Debates,* 22d Cong., 2d sess., appendix, 5-6.

24. Wellington, *Public Lands,* 5, 25-26; Feller, *Public Lands,* 111-12, 125-26; Hibbard, *Public Land Policies,* 171-73. Even Jackson proposed distribution in 1829-30 for internal improvements if authorized by a constitutional amendment. Richardson, *Messages and Papers,* 3:1015. And so did Calhoun, on the same basis. Memorandum, Mar. 18, 1831, James H. Hammond et al., "Letters on the Nullification Movement in South Carolina, 1830-1834," *American Historical Review,* 6 (July 1901): 743.

25. Robert Hayne, during the gathering crisis concerning the tariff in March 1830, worried about the connection. Hayne to James Hammond, in "Letters on Nullification," *American Historical Review,* 6 (July 1901): 738.

26. *Register of Debates,* 22d Cong., 1st sess., appendix, 112-18. The seven newer states were Ohio, Indiana, Illinois, Missouri, Alabama, Mississippi, and Louisiana.

27. Ibid., 625-38, 785-91, 870-84, 901-7; Public Lands Committee report, *Register of Debates,* 22d Cong., 1st sess., appendix, 118-26.

28. *Register of Debates,* 22d Cong., 1st sess., 1145-60, 1167-74.

29. Ibid., 1096-1118.

30. Ibid., 495.

31. Ibid., 1174.

32. Wellington, *Public Lands,* 40-42.

33. *Register of Debates,* 22d Cong., 2d sess., 5-6, 61-67.

34. Ibid., 67-79.

35. Ibid., 82-174, 204-235.

36. Feller, *Public Lands,* 164-69, believes there was such an understanding of Clay and Calhoun, at least that Calhounites would silently acquiesce in passage. If so, all that resulted was many absences in the House voting, but not enough to override a possible veto. Feller analyzes the Senate voting and finds party regularity: National Republicans for the bill and all but six Democrats opposed.

37. *Register of Debates,* 23d Cong., 1st sess., 77-82.

38. Clay contended that Jackson should have returned the bill before the close of the last session in March without his signature or with a veto, allowing Congress to vote on overriding. He asked Madison if the president's pocket veto was unconstitutional, to which Madison answered that there was no practical remedy, though Jackson ought to have given Congress an opportunity to react to his negative (HC to Madison, May 28, 1833, *CP* 8:643; Madison to HC, June 1833, *CP,* 8:646-47. The Constitution, art. 1, sec. 7, par. 1, provides that if the president does not return a bill within ten days, it shall become law "unless the Congress by their Adjournment prevent its Return, in which case it shall not be a law." Congress had adjourned only two days after Jackson received the bill. Clay theorized that the constitutional clause applied to a long session but not to a short session such as the one in March 1833. He was applying his own unwritten, dubious meaning to the provision.

39. HC to Francis Brooke, May 30, 1833, *CP,* 8:644; *Register of Debates,* 23d Cong., 1st sess., 1599-1606.

8. Jacksonian Ascendancy

1. *Register of Debates,* 23d Cong., 1st sess., 407-9, 413.
2. Ibid., 24th Cong., 1st sess., 615-29, 722-24, 802-3; *Register of Debates,* 24th Cong., 2d sess., 802-4, 806-7. Clay was urging federal aid for the Louisville canal at this time, and much was given in the long run. See his remarks in the Senate on May 25, 1836. *Register of Debates,* 24th Cong., 1st sess., 1673.
3. Hulbert, *Cumberland Road,* 85-90.
4. B. Hammond, *Banks and Politics,* 451.
5. *Register of Debates,* 24th Cong., 1st sess., 48-52.
6. Ibid., 1172-77, 1248-49, 1283, 1288-1373, 1742. The report by Ewing for the Committee on Public Lands, sketching background, exploring options of policy, and recommending passage of Clay's bill, is in *Register of Debates,* 24th Cong., 1st sess., appendix, 45-50.
7. Feller, *Public Lands,* 181-82; Wellington, *Public Lands,* 50-51.
8. Niven, *Calhoun,* 211-13; *Register of Debates,* 23d Cong., 2d sess., 367-92.
9. Wiltse, *Calhoun: Nullifier,* 263-67.
10. *Register of Debates,* 24th Cong., 1st sess., 1649-57.
11. Benton, *Thirty Years' View,* 1:653.
12. The debate is reported in *Register of Debates,* 24th Cong., 1st sess., 1793-1846. For Jackson's decision, see Swisher, *Taney,* 329-31. Taney had drafted a veto message, which the president did not issue. Provisions of the statute are in *U. S. Statutes at Large* 5 (1836): 52-56.
13. Wellington, *Public Lands,* 51-64; Turner, *United States, 1830-1850,* 444-49.
14. *Register of Debates,* 24th Cong., 2d sess., 774-77.
15. Baxter, *Webster,* 284-90.
16. *Register of Debates,* 24th Cong., 2d sess., 706, 753-60.
17. Ibid., 535-50.
18. Ibid., 661-67.
19. Ibid., 731-52.
20. Ibid., 778.
21. Ibid., 992-98.
22. Wiltse, *Calhoun: Nullifier,* 296-97.
23. *Register of Debates,* 24th Cong., 2d sess., 1024-25.
24. Ibid., 1005.
25. Ibid., 1034.
26. McFaul, *Jacksonian Finance,* 82-106, 114-16, 130-38, 143-77; *U. S. Statutes at Large* 5 (1836): 52-56.
27. *Register of Debates,* 23d Cong., 2d sess., 552, 576-82, 595-613, appendix, 414; Benton, *Thirty Years' View,* 1:550-53; McFaul, *Jacksonian Finance,* 128-30, 140.

28. Carl B. Swisher, *History of the Supreme Court of the United States,* vol. 5, *The Taney Period* (New York, 1974), 105-9. The case is reported in 8 Peters 118 (1834) and 11 Peters 257 (1837). The majority opinion drew extensively from Clay's argument.

29. Remini, *Jackson,* 3:327-28.

30. *Register of Debates,* 24th Cong., 2d sess., 21-68, 120-23, 327-40, 578-617.

31. Ibid., 8-17, 70-79, 89-103. 172-204.

32. Clay's principal speech of Jan. 11, 1837, is in *Register of Debates,* 24th Cong., 2d sess., 360-76. Rives's views are in *Register of Debates,* 24th Cong., 2d sess., 343-60.

33. Ibid., 778.

34. Remini, *Jackson,* 3:410-11.

35. *Register of Debates,* 24th Cong., 2d sess., 382-91.

36. Ibid., 429-40.

37. Ibid., 499-506.

38. Colton, *Life and Speeches,* 2:133-34.

9. Financial Problems

1. D.B. Cole, *Van Buren,* 294-97; James C. Curtis, *The Fox at Bay: Martin Van Buren and the Presidency, 1837-1841* (Lexington, 1970), 68-72; Major L. Wilson, *The Presidency of Martin Van Buren* (Lawrence, Kans., 1984), 52-60.

2. Smith, *Second BUS,* 184-88; Dewey, *Financial History,* 225; William G. Shade, *Banks or No Banks: The Money Issue in Western Politics, 1832-1865* (Detroit, 1972), 42-43.

3. HC to Alexander W. Stow, Apr. 26, 1837, *CP,* 9:43.

4. Baxter, *Webster,* 256-57; Benton, *Thirty Years' View,* 2:11-16.

5. Van Buren expressed the Democratic view in his message to Congress, Sept. 5, 1837, *Register of Debates,* 25th Cong., 1st sess., appendix, 1-2.

6. Bishop, *American Manufactures,* 2:409-10; Reginald C. McGrane, *The Panic of 1837: Some Financial Problems of the Jacksonian Era* (Chicago, 1924), 42-144; D.B. Cole, *Van Buren,* 292-93; Wilson, *Presidency of Van Buren,* 44-49.

7. Peter Temin, *The Jacksonian Economy* (New York, 1969), 22-176; George Macesich, "Sources of Monetary Disturbances in the United States, 1834-1845," *Journal of Economic History* 20 (Sept. 1960): 407-34; Jeffrey G. Williamson, "International Trade and United States Economic Development: 1827-1843," *Journal of Economic History* 21 (Sept. 1961): 372-83; Hugh Rockoff, "Money, Prices, and Banks in the Jacksonian Era," in *The Reinterpretation of American Economic History,* edited by Robert W. Fogel and Stanley L. Engerman (New York, 1971), 448-58.

8. McFaul, *Jacksonian Finance,* 1-201; Shade, *Banks or No*

Banks, 18, 57, 99, 151-67; James Rogers Sharp, *The Jacksonians versus the Banks: Politics in the States after the Panic of 1837* (New York, 1970), 122, 208-10, 284, 318-29; Harry Scheiber, "The Pet Banks in Jacksonian Politics and Finance, 1833-1841," *Journal of Economic History* 23 (June 1963): 196-214; Benton, *Thirty Years' View,* 2:42-43.

9. Curtis, *Fox at Bay,* 64-85; McFaul, *Jacksonian Finance,* 123-27; Turner, *United States, 1830-1850,* 456-60.

10. *Register of Debates,* 25th Cong., 1st sess., appendix, 1-9. D.B. Cole, *Van Buren,* 301-6, criticizes the president's call for detachment of government from the economy.

11. D.B. Cole, *Van Buren,* 105. For Benton's support of the specie amendment, see *Register of Debates,* 25th Cong., 1st sess., 188-208.

12. Buchanan's and Wright's speeches, *Register of Debates,* 25th Cong., 1st sess., 351-83, 441-69.

13. Ibid., 160-84, 247-50.

14. Ibid., 251-69. For Clay's general view of Whig strategy, see his letter to Waddy Thompson Jr., July 8, 1837, *CP,* 9:56-59, and another to Alexander Hamilton Jr., July 18, 1837, *CP,* 9:63.

15. *Register of Debates,* 25th Cong., 1st sess., 269-82.

16. Ibid., 311-31. For the Webster-Calhoun exchange, see *Register of Debates,* 25th Cong., 1st sess., 479, 485-92.

17. Ibid., 511; Wilson, *Presidency of Van Buren,* 76-77, analyzes the voting.

18. Benton, *Thirty Years' View,* 2:33-36.

19. *Congressional Globe,* 25th Cong., 1st sess., 17, 29-32; editorial summary of HC's speech, *CP,* 9:74; Benton, *Thirty Years' View,* 2:36-39.

20. *Register of Debates,* 25th Cong., 1st sess., 516-25.

21. Benton, *Thirty Years' View,* 2:42-56.

22. HC to Samuel P. Lyman, Nov. 22, 1837, *CP,* 9:93.

23. Congressional Globe, 25th Cong., 2d sess., 2-7; Curtis, *Fox at Bay,* 111-17; Wilson, *Presidency of Van Buren,* 100-101.

24. HC to Peter B. Porter, Dec. 5, 1837, *CP,* 9:96. See also HC to Alexander Hamilton Jr., Dec. 6, 1837, *CP,* 9:97.

25. See *Congressional Globe,* 25th Cong., 2d sess., appendix, 614-19, for Clay's speech. See *Congressional Globe,* 25th Cong., 2d sess., appendix, 151-54, 166, 170-71, 190-91, 228-30, 259, 264, for a report of the debate in the Senate.

26. The fullest source for this oratorical duel with Calhoun is Benton, *Thirty Years' View,* 2:101-23.

27. Ibid., 190-91, 259, 264; Wilson, *Presidency of Van Buren,* 110-11.

28. Wilson, *Presidency of Van Buren,* 126-28, 132-36.

29. *CP,* 9:336-39.

30. Curtis, *Fox at Bay,* 142-51; D.B. Cole, *Van Buren,* 355-61.

31. Colton, *Life and Speeches,* 2:60, 6:170-91.

32. HC to Francis Brooke, Aug. 28, 1838, *CP,* 9:239; *CP,* 9:203-4, editorial notes.

33. HC to Biddle, Feb. 3, 4, 20, 1838, *CP,* 9:139, 148-49.

34. *Congressional Globe,* 25th Cong., 2d sess., 396-97.

35. HC to Nathaniel Tallmadge, Apr. 12, 1839, *CP,* 9:305. Clay had shown his willingness to continue the state-bank deposit system at least temporarily during a discussion in the Senate in late June 1838. He supported some amendments continuing the system but making adjustments, as proposed by Webster. *CP,* 9:210-11.

36. Benton, *Thirty Years' View,* 2:83-94; Webster to Biddle, May 3, 29, 1838, Wiltse, *Webster: Correspondence,* 4:292-93, 301; McGrane, *Panic of 1837,* 177-204.

37. *Congressional Globe,* 25th Cong., 2d sess., 344, 352, 411. Webster wrote Biddle an unsigned letter and undated, but May 1838, headed "Private as murder," saying he had told Clay he intended to move for repeal of specie circular but had to leave town. When he returned, he continued, Clay had already moved for repeal (McGrane, *Biddle Correspondence,* 310-11). Clay wrote Peter Porter, June 3, 1838: "It was tweedle dum & tweedle dee, between his form and mine. Mine was indeed the more appropriate and more dignified shape for Legislation. . . . But this competition about the resolution was unworthy of either of us" (*CP,* 9:198). No doubt, correct.

38. *Congressional Globe,* 25th Cong., 2d sess., 5-6; Wellington, *Public Lands,* 66-70.

39. *Congressional Globe,* 25th Cong., 2d sess., 293-95, 303-5; *Congressional Globe,* 25th Cong., 3d sess., 98, 110-12, 127, appendix, 44-61, 350-54. See also *CP,* 9:265-69, 274, 409.

40. *Congressional Globe,* 25th Cong., 2d sess., 136-44, 462-63.

41. *CP,* 9:133-38; Colton, *Life and Speeches,* 6:87-93. Clay denied he had used terms such as *rabble* and *pirates* to describe preemptioners, but it is clear he had nothing good in mind when he described those who abused the system, if not others who observed the law. See HC to Alston B. Estes, Jan. 26, 1838, *CP,* 9:321-22.

42. *Congressional Globe,* 25th Cong., 2d sess., 463; Webster's speech supporting graduation on January 27, 1838, is in *Congressional Globe,* 25th Cong., 2d sess., 135-36; Peterson, *Triumvirate,* 281-82, comments on voting.

43. HC to Benjamin W. Leigh, Sept. 25, 1839, *CP,* 9:346; McGrane, *Panic of 1837,* 21-39; Wellington, *Public Lands,* 75-82; Baxter, *Webster,* 298; text of Webster's legal opinion, Wiltse, *Webster: Correspondence,* 4:401-2.

10. Log Cabin

1. D.B. Cole, *Van Buren,* 376-78; Temin, *Jacksonian Economy,* 148-70.

2. William J. Cooper, *The South and the Politics of Slavery*

(Baton Rouge, 1978), 101-3, 120-26, 132-33; Cooper, *Liberty and Slavery,* 53-63, 192-95.

3. Nancy N. Scott, ed., *A Memoir of Hugh Lawson White* (Philadelphia, 1856), 356-68, 375-401.

4. Michael Birkner, *Samuel L. Southard: Jeffersonian Whig* (Cranbury, N.J., 1984), 184-85; Baxter, *Webster,* 267-69.

5. Remini, *Clay,* 548-57.

6. Typical of much of the literature are Turner, *United States, 1830-1850,* 483-86; Remini, *Clay,* 561-66. The best description of the popular style of the campaign is Robert G. Gunderson's *The Log-Cabin Campaign* (Lexington, 1957).

7. Allan Nevins, ed., *The Diary of Philip Hone, 1828-1851* (New York, 1936), 487-88.

8. *Niles' Register,* vol. 59, Oct. 3, 1840, 70-71.

9. The quotation of Clay's letter to John Clayton from the Clayton Papers is in Eber Malcolm Carroll, *Origins of the Whig Party* (Durham, N.C., 1925), 168 n. 187. For the traditional interpretation of the election, see Carroll, *Whig Party,* 165-69.

10. William R. Brock, *Parties and Political Conscience: American Dilemmas, 1840-1850* (Millwood, N.Y., 1979), 5 and passim, finds an important ideological and economic character in this election and others of the era. Michael F. Holt, in *A Master's Due: Essays in Honor of David Herbert Donald,* by William J. Cooper et al. (Baton Rouge, 1985), 16-58, analyzes the elections of this time on the basis of quantitative data and finds a correlation with economic conditions. The Whigs fared better when the economy was in trouble, he reports. A thorough study of western politics during this election campaign by R. Carlyle Buley in *The Old Northwest,* 2 vols. (Bloomington, Ind., 1951), 2:259 and passim, concludes that "underneath the superficialities of the prolonged campaign lay solid and serious consideration of basic issues in politics and economics."

11. The itinerary is given in *CP,* 9:330 n. 1. The text of the Buffalo speech is in Colton, *Life and Speeches,* 6:161-64.

12. The text of the speech here is in Colton, *Life and Speeches,* 6:197-214.

13. The text of the speech, ibid., 215-19. For a description of the meeting and the subsequent exchange of Clay and Jackson, see *Niles' Register,* vol. 59, Sept. 5, 1840, 10.

14. Richard Chambers, ed., *Speeches of the Hon. Henry Clay* (Cincinnati, 1842), 501-2.

15. Baxter, *Webster,* 267-74; John A. Garraty, *Silas Wright* (New York, 1949), 200-201.

16. *Congressional Globe,* 26th Cong., 2d sess., 14, 19-23, 198.

17. HC to Harrison G. Otis, Dec. 28, 1840, *CP,* 9:468.

18. *Congressional Globe,* 26th Cong., 2d sess., 124.

19. Richard Gantz, "Henry Clay and the Harvest of Bitter Fruit: The Struggle with John Tyler, 1841-42" (Ph.D. diss., Indiana

University, 1986), 41.

20. *Congressional Globe,* 26th Cong., 2d sess., 20-21, 58-61, 78-80, 114-20.

21. Ibid., 52-56. There is a general discussion of this subject in Robbins, *Landed Heritage,* 81-85.

22. For the text of HC's full-scale speech, see Colton, *Life and Speeches,* 6:227-70.

23. *Congressional Globe,* 26th Cong., 2d sess., 23.

24. Ibid., 22.

25. Robbins, *Landed Heritage,* 83-85; Wellington, *Public Lands,* 87-93. Webster was one of the Whigs who voted for preemption, though he had strongly supported distribution.

26. HC to Cornelius C. Baldwin, Aug. 28, 1838, *CP,* 9:222.

27. *Congressional Globe,* 26th Cong., 1st sess., appendix, 737-38.

28. Woodbury responded with a partial report for raising some low rates up to the future maximum of 20 percent. Editorial note, *CP,* 9:479.

29. *Register of Debates,* 24th Cong., 1st sess., 55; *Register of Debates,* 24th Cong., 2d sess., 575-77, 874-94, 916-52, 965-82.

30. Binkley, "American System," 306-7; HC to Peter B. Porter, Dec. 8, 1840, *CP,* 9:459.

31. Richardson, *Messages and Papers* (1897 ed.), 4:5-21.

32. HC to John Clayton, Dec. 17, 1840, *CP,* 9:466.

33. George R. Poage, *Henry Clay and the Whig Party* (Chapel Hill, N.C., 1936), 15-21, 27-28; Remini, *Clay,* 570-76.

34. HC to Harrison and Harrison to HC, Mar. 13, 1841, *CP,* 9:514-16; HC to Harrison, Mar. 15, 1841, *CP,* 9:516-17; Baxter, *Webster,* 300-301.

35. Richardson, *Messages and Papers* (1897 ed.), 4:36-39.

36. HC to John L. Lawrence, Apr. 13, 1841, *CP,* 9:519.

37. HC to John M. Berrien, Apr. 20, 1841, *CP,* 9:521; HC to Waddy Thompson, Apr. 23, 1841, *CP,* 9:522.

38. Tyler to HC, Apr. 30, 1841, *CP,* 9:528.

39. Gantz, "Clay and Tyler," 78.

40. *Congressional Globe,* 25th Cong., 2d sess., 396-97.

41. HC to Ewing, Apr. 30, 1841, *CP,* 9:525; Ewing to HC, May 8, 1841, *CP,* 9:530.

42. In his letter to Ewing on April 30, cited above, Clay made the surprising remark that he might favor a uniform ad valorem rate, instead of specific ones, on all articles. He never made a serious move in the Senate for that policy.

43. HC to Francis Brooke, May 14, 1841, *CP,* 9:534.

11. Veto

1. *Congressional Globe,* 27th Cong., 1st sess., 11-12, 22.

2. Ibid., 13-14, 21-26, 31-36, 320-21; Hone, *Diary,* 546-47.

3. *Congressional Globe,* 27th Cong., 1st sess., 6-7.

4. Ibid., 22-23, 48-49; HC to Ewing, June 2, 1841, *CP,* 9:535.

5. HC to Robert Letcher, June 11, 1841, *CP,* 9:543.

6. Gantz, "Clay and Tyler," 109-12.

7. Ibid., 122; *Congressional Globe,* 27th Cong., 1st sess., appendix, 351-55.

8. *Congressional Globe,* 27th Cong., 1st sess., 145.

9. Ibid., 47-48.

10. Ibid., 198.

11. Ibid., 104-5; Baxter, *Webster,* 302-3.

12. *Congressional Globe,* 27th Cong., 1st sess., 163-78, 182-88, 191-200, 215-16, 234-37, 246-52.

13. Ibid., appendix, 362.

14. Oliver P. Chitwood, *John Tyler: Champion of the Old South* (New York, 1939), 222-23; Lyon G. Tyler, *Letters and Times of the Tylers* (Richmond, 1884-85), 2:55-70.

15. HC to Porter, July 21, 1841, *CP,* 9:570; Porter to HC, July 23, 1841, *CP,* 9:572. It appears that Porter did not originate this version of Clay's compromise but did communicate with others to facilitate its progress. Its provisions were similar to Bayard's proposed amendment.

16. *Congressional Globe,* 27th Cong., 1st sess., 256; *Congressional Globe,* 27th Cong., 1st sess., appendix, 362; Poage, *Clay and Whig Party,* 38-41, 61; *CP,* vol. 9, editorial summary of sources, 575-76.

17. Baxter, *Webster,* 304; Poage, *Clay and Whig Party,* 38-41, 61.

18. *Congressional Globe,* 27th Cong., 1st sess., 337-38.

19. Benton, *Thirty Years' View,* 2:350-53; *Congressional Globe,* 27th Cong., 1st sess., 338-39.

20. Hone, *Diary,* 551-53, illustrates Whig complaints. *Niles' Register,* vol. 60, Aug. 21, 1841, 390-92, reprints a number of editorials in newspapers.

21. Crittenden to HC, Aug. 16, 1841, *CP,* 9:585-86.

22. Brock, *Parties and Political Conscience,* 102, 106.

23. The text of HC's speech is in *Congressional Globe,* 27th Cong., 1st sess., appendix, 364-66.

24. Rives's rebuttal and another exchange of the two senators are in *Congressional Globe,* 27th Cong., 1st sess., appendix, 366-70.

25. Ibid., 366.

26. Gantz, "Clay and Tyler," 167-77; Baxter, *Webster,* 305-7. When stipulating no branches contrary to law, Tyler may have had in mind a recent Supreme Court decision upholding state power to exclude out-of-state corporations *(Alabama Bank Cases,* 15 Peters 519 (1839). But it did not concern nationally chartered corporations, such as the present proposal would establish.

27. *Congressional Globe,* 27th Cong., 1st sess., 372, 417-18, appendix, 344-45.

28. Ibid., 418.
29. Chitwood, *Tyler,* 266-68; Brock, *Parties and Political Conscience,* 97-98; Benton, *Thirty Years' View,* 2:348-50. Henry Wise, one of Tyler's "corporal's guard," to which he himself said he belonged, many years later recalled his participation in the decision to veto: the president "instructed a friend [probably Wise], who was familiar with his views and all the facts as to the preparation of the second bill, to prepare his second veto." No doubt his relations with Tyler were very close, but his memory of the incident might have been none too reliable. Henry A. Wise, *Seven Decades of the Union* (Philadelphia, 1881), 187-93.
30. Poage, *Clay and Whig Party,* 100-101; Baxter, *Webster,* 308-10; *Washington (D.C.) National Intelligencer,* Sept. 13, 15, 27, 1841.
31. Poage, *Clay and Whig Party,* and Remini, *Clay,* are representative of modern scholarly opinion. Gantz, "Clay and Tyler," rejects the interpretation of Clay as dictator. All are cited above. Two adversaries charging him with dictatorial behavior were Calhoun and Benton.
32. *Congressional Globe,* 27th Cong., 1st sess., 7. Among several useful accounts of adoption of distribution are Gantz, "Clay and Tyler," 205-18; Hibbard, *Public Land Policies,* 144-69; Robbins, *Landed Heritage,* 86-91. Clay often contended that his long effort for distribution was stimulated by an improper Jacksonian pocket veto of his bill in 1833. The senator considered it to be a part of the tariff compromise of that year.
33. *Congressional Globe,* 27th Cong., 1st sess., 313-14, 318-20, 332, 337, 357.
34. Ibid., 387-88; *U. S. Statutes at Large* 5 (1836): 453-58.
35. *Congressional Globe,* 26th Cong., 1st sess., 298, 345, 433, 444-46, 486-87; Clay's speech in this earlier session on June 4, 1840, is in *Congressional Globe,* 26th Cong., 1st sess., 816. The Supreme Court case, *Ogden v. Saunders* (1827), upheld his defense of a state insolvency law, but in a second hearing it held for Webster's party from another state. Regardless of Clay's lapse of memory, the ruling did demonstrate the need of a federal bankruptcy law to cover interstate questions. An earlier decision in *Sturges v. Crowninshield* (1819) had invalidated a state's retrospective relief law.
36. *Congressional Globe,* 27th Cong., 1st sess., 240-46, 348-49.
37. Benton, *Thirty Years' View,* 2:229-323; Gantz, "Clay and Tyler," 213-14.
38. *Congressional Globe,* 27th Cong., 1st sess., 364-65, 369-70, 388.
39. Ibid., 390-91, 400-405, 427-30, 433-37.
40. Benton, *Thirty Years' View,* 2:357-62.
41. Claude M. Fuess, *The Life of Caleb Cushing* (New York, 1923), 1:293-314.

12. Limited Success

1. HC to John Sloane, Oct. 23, 1841, *CP,* 9:614-16; HC to Nathaniel P. Tallmadge, Oct. 30, 1841, *CP,* 9:618-19.

2. *Congressional Globe,* 27th Cong., 2d sess., 69, appendix, 164-66.

3. Ibid., appendix, 166-68.

4. *Congressional Globe,* 27th Cong., 2d sess., 6-7.

5. Baxter, *Webster,* 313-14.

6. Fuess, *Cushing,* 1:340-45, 381-82.

7. Benton, *Thirty Years' View,* 2:376-95.

8. HC to James Clay, Dec. 24, 1841, *CP,* 9:625; HC to Robert Winthrop, Jan. 8, 1842, *CP,* 9:629.

9. Gantz, "Clay and Tyler," 277-79. See Gantz, "Clay and Tyler," 255-77, for an excellent treatment of this topic.

10. HC to Peter Porter, Jan. 16, 1842, *CP,* 9:632.

11. *Congressional Globe,* 27th Cong., 2d sess., appendix, 98-99. Clay well knew that imprisonment for debt had been largely abandoned.

12. HC to Robert Letcher, Jan. 6, 1842, *CP,* 9:628. The words of emphasis were those of Clay's own writing.

13. Gantz, "Clay and Tyler," 280-84.

14. *Congressional Globe,* 27th Cong., 2d sess., 199-200, appendix, 141-46, 322-29.

15. *Congressional Globe,* 27th Cong., 2d sess., 5-6; Stanwood, *Tariff Controversies,* 1:17-19.

16. Schlesinger, *Age of Jackson,* 422-23.

17. *Niles' Register,* vol. 60, Sept. 25, 1841, 49, Nov. 20, 1841, 183-87.

18. *Congressional Globe,* 27th Cong., 2d sess., 204-5.

19. Ibid., 235-36.

20. Colton, *Life and Speeches,* 6:320-21, 323-51.

21. *Congressional Globe,* 27th Cong., 2d sess., 270, 273-74, 277, 304-6, 309-11, 322-23.

22. Ibid., 352-53, 372. Clay's most fully reported speech, delivered on Mar. 23, 1842, is in *Congressional Globe,* 27th Cong., 2d sess., appendix, 322-29.

23. Ibid., 373. Not the appendix.

24. Colton, *Life and Speeches,* 6:353-58.

25. Ibid., 360-84.

26. Luther Bradish et al. to HC, Mar. 31, 1842, editorial summary in *CP,* 9:690; HC to Luther Bradish et al., Apr. 15, 1842, text in *CP,* 9:698-700; HC to Ebenezer Pettigrew, June 1, 1842, *CP,* 9:705; Willie Mangum to HC, June 15, 1842, *CP,* 9:717-19. Alexander Stephens, a prominent Whig in Georgia, endorsed Clay's candidacy in opposition to the Tyler administration (Thomas Brown,

Politics and Statesmanship: Essays on the American Whig Party
[New York, 1985], 198). In a later letter, Aug. 3, 1842, Justice
Joseph Story assured Clay he supported him and Whig principles.
CP, 9:749-50.

27. For Clay's perspective on the events in Congress during the
summer, see Gantz, "Clay and Tyler," 313-22.

28. Stanwood, *Tariff Controversies,* 1:20-21.

29. *Congressional Globe,* 27th Cong., 2d sess., 669-72, 676-79.
The text of the bill may be found in *Congressional Globe,* 27th Cong.,
2d sess., 688.

30. The text of the veto, ibid., 694-95. Though the House version
of the bill had a vague provision possibly abolishing the Berrien
amendment, the prevailing Senate version specified it was only *postponing* it for a month. See the preceding note. Debate and voting in
the House on the veto are reported in *Congressional Globe,* 27th
Cong., 2d sess., 696-702, 708-18. The effort to override failed to get
the necessary two-thirds, 114-97.

31. Crittenden to HC, July 2, 1842, *CP,* 9:722; HC to Crittenden, July 10, 1842, *CP,* 9:731; Crittenden to HC, July 15, 1842, *CP,*
9:734-35; HC to Crittenden, July 16, 1842, *CP,* 9:735-36. Though
southern Whigs opposed higher tariff rates, a sizable number would
accept them if distribution was attached to such a measure. Willie
Mangum to HC, July 4, 1842, *CP,* 9:725.

32. The volatile John Botts, member of the House from Virginia, who had risen to national visibility the preceding session by
charging the president with planning a new party, now pushed for
impeachment. HC to Crittenden, July 21, 1842, *CP,* 9:739-40; HC to
John Quincy Adams, July 24, 1842, *CP,* 9:742-43.

33. *Congressional Globe,* 27th Cong., 2d sess., 787, 797-98, 802,
807-10, 814, 820-37, 840-44, 849-52. The bill passed the Senate, 25-
23. Wiltse, *Calhoun, Sectionalist,* 84-85.

34. HC to John M. Clayton, Aug. 8, 1842, *CP,* 9:753.

35. HC to John Berrien, Aug. 15, 1842, *CP,* 9:755-56.

36. Stanwood, *Tariff Controversies,* 1:24-30; Eiselen, *Pennsylvania Protectionism,* 148-49.

37. *Congressional Globe,* 27th Cong., 2d sess., 922, 936-38, 941-
60, 963. Brock, *Parties and Political Conscience,* 104-6, provides a
useful analysis of the voting.

38. *Congressional Globe,* 27th Cong., 2d sess., 948, 968. Tyler
now sent a protest to the House against a critical committee report
about his vetoes, whereupon it rejected the protest in much the
same language used in 1834 to reject President Jackson's remon-
strance during the national-bank controversy. *Congressional Globe,*
27th Cong., 2d sess., 973-74.

39. During the short time that land proceeds were distributed,
January to September 1842, sales were quite low, totalling
$691,100. Even the more populous "older" states received only an

average of $26,700, and the "new" western states received an average of $19,800. Clay was arguing for principle rather than substance, unnecessarily, it seems. Paul W. Gates, *History of Public Land Development* (Washington, D.C., 1968), 17.

40. HC to Nathan Sargent, *CP*, 9:766. Clay did not mention losing distribution in a letter to Berrien, who had been a strong proponent of that restriction, Sept. 4, 1842, *CP*, 9:762-63.

13. Disappointments

1. *CP*, 9:773-77, editorial summary.
2. *CP*, 9:782-85, editorial summary.
3. HC to John Clayton, Nov. 2, 1842, *CP*, 9:787-88.
4. Brock, *Parties and Political Conscience*, 107-13.
5. *CP*, 9:808-10, editorial summary, and passim; Epes Sargent, *The Life and Public Service of Henry Clay* (Auburn, N.Y., 1852), 214. See also HC to Benjamin W. Leigh, Mar. 17, 1843, *CP*, 9:805-6, for Clay's favorable comment on an address by the Whig convention in Virginia.
6. *CP*, 9:833, editorial note on itinerary; Poage, *Clay and Whig Party*, 116-22.
7. *CP*, 10:8, 10-11, 13, 17-18, and passim, for other speeches in the South. See also an example of his views on the tariff before starting the travel: HC to S.F. Bronson, Sept. 13, 1843, *CP*, 9:850.
8. Speech at Raleigh, North Carolina, Apr. 13, 1844, *CP*, 10:25-31.
9. He had expressed his opinion on the need for home valuation of imports in a letter to James A. Meriwether, Oct. 2, 1843, *CP*, 9:863.
10. *CP*, 10:11, 35, editorial summary. On preemption, see HC to J.H. Clay Mudd, Sept. 25, 1843, *CP*, 9:860.
11. HC to Andrew Broaddus Jr., June 5, 1843, *CP*, 9:824-26; HC to Henry H. Brackenridge, Nov. 12, 1843, *CP*, supplement, 291; speech at Raleigh, North Carolina, Apr. 13, 1844, *CP*, 10:32-34.
12. HC to William A. Graham, Feb. 6, 1844, *CP*, 10:6.
13. Arthur C. Cole, *The Whig Party in the South* (Washington, D.C., 1913), 98-103; Cooper, *South and Politics of Slavery*, 161-66.
14. Baxter, *Webster*, 369-71. Webster had thought of negotiating a reciprocity treaty with Britain after leaving the cabinet in early 1843, an idea Clay strongly criticized, but the New Englander soon abandoned such a move (HC to John Clayton, June 21, 1843, *CP*, 9:827-28). Webster was also mentioned as a vice presidential candidate with Clay, but neither man had any interest in it whatsoever. Remini, *Clay*, 621.
15. Rives to HC, July 15, 1844, *CP*, 10:84-85; HC to Rives, *CP*, 10:98-99.
16. Remini, *Clay*, 658.

17. HC to Crittenden, Dec. 5, 1843, *CP,* 9:897-99.
18. Remini, *Clay,* 637.
19. Text of the letter of Apr. 17, 1844, in *CP,* 10:41-46.
20. *CP.,* 10:46-47.
21. Remini, *Clay,* 645.
22. For his comments on the two letters in his private correspondence, see HC to Stephen Miller, July 1, 1844, *CP,* 10:78-79, and to Thomas M. Peters and John M. Jackson, July 27, 1844, *CP,* 10:89-91.
23. Eiselen, *Pennsylvania Protectionism,* 161-63; Stanwood, *Tariff Controversies,* 2:39-41.
24. HC to Joseph Paxton, *CP,* 10:118-19.
25. Garraty, *Silas Wright,* 314-17.
26. Glyndon G. Van Deusen, *The Jacksonian Era, 1828-1848* (New York, 1959), 187-89.
27. Correspondence in *CP,* 10, passim.
28. Useful historical discussions are the following: Remini, *Clay,* 611-67; Peterson, *Triumvirate,* 350-63; Brock, *Parties and Political Conscience,* 152-55; Poage, *Clay and Whig Party,* 139-51; Cooper, *Liberty and Slavery,* 206-12; Turner, *United States, 1830-1850,* 223, 527-30. Although there are differences of interpretation, all of them emphasize the issue of Texas as the leading factor in causing Clay's defeat.
29. In *CP,* 10, his correspondence during late 1844 reflects these factors. See especially HC to John Clayton, Dec. 2, 1844, *CP,* 10:167-68. Colton, *Life and Speeches,* 2:423-43, represents his view also, particularly because of this biographer's close relationship to him.
30. HC to Philip S. Galpin et al., *CP,* 10:148, editorial summary.
31. Remini, *Clay,* 634 and passim, believes Clay's worst mistake was to adhere so closely to old political topics.
32. Ratner, *Tariff in American History,* 23-25; Peterson, *Triumvirate,* 421-22.
33. HC to Ladies of Tennessee, [late 1846], Colton, *Life and Speeches,* 3:45.
34. HC to Gibson and Farmer, Oct. 11, 1847, *CP,* 10:357, editorial summary.
35. HC to Daniel Ullman, Aug. 4, 1847, *CP,* 10:342-43.
36. Poage, *Clay and Whig Party,* 156, 176-77.
37. HC to Leslie Combs, Mar. 7, 1849, Colton, *Life and Speeches,* 4:585.
38. Peterson, *Triumvirate,* 471.
39. *CP,* 10:735.
40. *Congressional Globe,* 31st Cong., 2d sess., 114.
41. Ibid., 1st sess., 844-51, 869-74, 900-904.
42. HC's speech, ibid., 850-51.

43. William L. Dayton moved an amendment for distribution to all states, but it failed, thirty to twelve. Ibid., 900.

44. George R. Taylor, *The Transportation Revolution, 1815-1860* (New York, 1951), 96.

45. *Congressional Globe,* 31st Cong., 2d sess., 540-44. Speeches by Clay and Benton may be found in *Congressional Globe,* 31st Cong., 2d sess., appendix, 140-43, 173-79.

46. Colton, *Life and Speeches,* 3:208-13; *Congressional Globe,* 31st Cong., 2d sess., 329, 353, 359, 363, 368, 381. See also his proposal the preceding session to explore the practicality of reservoirs to maintain an adequate channel for shipping on the Ohio River. *Congressional Globe,* 31st Cong., 1st sess., appendix, 1381-82.

47. *Congressional Globe,* 31st Cong., 1st sess., 115-16.

14. Retrospect

1. Robert L. Heilbroner, ed., *The Essential Adam Smith* (New York, 1986), 258-98; Paul L. Conkin, *Prophets of Prosperity: America's First Political Economists* (Bloomington, Ind., 1980), 28-40, 312-14.

2. John R. Nelson Jr., *Liberty and Prosperity: Political Economy and Policymaking in the New Nation, 1789-1812* (Baltimore, 1987); Drew R. McCoy, *The Elusive Republic: Political Economy in Jeffersonian America* (Chapel Hill, N.C., 1980), 136-52, 222-55.

3. Edward Pessen, *Jacksonian America: Society, Personality, and Politics* (Urbana, Ill., 1985), 197-260; Remini, *Clay,* 456-64; Daniel W. Howe, *The Political Culture of the American Whigs* (Chicago, 1979), 22-28, 96-122, 181-209; Lawrence Frederick Kohl, *The Politics of Individualism: Parties and the American Character in the Jacksonian Era* (New York, 1991), 6-18, 50-99, 115-23, 155, 226-29; Daniel Feller, "Politics and Society: Toward a Jacksonian Synthesis," *Journal of the Early Republic* 10 (Spring 1990): 135-61.

4. Pitkin, *Statistical View,* 266, 272-88, 295; *Historical Statistics,* part 2, 905, 907.

5. Norman S. Buck, *The Development of the Organisation of Anglo-American Trade, 1800-1850* (New Haven, Conn., 1925), 2-3, 121-28, 136-70.

6. *Historical Statistics,* part 1, 205.

7. J.H. Clapham, *An Economic History of Modern Britain* (Cambridge, Eng., 1930), 1:476-79, 482-84, 495-505. For a comparison of British and American rates, see *Niles' Register,* vol. 42, Aug. 4, 1832, 414-16, vol. 43, Jan. 12, 1833, 316.

8. Smart, *Economic Annals,* vol. 2, passim, is a comprehensive source on the policy in Parliament.

9. Clapham, *Economic History,* 328, 331-34.

10. Previous notes give full citations to these references.

11. Examples of econometric articles surveyed are Robert W. Fogel and Stanley L. Engerman, "A Model for the Explanation of In-

dustrial Expansion during the Nineteenth Century: With an Application to the American Iron Industry," *Journal of Political Economy* 77 (May-June 1969): 306-28; Robert B. Zevin, "The Growth of Cotton Textile Production after 1815," in *American Economic History,* edited by Fogel and Engerman, 122-47.

Mark Bils, "Tariff Protection and Production in the U.S. Cotton Textile Industry," *Journal of Economic History* 44 (Dec. 1984): 1035-45, employs hypothetical models because of sparse, questionable data and believes tariffs did provide crucial help for low-quality cottons. This category was recognized as prohibitive at the time of enactment, 1816-24.

12. *Historical Statistics,* part 1, 201-2, 205, 207, 209, part 2, 886, 902, 904-7. See the Appendix for a correlation of tariff rates and commodity prices.

13. V.S. Clark, *Manufactures,* 1:308-12; Douglass C. North et al., *Growth and Welfare in the American Past: A New Economic History* (Englewood Cliffs, N.J., 1983), 4, among others.

14. Smith, *Second BUS,* 233-63, is a useful evaluation of the bank's role, generally picturing it as Clay saw it. The negative features are brought forward by Schlesinger, *Age of Jackson.* A recent view may be found in Stuart Bruchey, *Enterprise: The Dynamic Economy of a Free People* (Cambridge, Mass., 1990), 180-92.

15. David Kinley, *The History, Organization and Influence of the Independent Treasury of the United States* (New York, 1893), passim.

16. Taylor's *Transportation Revolution, 1815-1860,* is a notable book supporting this theme.

17. Extensions and spurs of the National Road were intrastate projects. And national subscription to stock of the Chesapeake and Ohio Canal was a mixture with private capital.

18. Phillip S. Paludan, *"A People's Contest": The Union and Civil War, 1861-1865* (New York, 1988), 127-50, is a recent, informative discussion of these policies, as summarized below.

19. Roy P. Basler, ed., *The Collected Works of Abraham Lincoln* (New Brunswick, N.J., 1953), 1:48.

20. He reasoned that "the legitimate object of government, is to do for a community of people, whatever they need to have done, but cannot do, *at all,* or can not, *so well do,* for themselves—in their separate and individual capacities." Clay would have concurred completely. Basler, *Works of Lincoln,* 1:220-21. The words emphasized were by Lincoln.

21. Remini, *Clay,* xiii, 692, 786.

Index

Adams, John, 2

Adams, John Quincy: and transportation improvements, 7-8, 53, 63, 108-10; and Treaty of Ghent, 14; relationship with HC, 14, 214 n 29; HC as secretary of state under, 17, 42, 55-56, 57-66; and tariffs, 33, 63-65, 75-76, 78, 85; in election of 1824, 33, 53, 55, 192; as secretary of state, 48, 58, 59, 61; Latin American policy, 56, 57-59, 62; and British West Indies trade, 61, 62; in election of 1828, 65; on public-land sales, 115

African Americans. *See* colonization of emancipated slaves; slavery

agriculture: HC's personal involvement with, 3, 5; and banking in Kentucky, 4; and tariffs, 23, 28, 29, 188, 202, 203; and economic depression, 34

Alien and Sedition Acts of 1798, 70-71, 224 n 12

American Colonization Society, 119

American Quarterly Review, 89

American Revolution, 14

American System: origin of term, 27, 57, 74; origin of policy, 73, 74; HC's conception summarized, 199

Anglo-American trade. *See* British-American commerce

Antimason party, 95-96

Argus of Western America, 42

Baldwin, Henry, 22-23

Baltimore Union Bank, 97-98

banking: Kentucky policy on, 3; policy under Jefferson, 12; and economic depression of 1820s, 22, 35, 37, 40, 42; private banks, 40; and panic of 1837, 132-35, 144; policies during Civil War, 210. *See also* Bank of Kentucky; Bank of the Commonwealth; Bank of the United States (BUS); national bank; state banks

Bank of Kentucky, 4, 12, 40, 41

Bank of the Commonwealth, 40-41, 89, 128, 219 n 25, 234 n 28

Bank of the United States (BUS): failure to recharter in 1811, 12-13, 36, 214 n 28; and economic depression, 22, 35, 37, 42; recharter in 1816, 35-37, 218 n 6; activity after

DATE			